Revolution!

Revolution!

The Atlantic World Reborn

NEW-YORK
HISTORICAL
SOCIETY
MUSEUM & LIBRARY

g
GILES

*New-York Historical Society, New York City
in association with D Giles Limited, London*

© 2011 New-York Historical Society

First published in 2011 by GILES
An imprint of D Giles Limited
4 Crescent Stables, 139 Upper Richmond Road,
London, SW15 2TN, UK
www.gilesltd.com

ISBN: 978-0-916141-24-0 (Softcover edition)
ISBN: 978-1-904832-94-2 (Hardcover edition)

For the New-York Historical Society:
Project Editor and Manager: Valerie Paley

For D Giles Limited:
Copy-edited and proof-read by David Rose
Designed by Mercer Design

Produced by GILES, an imprint of D Giles Limited, London
Printed and bound in China

All measurements are in inches and centimeters

Front cover: (DETAIL) Anne-Louis Girodet de Roussy-Trioson
(1767–1824). *J. B. Belley, député de Saint Domingue à la Convention*,
1797. Oil on canvas, 62 3/5 × 43 7/10 in. (159 × 111 cm). Châteaux
de Versailles et de Trianon, Versailles, France. Photo credit: Erich
Lessing/Art Resource, NY.

Back cover: Unidentified artist after Nicolas Eustache Maurin
(1799–1850). *Dominique Toussaint L'Ouverture (1743–1803)*, after 1832.
Watercolor on ivory, 2 3/4 × 3 3/4 in. (7 × 9.5 cm). New-York Historical
Society. Purchase, The Louis Durr Fund, 1956.123.

Frontispiece: James Sharples (ca. 1751–1811). *Médéric-Louis-Elie
Moreau de Saint-Méry*, 1798. Pastel and black chalk (or black pastel)
on toned (now oxidized) wove paper, 9 7/16 × 7 1/4 in. (24 × 18.4 cm).
Metropolitan Museum of Art, Bequest of Charles Allen Munn,
1924, 24.109.89/Art Resource NY.

Contents

Foreword

This catalogue, and the exhibition it accompanies, were inspired by a lunchtime conversation in 2004, just as the New-York Historical Society celebrated its bicentennial. The topic around the table was "revolution"—perhaps on some level of consciousness because the N-YHS had itself undergone a bit of a revolution after two hundred years, sharpening its focus on American history and mounting big "blockbuster" exhibitions as part of a strategy to engage the broadest possible public. As the conversation progressed, the perennial, and inevitable, question of why the American and French revolutions were so distinct was raised. But this time the discussion was different, because one of the conversation's participants insisted on introducing a third revolution into the mix: the revolution in Haiti.

I am indebted to James Oliver Horton for drawing my attention to the Haitian revolution, both as the first successful slave rebellion and as catalyst for events in France and the United States that profoundly affected the histories of both countries. It was Jim's idea to consider all three revolutions together and *Revolution!* might not otherwise ever have taken shape. N-YHS trustees James Basker, David Blight, and our visionary former Board Chairman Richard Gilder participated in that lunchtime conversation as well. Their collective intelligence and knowledge truly sowed the seeds for this project. They deserve tremendous credit and a huge vote of thanks. It was my good fortune at the time to have become acquainted with Richard Rabinowitz, a brilliant historian and curator, who needed no encouragement whatsoever to see the promise in, and importance of, an exhibition on revolution in America, France, and Haiti.

Serendipitously, all of the people I've mentioned so far were together at a 2005 dinner at which the Frederick Douglass Book Prize was awarded to historian Laurent Dubois, for his book on the struggle over slavery and citizenship in the revolutionary French Caribbean. Listening to Laurent's acceptance speech, all of us concluded that we must involve him in our project. We further

LEFT Agostino Brunias (1728–1796). *Free West Indian Creoles in elegant dress,* ca. 1780.
Oil on canvas, 12⅛ × 9¾ in. (30.8 × 24.8 cm). Yale Center for British Art, Paul Mellon Collection.
The Bridgeman Art Library International.

concluded that our "dream team" for the role of catalogue editors and project historians would be Laurent and Thomas Bender, whose extraordinary book on the Atlantic world all of us had just read. Happily, they agreed!

It has taken six years and a major renovation of the N-YHS—another revolution for us—to bring this project to fruition. But along the way, as we mounted exhibitions on slavery, the Marquis de Lafayette, Grant and Lee, and Lincoln and New York, we benefitted from thinking about the three revolutions and how they came to define notions of freedom, equality, and human rights. I am so grateful to N-YHS Board Chairman Roger Hertog, and to all of our trustees, for the support they have given so that we could explore these big and basic ideas.

I am grateful, too, for the luxury of having wonderful colleagues at the N-YHS, who give so much of their time, energy, and intellect, so that these projects can succeed. In particular I would like to thank Valerie Paley, whose great work on this catalogue is so much in evidence. I also thank Stephen Edidin, Kathleen Hulser, Jean Ashton, and the Museum and Library staffs for their individual efforts in helping to realize this ambitious exhibition. I extend my sincere gratitude to a dedicated group of funders who recognized the importance of this project with their support and partnership. The exhibition was made possible with grant funds from the U.S. Department of Education Underground Railroad Educational and Cultural (URR) program, by public funds from the New York City Department of Cultural Affairs, and with a grant from The Nathan Cummings Foundation.

As the N-YHS enters its next phase as New York's destination for history, I thank everyone who has believed in us and our vision of *Making History Matter*.

Dr. Louise Mirrer
President and CEO, New-York Historical Society

Introduction

The New-York Historical Society exhibition, *Revolution! The Atlantic World Reborn*, is indeed a milestone event, if not a revolution, in the annals of American historical museums and libraries. The exhibition is, for one thing, part of a major renovation of New York's oldest cultural institution. Founded in 1804, the N-YHS has grown into a superb repository of millions of treasured objects: books, manuscripts, prints, photographs, paintings, and the artifacts of ordinary life in the United States. It has also been a steadily evolving agency of public knowledge—offering lectures, publications, exhibitions, educational programs, and now a wide variety of new media. The reopening of the Society in 2011 expresses this public role by making its building much more hospitable to the diverse audiences that flock to its programs each year.

In another, more subtle way, this exhibition marks a real maturing of the world of history museums. Almost all American historical museums are regional or local in scope. The exceptions, like the Smithsonian, are dedicated to our national history. Aside from Holocaust memorials and museums around the nation, scarcely ever has an American history museum undertaken an interpretation of events beyond our shores. *Revolution!*, though it has plenty of American history in it, fundamentally situates itself in a transnational perspective. Globalization is a buzzword today, but it is a much older phenomenon. We hope that this exhibition encourages American visitors to see their national history as deeply intertwined with that of other peoples.

Over the past five years, dozens of archivists, librarians, scholars, curators, and educators from all around the Atlantic have contributed to shaping this particular *Revolution*, transnational in scope and international in its making. In all, nearly three hundred items have come from seventy public repositories and private collections in thirteen nations. Curatorial work—even in the age of the Internet—approximates the uncertainties of a picaresque adventure. We set out in search of one thing—a document, an image, an artifact—and discover that a whole complex historical world lies behind it. Who knew, for example, that there were three versions of the *Déclaration des droits de l'homme et du citoyen*? That images of Toussaint Louverture issued from French presses were in rhythm with the nineteenth-century politics of the French Caribbean? That a sober-looking 1763 broadside turns out to be a nearly treasonous satire? At these moments, when curiosity and humility go hand in hand, the exhibition curator blesses the wisdom of those who spend careers caring for and studying those collections. As exhibition deadlines approach, this appreciation turns to prayerful gratitude.

Our debt to research scholars is equally deep, if never quite so easily measured. The study of the eighteenth-century revolutions, of slavery and abolition, of African and African American history, of the Caribbean and the Atlantic, has been flowering amazingly in the past three decades. Every month, a list of completed dissertations reports the labors of another dozen young scholars in American universities in rewriting these histories—quite an increase since I drafted my own prospectus in 1970. As graduate students, we passed language exams for heaven knows what reasons, perhaps as a sort of vaccine against some future exposure. Forty years later, sitting in the reading rooms of archives in Port-au-Prince or Aix-en-Provence, I finally know why.

Perhaps most surprising in this intellectual evolution has been the steadily growing attention to the Haitian revolution. I am sure that there are dozens of historian/Rip Van Winkles who, busy with other areas of scholarship for decades, have been shocked to discover that events in Saint-Domingue, scarcely mentioned in R. R. Palmer's magisterial *The Age of the Democratic Revolution* (1959–64), now vie with those occurring in Philadelphia and Paris as the most important moments in the history of liberty. It has been challenging and exciting to clamber aboard this swift-moving train of scholarship, and we're grateful for the scholars, especially those in Haiti itself, who've been our conductors in this journey. This catalogue brings together many of the most creative contributors to this new historical synthesis.

Additionally, we have to acknowledge how much, to reverse a familiar phrase, "the past can learn from the present." This project has been constantly adumbrated by fast-moving events on the world stage. Recently, the horrors of human trafficking have once again become the subjects of magazine articles and political petitions, and a revived anti-slavery movement arises to combat them. Politics in the United States got a sudden jolt from an anti-tax crusade called the

"Tea Party" in 2009–10, complete with protestors in knee breeches and three-cornered hats.

This decade's news is a textbook of the history of revolutions. From Serbia in 2000 and Georgia in 2003, we've seen one after another: the Orange Revolution in Ukraine (2004), the Cedar Revolution in Lebanon and the Tulip Revolution in Kyrgyzstan (both 2005), failed revolutions in Burma in 2007 and in Moldova and Iran in 2009, and, most recently, the upheavals in Tunisia, Egypt, and other parts of the Arab world, in 2011. These events stimulate us to look again at the events in Boston, Liverpool, Paris, and Cap Français two hundred years ago. We ask, what is the relationship between street violence and the backroom negotiations between power brokers? How does the social media of our day (the claimed power of Twitter and Facebook) compare with those of the eighteenth century (broadsides, marches, and the very first "strikes" in history)? How does regime change redefine the sense of peoplehood? How does the drive for universal human rights intersect with resurgent nationalism—both children of the eighteenth-century revolutions?

Nothing has cast a darker shadow over this project than *le séisme*, the earthquake that devastated Haiti on January 12, 2010. It took the lives of a quarter-million legatees of the Haitian Revolution and destroyed so much of the already tattered physical legacy of the nation's past. On behalf of my colleagues at the New-York Historical Society and American History Workshop, I hope that this exhibition and catalogue, by widening our understanding of that past, can make a small contribution to repairing that loss.

Richard Rabinowitz
Chief Curator, *Revolution! The Atlantic World Reborn* exhibition
Brooklyn, New York, February 2011

A Season of Revolutions: The United States, France, and Haiti

Thomas Bender

DÉCLARATION

DES DROITS

DE L'HOMME ET DU CITOYEN.

LE peuple Français, convaincu que l'oubli & le mépris des droits naturels de l'homme, font les seules causes des malheurs du monde, a résolu d'exposer dans une déclaration solennelle ces droits sacrés & inaliénables, afin que tous les citoyens pouvant comparer sans cesse les actes du gouvernement avec le but de toute institution sociale, ne se laisse jamais opprimer & avilir par la tyrannie, afin que le peuple ait toujours devant les yeux les bases de sa liberté & de son bonheur, le magistrat la règle de ses devoirs, le législateur l'objet de sa mission.

En conséquence, il proclame, en présence de l'Etre suprême, la déclaration suivante des droits de l'homme & du citoyen.

ARTICLE PREMIER.

Le but de la société est le bonheur commun.

Le gouvernement est institué pour garantir à l'homme la jouissance de ses droits naturels & imprescriptibles.

II.

Ces droits sont l'égalité, la liberté, la sûreté, la propriété.

III.

Tous les hommes sont égaux par la nature & devant la loi.

IV.

La loi est l'expression libre & solennelle de la volonté générale; elle est la même pour tous, soit qu'elle protège, soit qu'elle punisse; elle ne peut ordonner que ce qui est juste & utile à la société, elle ne peut défendre que ce qui lui est nuisible.

V.

Tous les citoyens sont également admissibles aux emplois publics. Les peuples libres ne connoissent d'autres motifs de préférence dans leurs élections, que les vertus & les talens.

VI.

La liberté est le pouvoir qui appartient à l'homme de faire tout ce qui ne nuit pas aux droits d'autrui : elle a pour principe, la nature; pour règle, la justice; pour sauve-garde, la loi; sa limite morale est dans cette maxime : *Ne fais pas à un autre ce que tu ne veux pas qui te soit fait.*

VII.

Le droit de manifester sa pensée & ses opinions, soit par la voie de la presse, soit de toute autre manière, le droit de s'assembler paisiblement, le libre exercice des cultes, ne peuvent être interdits.

La nécessité d'énoncer ses droits, suppose ou la présence ou le souvenir récent du despotisme.

VIII.

La sûreté consiste dans la protection accordée par la société à chacun de ses membres pour la conservation de sa personne, de ses droits & de ses propriétés.

IX.

La loi doit protéger la liberté publique & individuelle contre l'oppression de ceux qui gouvernent.

X.

Nul ne doit être accusé, arrêté, ni détenu que dans les cas déterminés par la loi, & selon les formes qu'elle a prescrites. Tout citoyen appelé ou saisi par autorité de la loi, doit obéir à l'instant; il se rend coupable par la résistance.

XI.

Tout acte exercé contre un homme hors des cas & sans les formes que la loi détermine, est arbitraire & tyrannique; celui contre lequel on voudroit l'exécuter par la violence, a le droit de le repousser par la force.

XII.

Ceux qui solliciteroient, expédieroient, signeroient, exécuteroient ou feroient exécuter des actes arbitraires, sont coupables & doivent être punis.

XIII.

Tout homme étant présumé innocent jusqu'à ce qu'il ait été déclaré coupable, s'il est jugé indispensable de l'arrêter, toute rigueur qui ne seroit pas nécessaire pour s'assurer de sa personne, doit être sévèrement réprimée par la loi.

XIV.

Nul ne doit être jugé & puni qu'après avoir été entendu ou légalement appelé, & qu'en vertu d'une loi promulguée antérieurement au délit. La loi qui puniroit des délits commis avant qu'elle existât, seroit une tyrannie; l'effet rétroactif donné à loi seroit un crime.

XV.

La loi ne doit décerner que des peines strictement & évidemment nécessaires; les peines doivent être proportionnées au délit & utiles à la société.

XVI.

Le droit de propriété est celui qui appartient à tout citoyen, de jouir & de disposer à son gré de ses biens & de ses revenus, du fruit de son travail & de son industrie.

XVII.

Nul genre de travail, de culture, de commerce, ne peut être interdit à l'industrie des citoyens.

XVIII.

Tout homme peut engager ses services, son temps; mais il ne peut se vendre ni être vendu; sa personne n'est pas une propriété aliénable. La loi ne connoît point de domesticité; il ne peut exister qu'un engagement de soins & de reconnoissance, entre l'homme qui travaille & celui qui l'emploie.

XIX.

Nul ne peut être privé de la moindre portion de sa propriété, sans son consentement, si ce n'est lorsque la nécessité publique légalement constatée l'exige, & sous la condition d'une juste & préalable indemnité.

XX.

Nulle contribution ne peut être établie que pour l'utilité générale. Tous les citoyens ont droit de concourir à l'établissement des contributions, d'en surveiller l'emploi, & de s'en faire rendre compte.

XXI.

Les secours publics sont une dette sacrée. La société doit la subsistance aux citoyens malheureux, soit en leur procurant du travail, soit en assurant les moyens d'exister à ceux qui sont hors d'état de travailler.

XXII.

L'instruction est le besoin de tous. La société doit favoriser de tout son pouvoir les progrès de la raison publique, & mettre l'instruction à la portée de tous les citoyens.

XXIII.

La garantie sociale consiste dans l'action de tous, pour assurer à chacun la jouissance & la conservation de ses droits : cette garantie repose sur la souveraineté nationale.

XXIV.

Elle ne peut exister, si les limites des fonctions publiques ne sont pas clairement déterminées par la loi, & si la responsabilité de tous les fonctionnaires n'est pas assurée.

XXV.

La souveraineté réside dans le peuple; elle est une & indivisible, imprescriptible & inaliénable.

XXVI.

Aucune portion du peuple ne peut exercer la puissance du peuple entier; mais chaque section du souverain assemblée, doit jouir du droit d'exprimer sa volonté avec une entière liberté.

XXVII.

Que tout individu qui usurperoit la souveraineté, soit à l'instant mis à mort par les hommes libres.

XXVIII.

Un peuple a toujours le droit de revoir, de réformer & de changer sa constitution. Une génération ne peut assujettir à ses lois les générations futures.

XXIX.

Chaque citoyen a un droit égal de concourir à la formation de la loi, & à la nomination de ses mandataires ou de ses agens.

XXX.

Les fonctions publiques sont essentiellement temporaires; elles ne peuvent être considérées comme des distinctions ni comme des récompenses, mais comme des devoirs.

XXXI.

Les délits des mandataires du peuple & de ses agens, ne doivent jamais être impunis. Nul n'a le droit de se prétendre plus inviolable que les autres citoyens.

XXXII.

Le droit de présenter des pétitions aux dépositaires de l'autorité publique, ne peut en aucun cas être interdit, suspendu ni limité.

XXXIII.

La résistance à l'oppression est la conséquence des autres droits de l'homme.

XXXIV.

Il y a oppression contre le corps social lorsqu'un seul de ses membres est opprimé : il y a oppression contre chaque membre lorsque le corps social est opprimé.

XXXV.

Quand le gouvernement viole les droits du peuple, l'insurrection est pour le peuple, & pour chaque portion du peuple le plus sacré des droits & le plus indispensable des devoirs.

Se trouve à la Manufacture Républicaine de papiers peints, rue Saint-Nicaise, maison de Longueville.

OPPOSITE Broadside for *Déclaration des Droits de l'Homme et du Citoyen*, ca. 1793–95. New-York Historical Society, SY DC1789 no.5 oversize.

istorical memory tends to remember the great revolutions of the eighteenth century quite separately. The French might be contrasted with the American, and the Haitian too often is overlooked beyond the Caribbean. While separate they were, they were collectively a single world-shaping event. French financial and military assistance made possible the American victory, and the resulting French debt compelled the French king to call the Estates General, which triggered the revolution there. And that revolution provided the spark that ignited freedom claims in Saint-Domingue, today's Haiti. And the success of the Haitian Revolution prompted Napoleon to sell Louisiana to the United States, enabling for the first time a continental vision for the new United States.

The Haitian Revolution is rarely associated with the founding era of the American republic. Yet there are traces here and there. Popular fiction has a better memory of the significance of the Haitian Revolution than does popular history. On the first page of the novel *Gone with the Wind* (1936), Margaret Mitchell began her description of Scarlett O'Hara by pointing out that Scarlett's mother was "a Coast aristocrat of French descent," a reference, lost perhaps to readers outside of the South, that her family were slaveholders who fled with their slaves during the black Haitian struggle for freedom and independence.

The Atlantic Ocean was a locus of movement in the age of revolution: for people, ideas, and goods. People on the different continents—Africa, the Americas, and Europe—had knowledge of and interest in the other continents, and the emerging culture of print provided a substantial diet of information. For instance, within two months of its signing, the Declaration of Independence was being widely read in Europe, as far east as Warsaw, Poland. Surreptitious copies were circulating in Spanish America, and planters in Jamaica believed that the North American rhetoric of freedom was one of the causes of a slave revolt on the island in 1776.

People as well as ideas were in motion. Francisco de Miranda, a Venezuelan, was a witness and sometime participant in the great events of the era, and he provides a particularly interesting example. A sometime collaborator with the revolutionary leader Simon Bolívar, de Miranda's circle of friends populated the whole Atlantic world.[1] They included Benjamin Franklin, Alexander Hamilton, Thomas Paine, and George Washington in North America, but many Europeans as well: the Marquis de Lafayette, the English philosophers Jeremy Bentham and James Mill, the composer Joseph

Haydn, the German-Jewish philosopher Moses Mendelssohn, and the historian Edward Gibbon. He was even granted an aristocratic title by Catherine the Great, Empress of Russia. A minor participant in the Enlightenment, he is best described as an enthusiastic consumer of the liberal and liberating ideas of the age. His embrace of the Enlightenment and his cosmopolitan experience helped shape his anti-colonial commitments, and he became an early leader of the Venezuelan movement for independence.

His father purchased a captaincy in the Spanish army for him, and he served in North Africa, where he caused some distress because of his open sympathy with the desire of his Moorish opponents to rid their land of foreign military forces. Stationed afterward in Cuba, he was part of the Spanish expedition that, allied with France, aided the rebelling Thirteen Colonies. He took part in the recapture of Pensacola, Florida from the British, and he had a role in assisting the French fleet that made possible the American victory at Yorktown in 1782. In the next year, he left the Spanish army (under a cloud of suspicion of being a spy) and traveled north to see the new American republic.

From the United States he went to Paris, arriving on the eve of the storming of the Bastille. His sympathies were with the revolution, and he commanded a contingent of revolutionary troops in Belgium. But as the revolution turned more radical, his moderation made him suspect. Challenged by Robespierre, a dominant figure in the Terror (1794–95), he was charged with treason. He escaped the guillotine but spent two years in prison. After his release he went to Britain seeking support for a Venezuelan revolution. Nothing came of his effort, and he sailed to the United States, where he solicited help from Thomas Jefferson and James Madison, again without success. In New York, however, he found both volunteers and funds for an expedition, which sailed in 1806. The landing in Venezuela was a disaster; many of his volunteers were taken prisoner by the Spanish authorities, but he escaped to London.

A revolutionary moment arrived for Spanish America when Napoleon invaded Spain and deposed the king. Miranda returned to Venezuela and joined the short-lived independent Venezuelan government. He was at its head in 1812 when Caracas was devastated by an earthquake that killed 10,000 people. Simultaneously the city was besieged by superior Spanish forces. Without consulting anyone, he surrendered. That angered Simon Bolívar, the military leader of the anti-colonial movement in South America, who handed Miranda over to the Spanish authorities. They imprisoned him in Spain, and he died in prison six years later.

For all of his fervor, he was a moderate. Independence meant more to him than revolution. He preferred the American to the more radical French Revolution. And like nearly all white revolutionaries in North America, France, and Latin America, he believed freedom had a boundary. Blacks need not apply. He preferred no revolution at all than to suffer the revolution on Saint-Domingue:

> I confess that much as I desire liberty and independence in the New World, I fear anarchy and revolution even more. God forbid that the other countries suffer the same fate as Saint Domingue…better that they should remain another century under the barbarous and senseless oppression of Spain.[2]

A man of grand ambition, middling talent, and few accomplishments, he is remembered in his native Venezuela by the title "Precursor."

Though he was not a central figure in the eighteenth-century Atlantic revolutions, I begin with Miranda because he exemplifies three of the main themes (and some smaller ones) of this chapter. First, the three great eighteenth-century revolutions were not only close in chronology, but they also were part of a larger and interconnected history of the Atlantic world. Although historians generally treat these revolutions as separate and self-contained entities, their histories were in reality entangled with each other, just as Miranda was caught up in all three revolutions, as well as Venezuela's. Another central theme we see in Miranda's story is a pattern of noble words and results that fall short of the rhetoric. While one might fairly charge these leaders with hypocrisy, a longer term perspective reveals that the words had an enduring and important afterlife.

The long view points to my third and perhaps my most important proposition. If the eighteenth-century Atlantic revolutions did not bring forth egalitarian and democratic polities, they made such polities possible, perhaps even inevitable—in the long term. They established new expectations in politics and society: equality and dignity rather than a world of inequality and privilege became an aspiration that would develop over time into a global universal. It was this historical shift that drove Alexis de Tocqueville's study of the French Revolution and his *Democracy in America* (1835–40).[3]

The "Great Seal" of the new United States may have overstated the actual circumstances at the moment of its adoption, but it captured a larger historical truth: *novus ordo seculorum*—"New

In CONGRESS, July 4, 1776.

A DECLARATION

By the REPRESENTATIVES of the

UNITED STATES OF AMERICA,

In GENERAL CONGRESS ASSEMBLED.

WHEN in the Course of human Events, it becomes neceſſary for one People to diſſolve the Political Bands which have connected them with another, and to aſſume among the Powers of the Earth, the ſeparate and equal Station to which the Laws of Nature and of Nature's God entitle them, a decent Reſpect to the Opinions of Mankind requires that they ſhould declare the Cauſes which impel them to the Separation.

We hold theſe Truths to be ſelf-evident, that all Men are created equal, that they are endowed by their Creator with certain unalienable Rights, that among theſe are Life, Liberty and the Purſuit of Happineſs.---That to ſecure theſe Rights, Governments are inſtituted among Men, deriving their juſt Powers from the Conſent of the Governed, that whenever any Form of Government becomes deſtructive of theſe Ends, it is the Right of the People to alter or to aboliſh it, and to inſtitute new Government, laying its Foundation on ſuch Principles, and organizing its Powers in ſuch Form, as to them ſhall ſeem moſt likely to effect their Safety and Happineſs. Prudence, indeed will dictate that Governments long eſtabliſhed ſhould not be changed for light and tranſient Cauſes; and accordingly all Experience hath ſhewn, that Mankind are more diſpoſed to ſuffer, while Evils are ſufferable, than to right themſelves by aboliſhing the Forms to which they are accuſtomed. But when a long Train of Abuſes and Uſurpations, purſuing invariably the ſame Object, evinces a Deſign to reduce them under abſolute Deſpotiſm, it is their Right, it is their Duty, to throw off ſuch Government, and to provide new Guards for their future Security. Such has been the patient Sufferance of theſe Colonies; and ſuch is now the Neceſſity which conſtrains them to alter their former Syſtems of Government. The Hiſtory of the preſent King of Great-Britain is a Hiſtory of repeated Injuries and Uſurpations, all having in direct Object the Eſtabliſhment of an abſolute Tyranny over theſe States. To prove this, let Facts be ſubmitted to a candid World.

He has refuſed his Aſſent to Laws, the moſt wholeſome and neceſſary for the public Good.

He has forbidden his Governors to paſs Laws of immediate and preſſing Importance, unleſs ſuſpended in their Operation till his Aſſent ſhould be obtained; and when ſo ſuſpended, he has utterly neglected to attend to them.

He has refuſed to paſs other Laws for the Accommodation of large Diſtricts of People, unleſs thoſe People would relinquiſh the Right of Repreſentation in the Legiſlature, a Right ineſtimable to them, and formidable to Tyrants only.

He has called together Legiſlative Bodies at Places unuſual, uncomfortable, and diſtant from the Depoſitory of their public Records, for the ſole Purpoſe of fatiguing them into Compliance with his Meaſures.

He has diſſolved Repreſentative Houſes repeatedly, for oppoſing with manly Firmneſs his Invaſions on the Rights of the People.

He has refuſed for a long Time, after ſuch Diſſolutions, to cauſe others to be elected; whereby the Legiſlative Powers, incapable of Annihilation, have returned to the People at large for their exerciſe; the State remaining in the mean time expoſed to all the Dangers of Invaſion from without, and Convulſions within.

He has endeavoured to prevent the Population of theſe States; for that Purpoſe obſtructing the Laws for Naturalization of Foreigners; refuſing to paſs others to encourage their Migrations hither, and raiſing the Conditions of new Appropriations of Lands.

He has obſtructed the Adminiſtration of Juſtice, by refuſing his Aſſent to Laws for eſtabliſhing Judiciary Powers.

He has made Judges dependent on his Will alone, for the Tenure of their Offices, and the Amount and Payment of their Salaries.

He has erected a Multitude of new Offices, and ſent hither Swarms of Officers to harraſs our People, and eat out their Subſtance.

He has kept among us, in Times of Peace, Standing Armies, without the Conſent of our Legiſlatures.

He has affected to render the Military independent of and ſuperior to the Civil Power.

He has combined with others to ſubject us to a Juriſdiction foreign to our Conſtitution, and unacknowledged by our Laws; given his Aſſent to their Acts of pretended Legiſlation:

For quartering large Bodies of armed Troops among us:

For protecting them, by a mock Trial, from Puniſhment for any Murders which they ſhould commit on the Inhabitants of theſe States:

For cutting off our Trade with all Parts of the World:

For impoſing Taxes on us without our Conſent:

For depriving us, in many Caſes, of the Benefits of Trial by Jury:

For tranſporting us beyond Seas to be tried for pretended Offences:

For aboliſhing the free Syſtem of Engliſh Laws in a neighbouring Province, eſtabliſhing therein an arbitrary Government, and enlarging its Boundaries, ſo as to render it at once an Example and fit Inſtrument for introducing the ſame abſolute Rule into theſe Colonies:

For taking away our Charters, aboliſhing our moſt valuable Laws, and altering fundamentally the Forms of our Governments:

For ſuſpending our own Legiſlatures, and declaring themſelves inveſted with Power to legiſlate for us in all Caſes whatſoever.

He has abdicated Government here, by declaring us out of his Protection and waging War againſt us.

He has plundered our Seas, ravaged our Coaſts, burnt our Towns, and deſtroyed the Lives of our People.

He is, at this Time, tranſporting large Armies of foreign Mercenaries to compleat the Works of Death, Deſolation and Tyranny, already begun with Circumſtances of Cruelty and Perfidy, ſcarcely paralleled in the moſt barbarous Ages, and totally unworthy the Head of a civilized Nation.

He has conſtrained our fellow Citizens taken Captive on the high Seas to bear Arms againſt their Country, to become the Executioners of their Friends and Brethren, or to fall themſelves by their Hands.

He has excited Domeſtic Inſurrections amongſt us, and has endeavoured to bring on the Inhabitants of our Frontiers, the merciless Indian Savages, whoſe known Rule of Warfare, is an undiſtinguiſhed Deſtruction, of all Ages, Sexes and Conditions.

In every Stage of theſe Oppreſſions we have petitioned for Redreſs, in the moſt humble Terms: Our repeated Petitions have been anſwered only by repeated Injury. A Prince, whoſe Character is thus marked by every Act which may define a Tyrant, is unfit to be the Ruler of a free People.

Nor have we been wanting in Attentions to our Britiſh Brethren. We have warned them from Time to Time of Attempts by their Legiſlature to extend an unwarrantable Juriſdiction over us. We have reminded them of the Circumſtances of our Emigration and Settlement here. We have appealed to their native Juſtice and Magnanimity, and we have conjured them by the Ties of our common Kindred to diſavow theſe Uſurpations, which would inevitably interrupt our Connections and Correſpondence. They too have been deaf to the Voice of Juſtice and of Conſanguinity. We muſt, therefore, acquieſce in the Neceſſity which denounces our Separation, and hold them, as we hold the reſt of Mankind, Enemies in War, in Peace, Friends.

We, therefore, the Repreſentatives of the UNITED STATES OF AMERICA, in GENERAL CONGRESS aſſembled, appealing to the Supreme Judge of the World for the Rectitude of our Intentions, do, in the Name and by the Authority of the good People of theſe Colonies, ſolemnly Publiſh and Declare, That theſe United Colonies are, and of Right ought to be, FREE AND INDEPENDENT STATES; that they are abſolved from all Allegiance to the Britiſh Crown, and that all political Connection between them and the State of Great-Britain, is and ought to be totally diſſolved; and that as FREE AND INDEPENDENT STATES, they have full Power to levy War, conclude Peace, contract Alliances, eſtabliſh Commerce, and to do all other Acts and Things which INDEPENDENT STATES may of right do. And for the Support of this Declaration, with a firm Reliance on the Protection of divine Providence we mutually pledge to each other our Lives, our Fortunes, and our ſacred Honor.

Signed by ORDER *and in* BEHALF *of the* CONGRESS,

JOHN HANCOCK, President.

ATTEST.
CHARLES THOMSON, SECRETARY.

NEW-YORK: Printed by HUGH GAINE, in Hanover-Square.

A

DEFENCE.

OF THE

CONSTITUTIONS of GOVERNMENT

OF THE

UNITED STATES of AMERICA.

By JOHN ADAMS, L.L.D.

AND A MEMBER OF THE ACADEMY OF ARTS AND SCIENCES AT BOSTON.

All nature's difference keeps all nature's peace. POPE.

LONDON, Printed,

BOSTON, Re-printed and sold by EDMUND FREEMAN, opposite the NORTH Door of the STATE-HOUSE.

M,DCC,LXXXVIII.

DÉFENSE

DES

CONSTITUTIONS

AMÉRICAINES,

OU

De la nécessité d'une balance dans les pouvoirs d'un gouvernement libre.

Par M. JOHN ADAMS, ci-devant Ministre Plénipotentiaire des États-Unis près la cour de Londres, et actuellement Vice-Président des États-Unis, et Président du Sénat.

Avec des Notes et Observations de M. DE LA CROIX, Professeur de Droit Public au Lycée.

All nature's difference keeps all nature's peace.
L'opposition de toute la nature tient toute la nature en paix. POPE.

TOME PREMIER.

A PARIS,
Chez BUISSON, Libraire et Imprimeur, rue Hautefeuille, Nº. 20.
1792.

Order of the Ages." And the expansion of the means of public discussion—new places of public assemblage, widened literacy, and a massive increase in printed materials—facilitated a broad Atlantic-wide discussion of human rights, the idea of popular sovereignty, and citizenship.

Seeds were planted, and we are still tending their shoots. The seeding was the work of all three revolutions, not any single one. This age of revolution was that special moment when, as Hannah Arendt put it, "men began to be aware that a new beginning could be a political phenomenon, that it could be the result of what men had done and what they could consciously set out to do."[4] Before this historical moment, the word "revolution" referred to impersonal events, like the revolution of the earth on its axis or the planets around the sun. The eighteenth century, however, came to understand revolution as something humanly willed. John Adams, upon finishing his and Benjamin Franklin's final edit of Thomas Jefferson's draft of the Declaration of Independence, was among the first to articulate this notion of revolution in a letter to his wife, Abigail, dated July 3, 1776:

> When I look back to the Year 1761 ... and run through the whole Period from that Time to this, and recollect the series of political Events, the Chain of Causes and Effects, I am surprised at the Suddenness, as well as the Greatness of this Revolution.[5]

A properly capacious framework for understanding the eighteenth-century revolutions goes beyond even the Atlantic world. The defining context that accounts for the conjuncture of the three late eighteenth-century Atlantic revolutions (and the early nineteenth-century ones in Spanish America) was the global competition of the British, French, and Spanish empires. That competition, particularly between France and Britain, was long lasting. An almost continuous war began in 1689, and it did not end until 1815, with the final defeat of Napoleon. The competition produced, among other wars, the hugely expensive Seven Years' War, the world's first war fought on every continent. Britain's victory in that war was overwhelming. France lost Canada as well as much-valued trading posts in India and Africa. Britain consolidated its territory in India and more than doubled its American empire.

The acquisition of vast new territories increased the cost of empire. Needing new sources of revenue, the imperial authorities looked to the colonies. They also undertook administrative reforms,

The able Doctor, or America Swallowing the Bitter Draught.

which tended to centralize power and weaken the local colonial institutions of governance, most notably representative bodies, like the lower houses of assembly in the British Colonies, and the judiciary. This was true of Spanish America as well as of the British colonies. There was resistance to these changes in both North America and South. Spanish America did not achieve independence in the eighteenth century, as did the North Americans, and the Haitians in 1804. But there were significant rebellions in the 1780s in New Granada (Colombia) and the revolt led by Tupac Amaru, the descendant of the last Inca king, in Peru. His insurgency, which was inspired more by indigenous political theories than by the Enlightenment ones that were more prevalent elsewhere, nearly cost Spain the vast territory of the Rio de la Plata Vice-Royalty, from Buenos Aires to Peru and Bolivia, or so a former Spanish colonial official later wrote.[6]

ABOVE *The Able Doctor or Swallowing the Bitter Draught*, 1774. Engraving, 3.6 × 5.8 in. (9.1 × 14.8 cm). The John Carter Brown Library at Brown University, 29836.

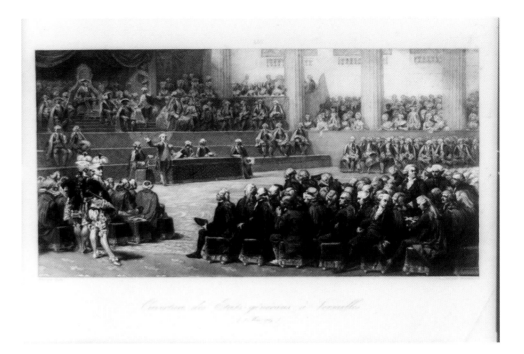

The removal of France from North America also weakened the position of Native Americans, who had previously been able to play the two European empires against each other. At the same time, the new territories in the Ohio Valley whetted the voracious British American appetite for land. In an effort to concentrate settlers nearer the coast and to maintain peace with the Indians, the British Proclamation of 1763 established a line following the ridge of the Appalachian Mountains. Settlement west of it was prohibited, a policy that infuriated the colonists. Another policy concerning the newly acquired territories produced further anger, especially in the New England colonies: the British protected the rights of the Catholics of Québec to practice their religion. These policies organizing the former French colony to the north and west of the thirteen colonies, along with the more familiar ones concerning taxation, trade regulations, and the abuse of traditional political and legal rights by the British government, were major causes of the American Revolution.

There were other important outcomes of the Seven Years' War, but the most important was the French desire for revenge. That was fortunate for the Thirteen Colonies, for it is the reason the French provided the financial and military aid that was decisive for the achievement of independence. Ironically, the French assistance to the republican Americans brought a monarchy already deeply in debt to the brink of bankruptcy. In order to stave off bankruptcy, the French

OBSERVATIONS

SUR

LA VIRGINIE,

PAR M. J***. *Jefferson*.

TRADUITES DE L'ANGLOIS.

À PARIS,

Chez BARROIS, l'aîné, Libraire, rue du
Hurepoix, près le pont Saint-Michel.

1786.

NOTES on the ſtate of VIRGINIA;

written in the year 1781, ſomewhat cor-
rected and enlarged in the winter of 1782,
for the uſe of a Foreigner of diſtinction, in
anſwer to certain queries propoſed by him
reſpecting

MDCCLXXXII.

[Paris]
1785

king, Louis XVI, decided to call the Estates General, which had not met since 1614, to convene May 1, 1789. When in mid-June the Third Estate transformed itself into a National Assembly and began drafting a constitution, they were in effect assuming the national sovereignty that historically had belonged to monarchs. Thus began the sequence of events that led to the storming of the Bastille on July 14, 1789, with much more to follow.

There was more than a financial connection between the American and French revolutions. The leaders in both shared the ideas of the Enlightenment, including a commitment to liberty, contempt for feudalism, preference for a free economy, and a belief in the virtue of a secular state. A French noble, the Vicomte de Noailles, who had fought with the Americans at Yorktown and who was asked by Washington to accept the British surrender on behalf of France, introduced the legislation that ended feudalism in France.[7]

The French Declaration of the Rights of Man and Citizen was prompted by the American Declaration of Independence. Lafayette, who had fought in the American Revolution, was one of the drafters of the French document, and in that role he consulted with his friend Thomas Jefferson, the minister of the United States residing in Paris. But the French fully understood that there was a difference in situation.[8] They were in the capital of a powerful monarchy, not a distant colony. They also understood that making a claim for equality was more radical in the very hierarchical French society than in the thirteen colonies where, with the very large exception of the enslaved population, there was much greater equality. But neither the American nor the French declaration was intended to include women. Nor did either declaration address the question of slavery. But in France, unlike America, there was a public discussion of both issues in the course of the revolution, and during the radical years of Jacobin dominance, slavery was abolished. Olympe de Gouges raised the issue of equality for women. As American women would later do with the American Declaration of Independence at Seneca Falls in 1848, she rehearsed the language of the Declaration of the Rights of Men with women included: "Woman is born free and lives equal to men in her rights."[9] Haiti's revolution was all about slavery and the color line. As Laurent Dubois has noted, the birth of the new republic was "premised on the self-evident truth that no one should be a slave."[10]

For that reason the Haitian Revolution, the largest slave revolt in history, was celebrated by blacks throughout the Americas. In the 1820s, African Americans regularly celebrated the anniversary of Haitian independence, and David Walker, a free black in Boston,

ABOVE *Toussaint Louverture Chef des Noirs Insurgés de Saint Domingue*, ca. 1800. Hand-colored engraving, 13⅞ × 10⅛ in. (35.2 × 25.8 cm). The John Carter Brown Library at Brown University, 63-149.

OVERLEAF Illman Brothers, engravers, after Edouard-Armand Dumaresq (1826–1895). *The Surrender of Cornwallis at Yorktown*, ca. 1850. Engraving, 19 × 26 in. (48.3 × 66 cm). New-York Historical Society, PR 68.

THE SURRENDER OF CORNW

LIS AT YORKTOWN, A. D. 1781.

OPPOSITE *Cahier des doléances de la Colonie de Saint Domingue, a présenter au Roi, dans l'assemblée des États Généraux de la Nation par MM les députés de cette Colonie.* Archives nationales—D XXV 13, liasse 122, pièce 8.

declared in his *Appeal to the Colored Citizens of the World* (1829): "Hayti [is] the glory of the blacks and terror of tyrants."[11] No one was more frightened than Thomas Jefferson, who wrote to James Monroe in 1793 that he was "more & more convinced" that "all the West India Islands will remain in the hands of the people of color; & a total expulsion of the whites [will] sooner or later take place. It is high time we should foresee the bloody scenes which our children certainly and possibly ourselves (south of the Potomac) [will] have to wade through & try to avert them."[12] Four years later, in a letter to another Virginian, he elaborated: "Unless something is done, and soon done, we shall be the murderers of our own children…; the revolutionary storm, now sweeping the globe will be upon us."[13]

The creation of a black republic in the Americas frightened and haunted white planters everywhere. If Jefferson lapsed into hysteria, most planters simply opted for denial. Senator Robert Y. Hayne of South Carolina declared on the Senate floor that "Our policy with regard to Haiti is plain." It was that "we can never acknowledge her independence."[14] And the United States did not recognize Haiti until Abraham Lincoln did so in the course of the Civil War.

The United States also dissociated itself from the French Revolution. At first the citizens of the new republic celebrated their former ally's challenge to European feudalism and monarchism. But the rise of the radical Jacobins and the violence of the "Terror" in 1794–95, along with the revolution's "godlessness" and strongly anti-clerical policies, turned most Americans against it.

For the blacks of Saint-Domingue, the outbreak of revolution in France—and the rights talk that it stimulated—presented an opportunity. If, as the French Declaration of Rights announced, "men are born free and remain free and equal in rights," the free colored of Saint-Domingue—*gens de couleur*—were prepared to make that claim. Planters tended to grant freedom to mixed-race slaves, many of whom were, of course, their own children, sometimes from legitimate marriages. By 1789, the number of these *gens de couleur* had increased dramatically, nearly equaling the number of whites (27,548 blacks to 30,820 whites)—all within a vast sea of enslaved Africans. (At least two-thirds of the enslaved blacks had been born in Africa.) Many of the *gens de couleur* were educated and wealthy, and those in Paris during the early days of the revolution used their wealth and standing to advocate for citizenship, which in 1791 was granted to mulattoes born of two free parents. This was obviously important to the *gens de couleur*, but it is significant in another way: citizenship crossed the color line. In revolutionary France, at least, color alone no longer defined the limits of European citizenship.

n° 5.

N° 252

f. 13. 10.

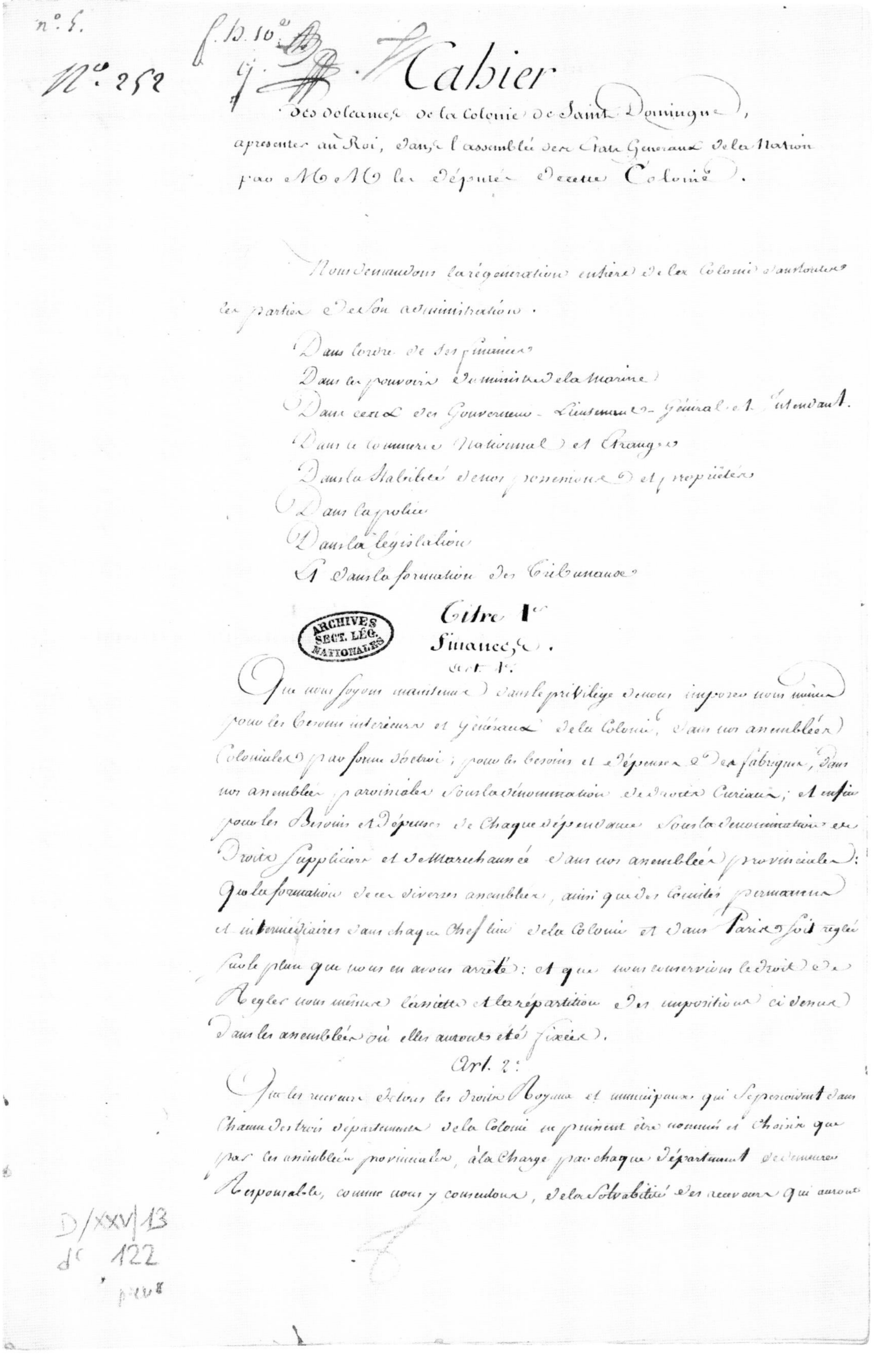

Cahier

des doléances de la Colonie de Saint Domingue, a presenter au Roi, dans l'assemblée des États Generaux de la Nation par M.M. les députés de cette Colonie.

Nous demandons la régéneration entiere de la Colonie dans toutes les parties de son administration.

Dans l'ordre de ses finances

Dans les pouvoirs du ministre de la Marine

Dans ceux des Gouverneurs Lieutenants Généraux et Intendants.

Dans le commerce National et Etranger

Dans la stabilité de nos possessions et propriétés

Dans la police

Dans la législation

Et dans la formation des Tribunaux

Titre 1er

Finances.

Art. 1er

Que nous soyons maintenus dans le privilege de nous imposer nous mêmes pour les besoins intérieurs et généraux de la Colonie, dans nos assemblées Coloniales par forme d'octroi; pour les besoins et dépenses des fabriques, dans nos assemblées paroissiales sous la dénomination de droits Curiaux; et enfin pour les besoins et dépenses de chaque dépendance sous la dénomination de Droits supplices et de Maréchaussée dans nos assemblées provinciales: Que la formation de ces diverses assemblées, ainsi que des Comités permanents et intermédiaires dans chaque Chef lieu de la Colonie et dans Paris, soit reglée sur le plan que nous en avons arrêté: et que nous conservions le droit de Regler nous mêmes l'assiette et la répartition des impositions ci dessus dans les assemblées où elles auront été fixées.

Art. 2.

Que les receveurs de tous les droits Royaux et municipaux qui se percoivent dans chacun des trois départements de la Colonie ne puissent être nommés et choisis que par les assemblées provinciales, à la charge par chaque département de demeurer Responsable, comme nous y consentons, de la solvabilité des receveurs qui auront

ARCHIVES SECT. LÉG. NATIONALES

D/XXV/13

d° 122

VUE DES 40. JOURS D'INCENDIE DES HABITATIONS DE LA PLAINE DU CAP F

Arrivée le 23. Aout 1791. Vieux style.

ABOVE J. B. Chapuy (1760–1802) after J. L. Boquet. *Vue des 40 Jours d'Incendie des Habitations de la Plaine du Cap Français*, 1793. Colored copper-plate engraving. 27 × 35 in. (68.58 × 88.9 cm). Collection of Dr. Fritz Daguillard.

Saint-Domingue in the late eighteenth century was per square mile unquestionably the wealthiest place on earth, a wealth that depended upon slave labor cultivating coffee and sugar. The logic of freedom in the rhetoric of the French Revolution threatened that profitable regime. While the French in the metropole wavered on the matter of slavery, the enslaved people of Saint-Domingue took matters into their own hands. In the summer of 1791, about two hundred slaves had begun assembling and plotting in spaces associated with traditional religious practices, where bonds of solidarity were formed. While the *gens de couleur* made their case in the language of the Enlightenment, these revolutionaries sealed their oath of secrecy in a ritual that was probably of African origin. In mid-August the plot unfolded, with many nights of fire. Together perhaps a hundred thousand slaves revolted and torched more than three hundred plantations in the northern region of Le Cap. Houses were burned, whites were killed. A planter described the scene: "the fire … covered the sky with churning smoke, during the day, and at night lit up the horizon with aurora borealis … and gave all objects a livid tint of blood." [15]

The island became a focal point of the continuing battle between France and England. Toussaint Louverture, the great leader of the revolution, at first sided with the Spanish to fight off the British. He wanted freedom within the French empire rather than independence, but freedom alone required a battle with the French army sent by Napoleon and commanded by his brother-in-law, Charles-Victor-Emmanuel Leclerc. Leclerc would die in Saint-Domingue, but not until after he made an agreement with Toussaint that ended the fighting. Toussaint may have agreed to end the war because the peace of Amiens between England and France, ratified in March 1802, meant he could not hope for a British alliance. Toussaint also agreed to go to France for further negotiations, but he was arrested upon arrival and jailed, where he soon thereafter died.

John Adams, the second president of the United States and leader of a party hostile to France, had earlier provided Toussaint with essential supplies, including military items. Through a special envoy to Toussaint, he indicated that the United States would not oppose a declaration of independence. By the time Jean-Jacques Dessalines, a successor to Toussaint, did declare the independence of Haiti in 1804, Adams's successor, Thomas Jefferson, was president. He not only refused recognition, but he embargoed all trade with Haiti to restrict black sailors from spreading the word of a successful slave revolt. The events in Haiti also moved Jefferson to urge legislation ending the importation of slaves in 1808,

OPPOSITE News of the revolution in Saint-
Domingue came to Americans quickly through
newspaper accounts like this one. *Aurora
General Advertiser* (Philadelphia), October 11,
1791. Library Company of Philadelphia.

the earliest date allowed by the Constitution. Ironically, Jefferson's greatest achievement as president was the gift of Haiti's Toussaint Louverture: the opportunity to purchase Louisiana at a bargain price. In Napoleon's mind Louisiana was the breadbasket that would supply foodstuffs for the enormously profitable colony of Saint-Domingue. Without the island, there was little need for Louisiana.

The historian Henry Adams, grandson of one president, and great-grandson of another, wrote in his study of the Jefferson and Madison administrations that this purchase equaled in importance the framing and ratification of the Constitution. And it was, he declared, a gift of the Haitian Revolution, adding that "prejudice of race alone blinded the American people to the debt they owed to the desperate courage of five hundred thousand Haytian negroes who would not be enslaved."[16]

The sequence of eighteenth-century revolutions that began with the revolt of the thirteen American colonies came to a close with Haiti. But the anti-colonial and republican aspirations of the eighteenth century persisted, and the ultimately successful Spanish American moves for independence began in the context of Napoleon's invasion of Spain in 1808. His removal of the Spanish king, to whom the colonies had owed their loyalty, opened the door to independence for all of Spain's continental colonies between 1810 and 1825. So the last phase of the Atlantic Revolutions, like the first, was framed and prompted by the circumstances of the prolonged global war between France and England, which came to an end only in 1815, with the final defeat of Napoleon. And it was not until then that the United States itself achieved practical independence from Great Britain. Before that the English had maintained forts in the Ohio Valley and, along with Spain in Florida, had encouraged Indian attacks and sought to lure western settlements away from the union.

The idea that the American Revolution and early American history generally was part of a larger age of revolutions is both an old but lost idea and a re-emerging one. The classic nineteenth-century historians of the United States—George Bancroft, Francis Parkman, and Henry Adams—were aware of the North Atlantic connections of American history generally, though compared to current scholarship they slighted Africa and South America. Some historians carried on this cosmopolitan historiography: W. E. B. DuBois in particular understood the larger dimensions of American history, beginning with his Harvard dissertation on the suppression of the Atlantic slave trade and in his later interest in Pan-Africanism.[17] Similarly, the historian Herbert E. Bolton in his presidential address which the French papers attribute the journey of that Sovereign to Aix-la-Chapelle.

RICHMOND, Oct. 1.

Extract of a letter from a gentleman in Bourdeaux, to his friend in this city, dated July 29, 1791.

"We refer you to our last, of 1st ult. since which, capt. Corran, of the Mary, delivered us a letter from you, of the 13th do. covering bill of lading, and invoice for 279 hogsheads of tobacco, and a parcel of staves, we are sorry to inform you, that the sale of the tobacco will meet with some difficulty. Mr. Fenwick, the American Consul, has informed officially against the Mary, as by not coming direct from America, he thinks her cargo should not be admitted to entry for home consumption ; in consequence, the director of the custom house has refused to accept the inward duties thereon, and we have landed it under bond, for exportation ; the whole lies in the interpretation of a clause in the new law, which says, that American tobacco can only be imported in French or American bottoms coming *direct* from America ; the question is, whether a vessel from the United States, that touches at an out port for orders, or advices, without breaking bulk is not to be considered as coming direct from America ? We are within the pale of the law, but the American Consul differs widely with us, and pretends, that the cargo of an American vessel, which from any motive whatsoever, may have touched at an out port, ought not to be admitted to a sale in France; it is strange, and we cannot help expressing our astonishment, that it should be your Consul, who is so very strenuous in creating and multiplying these difficulties to his countrymen, whereas we think his business should be to remove them. He has upon these late occasions, summoned at different times, the captains and crews of the same vessels, and has made them undergo a kind of inquisitorial examination—he has even called for the bills of lading and log-book, he says he acts by order of Mr. Jefferson. The matter cannot remain long in suspense—we have not been inactive in the business, and will push it on with all the spirit in our power : we have already petitioned the National Assembly on the subject, have protested against the director of the customs, and made him responsible for the consequences of the delay. There are two other vessels in the same predicament, one of which is to our address, you shall in course be advised the result.

Philadelphia, (Tuesday,)
OCTOBER 11.

St. DOMINGO DISTURBANCES.

The following concise and connected account of the late disturbances at St. Domingo, from their origin down to the latest intelligence recived from that island, is taken from a Journal kept there, handed to us by an obliging Correspondent, and translated for the GENERAL ADVERTISER.

(Concluded from our last.)

Sept. 1. There has been an engagement in the upper part of the Cape. About 60 negroes were killed. A mulatto and two negroes, after the engagement, advanced, and asked to parley with the General.—He came forward, and they were asked what they wanted. They answered that they required perfect liberty for all the negroes ; —the two negroes were killed, and the mulatto was suffered to escape.

A free negro, named Cappe, made his appearance on the plantation *Lambert* near the city, to encourage the negroes to revolt. He has been seized, and it is expected much will be learnt from him.

2. Two whites have been stopped, together with a Spanish mulatto. Their names were given up by Cappe ; who has given an account of the intended plot. He says that in the night of the 25th ult. all the negroes in the plain were to attack the city in different parts ; to be seconded by the negroes in the city, who were to set fire to

---

fired with effect ; but unfortunately their firing was stopped by a ball which was not perfectly round sticking in the piece. They were in danger of being taken and sent to camp for assistance. They received it with difficulty and with some loss retired.

A detachment of 60 dragoons having set out upon an expedition, the commander was killed, having fallen in with a powerful body of negroes. —The dragoons thought fit to retire.

6. An instance of unexampled courage.——A dragoon in the Army of M. de Rouvray, in the midst of action perceived a negro carrying off a standard belonging to the whites, he pursues him full speed, darts through the body of negroes, who were flying, striking to the right and left, follows up his man, perceives him enter a house filled with negroes, he does not desist, pursues, arrives. Eight steps at the entrance of the house do not stop him, he ascends them and enters on horseback, sword in hand, and in the midst of a croud, singles out the negro he was pursuing, kills him on the spot, and returns to camp with the standard. ——Another instance of great courage.—A mulattoe belonging to the army of the upper part of the Cape, sets off alone, arrives at a large house crouded with negroes, perceives a number assembled in a hall, he lifts up the blind, fires his pistols ; —he is attacked by a number, he cuts his way through them and arrives at camp.

The negroes have several pieces of Artillery in their camp on the heights of the Cape. The negroes of four plantations in the quarter *Morin*, who hitherto had remained quiet, yesterday revolted, in the engagement at *Petite Ance*, and have joined the body of insurgents.

7. An engagement in the heights of the Cape, in which the mulattoes killed 15 negroes and took several horses.

8. A detachment of 120 men of the army returned from *Mornet*, 5 leagues from the Cape. They brought with them several carts full of women and goods. In their route they had several engagements with the negroes, in which they were generally successful. On the 7th they killed several negroes and a white chief, and also took a white man, who was said to be a deserter from the regiment of Port-au-Prince, and the son of a former President of Parliament in France.

A mulatto girl and four negroes were also taken in this engagement. The girl was questioned—She says that those at the head of government in the island are concerned in the plot. The negroes declared the same thing. Their declarations make no impression. They have been executed.

10. In the night the negroes set fire to an outhouse in the plantation *Breda*. They attacked the camp in three different places ; they were with difficulty driven back—three whites were wounded. Ten of their number were killed, and fifteen taken prisoners. Two whites taken yesterday among the negroes at *Pont Margot* have been brought to town.

11. A negro taken yesterday in the heights of the Cape, has declared, that the rebels in that quarter, have eight pieces of artillery.

The armed boat sent to dislodge the negroes who had taken possession of a battery on the seashore, returned to day. She fired 250 times without effect, because her pieces were not of heavy metal enough. The negroes made use of the bullets fired at them—they fired them back from their 24 pounders with effect, struck the armed boat, which was obliged to retire, in a very leaky condition. No lives were lost.

12. The Spaniards of St. Domingo, have just returned an answer to the General's request : they are unwilling to lend any assistance. They advise that they have stopped a white man who was flying. They suspect him to be guilty—have confined him, and offer to give him up.

M. de Rouvray writes, that in an engagement he has killed a number of negroes, and among the rest one of their first leaders. He had him buried ; but the negroes took him up and buried him again with great pomp. They wear mourning. He thinks he will soon be able to overcome

---

I have the honor to be, with the most cordial affection, sir, your most obedient, humble servant,
(Signed) Pl. de Caduſch, president.

Letter from the President of the General Assembly of the General Assembly of Jamaica.

Cap-Francois, Aug. 31, 1791.

Gentlemen,

WE hope you have felt yourselves interested in our misfortunes. Each day we expect the arrival of the succours, which we have requested of you ; and still we fear they will arrive too late. We feel, indeed, for some persons, who present themselves, to defend us, and we hope that others will do the same, when our neighbours are acquainted with our distresses ; but we are in want of arms. This circumstance has induced the Assembly to pass a decree, authorizing me to entreat you, gentlemen, to endeavour to procure them for us. Fifteen thousand muskets would not be too many. Come to our assistance, and, by your protection, preserve this beautiful country from being laid entirely waste with fire and sword. The inhabitants of St. Domingo expect every thing from you, as from brethren.

I have the honor to be, with the most cordial and brotherly affection, gentlemen, your most obedient servant,
(Signed)
Pl. de Caduſch, president.

Aug. 28. It being represented to the General Assembly, that the Captains of vessels bound to Cape-Francois might, by the informations of the pilots, be induced to proceed to the lower parts of the island ;—the Assembly decreed, that the Lieut. Governor should be requested to send an armed vessel, of sufficient force, to cruise at the head of the island, and oblige all vessels, bound for St. Domingo, punctually to follow their original destination.

Cape-Francois, Sept. 2.

Several merchants who had previous to the disturbances shipped produce, and dollars, for France, finding themselves suddenly reduced to such a situation, as to be unable to wait for the usual returns, wished to have their produce relanded. Their desire not being complied with, they petitioned the General Assembly, who passed a decree, authorizing the Captains of the vessels to deliver up the property to the owners, on receiving payment for loading the same.

John Baptiste Cap, one of the chiefs of the insurgents, was arrested by a Negro, of the name of John, who, in return for this service, was rewarded with his liberty, and a medal with an honorable inscription, and a pension of 300 livres a year, for life.

Sept. 3. On a representation of the evil produced in St. Domingo, by the licentiousness of the press, the Assembly passed a provisional decree, prohibiting the sale, importation, or distribution of any pieces relative to the political revolution of France,—until their body should form a definitive decision respecting the liberty of the press.

Sept. 4. A letter from the municipality of the Quarter of Ennery, gave the most satisfactory account of the courage and activity of the inhabitants of that quarter, which with two hundred men of the troops of Port-au-Prince, had prevented the enemy from penetrating to the Westward.

Sept. 9. A letter from France, was read in the General Assembly, giving information that fifty armed ships were coming to St. Domingo, to raise insurrections among the slaves ; and that Mr. Raymond, the promoter of the decree of the 15th of May, was making numerous levies of rogues and ragamuffins in the streets of Paris. The letter severely taxed Messieurs Petion, Robertspierre, Gregoire, members of the National Assembly, as dangerous enemies to the colonies.

The Assembly thereupon passed a decree, ordaining that every emigrant from France should be sent back to the mother country, at the expense of the colony, unless he possessed a property in the island, or was the father, brother, son, or nephew of some person possessed of property in it.

An aged planter having petitioned for leave to remove to New-England, with his family, and some domestics, obtained permission, except that his niece was prevented to embark with him, as she was the wife of another citizen.

Some of the insurgents, who have been made prisoners, charge certain of the executive officers, as accomplices in the insurrection.

Translated from the COURIER de L'EUROPE.

Extract of a letter from Vienna, July 11.

" Since the project of the King of France's invasion has failed, it is very possible that the Emperor will see in an attack against France, a measure contrary to sound policy, and to the administration of our finances.

" Before the war against the Turks the national debt amounted to about 360 millions of florins. This sum, however enormous for the Austrian monarchy it may appear, has been augmented according to the statement I have seen, by 250 millions of florins. It appears therefore that it would prove prejudicial to our interest to engage in a war with the French, who would undoubtedly find within themselves, every means of resistance, and perhaps of attack, whilst we should be obliged to transport our troops, our ammunition, and all other implements of war, at an immense ex-

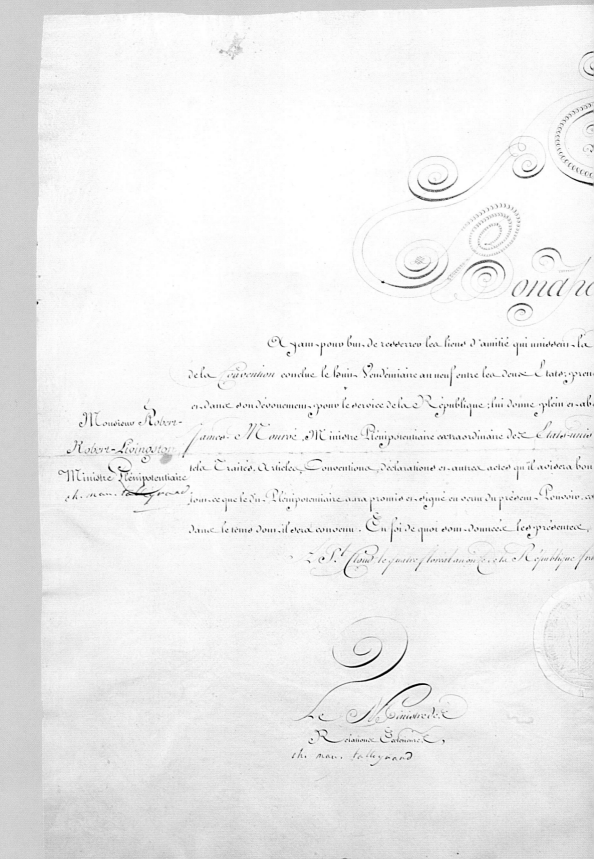

Monsieur Robert-
Robert-Livingston
Ministre Plénipotentiaire
ch. mau. talleyrand

Bonaparte

Ayant pour but de resserrer les liens d'amitié qui unissent la ...

de la Convention conclue le huit Vendémiaire an neuf entre les deux États; pren...

... dame son dévouement pour le service de la République; lui donne plein et ab...

... James Monroe, Ministre Plénipotentiaire extraordinaire des États-unis ...

... de la France, Traités, Articles, Conventions, déclarations et autres actes qu'il avisera bon ...

... pour ce que le dit Plénipotentiaire aura promis et signé en vertu du présent Pouvoir, a...

... dame le tems dont il sera convenu. En foi de quoi sont données les présentes...

... à S.t Cloud le quatre floréal an onze de la République fra...

Le Ministre des
Relations Extérieures,
ch. mau. talleyrand

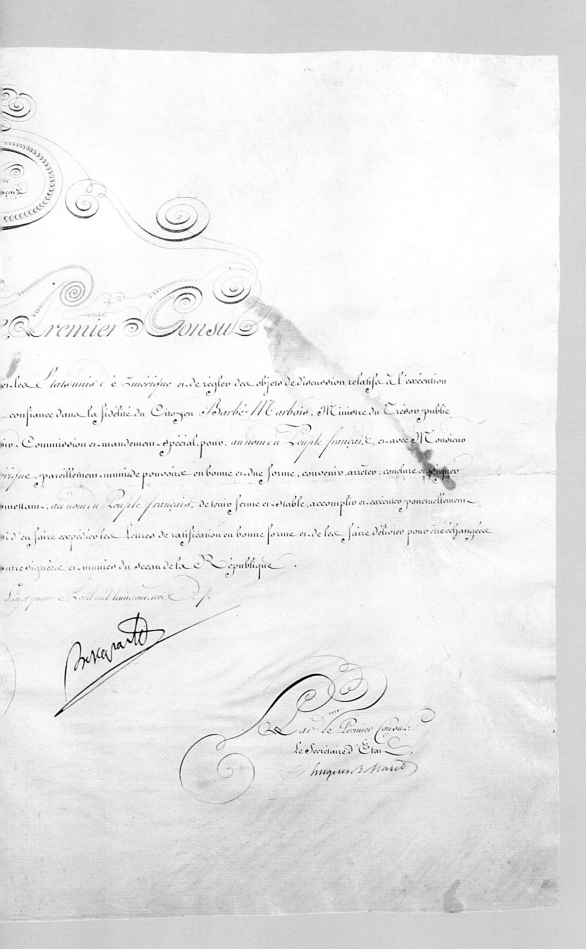

... Premier Consul

... les Etatsunis d'Amérique et de régler des objets de discussion relatifs à l'exécution

... confiance dans la fidélité du Citoyen Barbé-Marbois, Ministre du Trésor public

... Commission et mandement spécial pour, au nom du Peuple français, et avec Monsieur

... pareillement muni de pouvoirs en bonne et due forme, convenir, arrêter, conclure et signer

... mettant au nom du Peuple français, de tenir ferme et stable, accomplir et exécuter ponctuellement

... et en faire expédier les Lettres de ratification en bonne forme et de les faire délivrer pour être échangées

... être signées et munies du sceau de la République.

... Vingt quatre avril mil huit cent trois.

Bonaparte

Par le Premier Consul:
le Secrétaire d'État
Hugues B. Maret

to the American Historical Association in 1932 envisioned a common history of the Americas, "The Epic of Greater America."[18] In the 1940s, recognizing the emergence of the United States as the dominant power in the world, two different committees of historians, with the encouragement and support of the U.S. government and the Rockefeller Foundation, proposed that American history be taught in a way that engaged students in its interconnection with world history. A campaign mounted by various organizations—ranging from the Daughters of the American Revolution, to the National Association of Manufacturers, to more than half of the college presidents in the country—opposed what they considered a dilution of American history by including material beyond the territorial borders of the United States. The critics, aided and abetted by the *New York Times*, felt this more cosmopolitan American history would weaken both American identity and resolve during the perilous times of World War II and the subsequent Cold War.[19]

These concerns produced a trend in American historical writing that celebrated "American exceptionalism."[20] The United States, it was presumed, did not share a history with the rest of the world. It was thus exceptional, against the norm. Unlike other nations, there were supposedly no class issues and social conflict. The scholarship of the 1950s and early 1960s was thus given the name "consensus" history by its critics.[21] Exceptionalism and consensus history had the effect of isolating United States history from the larger history it in fact shared with other nations.

It should be said that the idea that history and the nation were somehow fused dates from the invention of the modern nation-state and the professionalization of historical study in universities in the nineteenth century. Not only did the two develop simultaneously, but they were partners in Germany, where the first generation of American professional historians was trained. History served to make national citizens by providing a past and a collective memory that all could share, thus sustaining the notion of a national community as a source of one's identity. That the nation was the natural subject and carrier of history was part of the professional culture of the discipline of history. This understanding was evident in historical scholarship on both sides of the Atlantic, and those parts of the world (then the greater part) that were colonized were thus outside of history as defined by the profession. They were the domain of anthropology. Thus the peoples of most of Asia, Africa, and the Caribbean were excluded from history as understood in academe, as they were ruled as colonies by European nation-empires and thus not themselves nations.

However, in the 1950s a specific interest in Atlantic history emerged. Partly the reasons were internal to the historical profession. The great work of the French historian Fernand Braudel on *La Méditerranée et le monde méditerranée à l'époque de Philippe II* (1949) prompted the idea of a history of the Atlantic to match that of the Mediterranean.[22] But the immediate impetus for the emergence of an Atlantic perspective in history was the Cold War. The North Atlantic Treaty Organization, a Euro-American Cold War alliance, was created in 1949, and it encouraged both political scientists and historians to think about a North Atlantic community as sharing a common history.[23]

A distinguished American historian of the French Revolution, Robert R. Palmer, took up the challenge, as did his French colleague and friend Jacques Godechot.[24] Palmer's was the more ambitious effort, a two-volume work, *The Age of Democratic Revolution* (1958–64).[25] These pioneering works were limited in their geographies, which, like NATO, embraced only the North Atlantic—Europe and North America. Palmer's volumes, with more than 1000 pages, had no entry in the index for Haiti.[26] This did not surprise the Haitian anthropologist Michel-Rolfe Trouillot, who insightfully observed that Haiti "entered history with the peculiar characteristic of being unthinkable even as it happened."[27] The new scholarship on the Atlantic world and the Atlantic revolutions has recognized that the three revolutions had both a common history and unique individual histories. With this new perspective it has become easier to grasp the importance of the Haitian Revolution for American history.[28]

Until the 1990s, Palmer's work was admired more than it was emulated, but then large changes ramified through the discipline. Today, scholarship on the Atlantic world flourishes, and it embraces all four continents with Atlantic shores.[29] European colonizers, once the whole story, are now less central. The study of indigenous peoples in both Africa and the Americas has vastly increased, and even the story of the Atlantic transit has changed. It has been recognized that it was not primarily a European experience. Before 1820, five times more Africans than Europeans made the crossing to the Americas.[30] Palmer's focus on the democratic character of the revolutions has also been challenged, or, better, modified. The three eighteenth-century Atlantic revolutions were not democratic in their immediate outcomes, and none of the leading figures who consolidated the new nations wanted to establish democracies. None had universal suffrage. Yet the logic of the age of revolution pointed to a rejection of hierarchy in favor of equality and an embrace of citizenship rather than subjecthood.

What accounts for the historiographical shift? Developments in the United States and around the world in the 1980s and 1990s changed the historical imagination. A new way of thinking about history crystallized, a way that realistically recognized that national histories were internally differentiated or diverse and they were part of larger histories. This understanding was prompted by simultaneous discussions of multiculturalism and globalization in the closing years of the twentieth century. In the context of those discussions, it seemed that for the sake of verisimilitude national histories should be comprised of histories smaller than the nation (the complex play of class, regions, racial and ethnic groups, gender difference, and so on) *and* histories larger than the nation, extending in some cases to encompass the globe.[31] Just as history includes long durations as well as immediate events, it is constituted by the interplay of multiple geographical scales. The point here is not to abandon or dilute national history, but rather to enrich it by revealing the ways in which historical causation operates across space as well as through time. The age of revolution as presented here reflects these changes in historical scholarship.

Notes

1   Biographical information from Karen Racine, *Francisco de Miranda: A Transatlantic Life in the Age of Revolution* (Wilmington, Del.: SR Books, 2007).

2   Quoted in John Lynch, "The Origins of Spanish American Independence," in Leslie Bethel, ed., *Independence of Latin America* (Cambridge History of Latin America, Vol. 3; Cambridge, Eng.: Cambridge Univ. Press, 1987), 46.

3   Thomas Bender, Introduction, Alexis de Toqueville, *Democracy in America*, ed. Thomas Bender (New York: Modern Library College Edition, 1981).

4   Hannah Arendt, *On Revolution* (New York: Penguin, 1975), 46.

5   Quoted in Horst Dippel, "The American Revolution and the Modern Concept of 'Revolution'," in Eric Angermann, ed., *New Wine in Old Skins: A Comparative View of Socio-Political Structures and Values Affecting the American Revolution* (Stuttgart, 1976), 117–18.

6   Jeremy Adelman, *Sovereignty and Revolution in the Iberian Atlantic* (Princeton: Princeton Univ. Press, 2006), 50.

7   Wim Klooster, *Revolutions in the Atlantic World: A Comparative History* (New York: NYU Press, 2009), 57.

8   On the global circulation of the U.S. Declaration of Independence, see David Armitage, *The Declaration of Independence: A Global History* (Cambridge: Harvard Univ. Press, 2007).

9   Ibid., 59.

10   Laurent Dubois, *Avengers of the New World: The Story of the Haitian Revolution* (Cambridge: Harvard Univ. Press, 2004), 1.

11   David Walker, *Appeal to the Colored Citizens of the World* (orig. 1829; New York: Hill & Wang, 1965), 21.

12   Thomas Jefferson to James Monroe, July 14, 1793, in Paul L. Ford, ed., *The Writings of Thomas Jefferson* (New York: G. P. Putnam, 1892–99), 6:349–50. One cannot help speculating whether it is relevant that these thoughts appeared on the fourth anniversary of Bastille Day.

13   Quoted in Winthrop Jordan, *White Over Black: American Attitudes Toward the Negro, 1550–1812* (Chapel Hill: Univ. of North Carolina Press, 1968), 386.

14   Quoted in Charles C. Tansill, *The United States and Santo Domingo* (Baltimore: Johns Hopkins Univ. Press, 1938), 121–22.

15   Quoted in DuBois, *Avengers of the New World*, 95.

16   Henry Adams, *History of the United States During the Administration of Jefferson and Madison* (orig. ed. 1889–91; New York: Library of America, 1986), 1:311. In the twentieth century, the connection between the Haitian Revolution and the Louisiana Purchase was obscured and forgotten, beginning with an article by William M. Sloan, "The World Aspects of the Louisiana Purchase," *American Historical Review*, 9 (1904), 507–21.

17   W. E. B. DuBois, *The Suppression of the African Slave-Trade to the United States of America, 1628–1870* (New York: Longmans, Green & Co., 1896).

18   Herbert E. Bolton, "The Epic of Greater America," *American Historical Review* 38 (1933): 448–74.

19   See Ian R. Tyrrell, "The Threat of Deprovincializing U.S. History in World War II: Allan Nevins and the *New York Times* to the Rescue," *Amerikanstudien/American Studies*, I (2003), 41–59; Thomas Bender, "Can National History be De-Provincialized? U.S. History Textbook Controversies in the 1940s and 1990s," *Contexts* 1 (2009): 28–41.

20   Daniel T. Rodgers, "Éxceptionalism," in Anthony Mohlo and Gordon S. Wood, eds., *Imagined Histories: American Historians Interpret the Past* (Princeton: Princeton Univ. Press, 1998), 21–40.

21   John Higham, "The Cult of the 'American Consensus': Homogenizing Our History," *Commentary* 27 (1959): 93–100; Higham. "Beyond Consensus: The Historian as Moral Critic," *American Historical Review* 67 (1962): 609–25.

22   His classic was published in English as *The Mediterranean and the Mediterranean World in the Age of Philip II* (New York: Harper, 1972).

23   On the postwar beginnings of a historiography of the Atlantic World, see Bernard Bailyn, *Atlantic History* (Cambridge: Harvard Univ. Press, 2005). There have been many recent critiques of Bailyn's own understanding of and practice of Atlantic history, but he was there at the creation and his account of the origins is sound.

24   Jacques Godechot, *Les Révolutions (1770–1799)* (Paris: Presses universitaires de France, 1963), translated as *France and the Atlantic Revolutions of the Eighteenth Century*, trans. Herbert Rowan (New York, 1965).

25   Robert R. Palmer, *The Age of Democratic Revolution: A Political History of Europe and America, 1760–1800*, 2 vols. (Princeton: Princeton Univ. Press, 1959–64).

26   Palmer's second volume had two unindexed paragraphs mentioning Haiti. In Godechot's *Les Révolutions* Saint-Domingue is discussed *inter alia* in four paragraphs (pp. 380–81) as part of a general discussion of the Caribbean. Haiti does not appear in the index for the English edition, but the same passages, reduced to one long paragraph, are there.

27   Michel-Rolfe Trouillot, *Silencing the Past: Power and the Production of History* (Boston: Beacon, 1995), 73. One should take note of the broadly framed history of the Haitian Revolution by the brilliant Afro-Trinidadian essayist, socialist theorist, and historian C. L. R. James, *Black Jacobins: Toussaint L'Ouverture and the Santo Domingo Revolution* (New York: Vintage Books, 1989), originally published in 1938, but only recognized as a classic by the mainstream of the profession in our own time.

28   Thomas Bender, "The Age of Revolution," *New York Times*, July 1, 2001.

29   There are even textbooks. See Douglas R. Egerton, Alison Games, Jane G. Landers, Kris Lane, and Donald R. Wright, *The Atlantic World* (Wheeling, Ill.: Harlan Davidson, 2007); Jorge Cañizares Esquerra and Erik Seeman, eds., *The Atlantic in Global History, 1500–2000* (Englewood Cliffs, N.J.: Prentice-Hall, 2006).

30   Howard Temperly, "Wealth of a Nation," *Times Literary Supplement*, April 9, 2004, 7.

31   Thomas Bender, "Historians, the Nation, and the Plentitude of Narratives," in Thomas Bender, ed., *Rethinking American History in a Global Age* (Berkeley: Univ. of California Press), 1–21. For two synthetic narratives using a global framework for American history, see Thomas Bender, *A Nation Among Nations: America's Place in World History* (New York: Hill & Wang, 2006); Ian R. Tyrrell, *Transnational Nation: United States History in Global Perspective since 1789* (Basingstoke, Hants., Eng.: Palgrave Macmillan, 2007). For the first textbook, see Carl Guarneri, *America in the World: United States History in Global Context* (Boston: McGraw Hill, 2007).

Insurgents before Independence: The Revolution of the American People

T. H. Breen

COMMON SENSE,

ADDRESSED TO THE

INHABITANTS

OF

AMERICA,

On the following interesting

CATO.

ACT I. SCENE I.

Portius, Marcus.

Por. THE Dawn is over-caft, the Morning low'rs,
And heavily in Clouds brings on the Day,
The great, th' important Day ; big with the Fate
Of *Cato* and of *Rome.*——Our Father's Death
Would fill up all the Guilt of Civil War,
And clofe the Scene of Blood.   Already *Cæfar*
Has ravaged more than half the Globe, and fees
Mankind grown thin by his deftructive Sword :
Should he go further, Numbers would be wanting
To form new Battels, and fupport his Crimes.
Ye Gods, what Havock does Ambition make
Among your Works !
  Marc. Thy fteddy Temper, *Portius,*
Can look on Guilt, Rebellion, Fraud, and *Cæfar,*
In the calm Lights of mild Philofophy ;
I'm tortured, ev'n to Madnefs, when I think
On the proud Victor : ev'ry Time he's named
Pharfalia rifes to my View——I fee

B

Th' In-

ithout the sacrifices of ordinary Americans, the Revolution would not have succeeded. Their mobilization in support of radical change reminds us that the origins of our political culture involved more than the writings and experiences of a few privileged gentlemen whom we identify as founding fathers.[1] This claim is not intended to discount the leadership of men such as George Washington, John Adams, and Thomas Jefferson. Rather, as we think comparatively about the revolutions that transformed Europe and America during the last decades of the eighteenth century, we should restore the people to the history of opposition to imperial rule and the birth of new republics. Americans—like the French and Haitians a few years later—insisted that the people themselves possessed fundamental political rights. These rights came not as a gift from traditional rulers, and certainly not from monarchs such as George III or Louis XVI. They were a birthright. This powerfully liberating doctrine, which we often take for granted, energized popular resistance to entrenched authority throughout the Atlantic world.[2]

Hints of tension between Great Britain and its mainland colonies came initially from an unlikely source. The early years of the eighteenth century witnessed the development of a highly self-confident, prosperous provincial elite. In each colony the composition of the ruling group varied. In some areas wealthy planters dominated the political culture. In other regions one encountered successful merchants and lawyers. But whatever their economic interests, the members of these local elites effectively ran the colonial governments, often with the full cooperation of appointed royal governors. Crown administrators quickly learned that American gentlemen elected to colonial assemblies richly rewarded British officials who chose not to interfere in local matters such as the granting of western land. Cozy political relationships of this sort helped promote a local sense of self-government within an imperial framework.[3]

Ordinary white Americans generally shared the political values of the ruling gentry. They, too, believed that in comparison with people who lived in New Spain or French Canada, they enjoyed greater prosperity and freedom. Moreover, they praised Great Britain for championing the Protestant faith in the contest against the world's Catholic powers. Colonial Americans wove these political assumptions into a compelling political identity known as imperial nationalism or provincial patriotism. They came to

OPPOSITE Joseph Addison, *Cato: A Tragedy.* London: Printed for J. Tonson, 1713. New-York Historical Society, PR 3304.C36 1713.

believe that they were just as important to the empire as were the king's subjects who happened to reside in other parts of the world, including England. Americans showed no reluctance in running up huge debts by purchasing consumer goods from the mother country; they generously contributed money and manpower to Britain's wars against France.[4] The first issue of a New Hampshire newspaper published in 1764 captured the defiant spirit of provincial patriotism. The editor insisted that his new journal provided the means by which "the spirited *Englishman*, the mountainous *Welshman*, the brave *Scotchman*, and *Irishman,* and the loyal *American*, may be firmly united and mutually RESOLVED to guard the glorious Throne of BRITANNIA …. Thus Harmony may be happily restored, Civil War disappointed, and each agree to embrace, as *British Brothers*, in defending the Common Cause."[5]

The powerful attraction of Britishness at mid-century, and the contributions that the colonists willingly made for the empire during the long wars against France, help explain the fury unleashed when Americans discovered that their "*British Brothers*" actually regarded them as lesser beings. The resentment fueled by finding themselves treated as second-class subjects initially angered elite colonists more than it did their ordinary neighbors.[6] Parliament most certainly did not anticipate such a stormy reaction. Deeply troubled by a rapidly rising national debt after the Seven Years' War, British leaders vowed to find ways to generate new revenue in America. They passed taxes—the most objectionable being the Sugar Act (1764), the Stamp Act (1765), and the Townshend Acts (1767)—and then enforced their collection with unprecedented vigor. The claim that Parliament held undisputed sovereignty over the Americans sparked several violent urban protests, but during the 1760s, educated, wealthy gentlemen voiced the loudest protests against the imperial structure.

For the members of the colonial gentry, the deepest pain resulted from a profound sense of rejection. British administrative reforms threatened their comfortable existence. Unless one comprehends the growing conviction that taxation without representation amounted to a form of cultural humiliation, one cannot understand the hyperbolic rhetoric uttered during this period by American leaders. These expressions of a political identity, born of perceived discrimination, contained the seeds of revolutionary nationalism: in other words, the origins of a belief that Americans were in fact different from their British brothers and that this difference warranted pride. "We won't be their Negroes," announced the promising young lawyer John Adams, writing as "Humphrey Ploughjogger." Like other educated and ambitious colonial leaders of

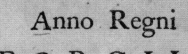

Anno Regni

GEORGII III.

REGIS

Magnæ Britanniæ, Franciæ, & Hiberniæ,

QUINTO.

At the Parliament begun and holden at *Westminster*, the Nineteenth Day of *May, Anno. Dom.* 1761, in the First Year of the Reign of our Sovereign Lord *GEORGE* the Third, by the Grace of God, of *Great-Britain, France,* and *Ireland,* King, Defender of the Faith, *&c.*

And from thence continued by several Prorogations to the Tenth Day of *January,* 1765, being the Fourth Session of the Twelfth Parliament of *Great-Britain.*

LONDON:

Printed by *Mark Baskett,* Printer to the King's Most Excellent Majesty: And, re-printed by *James Parker,* in the Province of *New-Jersey.*

from feveral Counties to them referred, and had come to two Refolutions thereon, which he read in his Place, and then delivered in at the Table, where they were again read, and are as follow:

Refolved, That it is the Opinion of this Committee that the feveral Petitions of fundry Inhabitants of the Counties of *King* and *Queen, Caroline,* and *Effex,* complaining of the great Expenfe, Trouble, and Lofs of Time, Suitors are put to in attending the Trial of their Caufes in the General Court, and alfo of the great Expenfe and Trouble occafioned by carrying Criminals with their Venires and Witneffes for Trial at the General Court, and praying that the Bill prefented to a former Seffion of Affembly To eftablifh a more eafy and expeditious Method for the Trial of Criminals, and of Caufes depending in the General Court, or fome other of the fame Nature, may pafs into a Law, be rejected.

Refolved, That it is the Opinion of this Committee that that Part of the Petition of Capt. *Richard Pearis,* praying to be allowed for Horfes and Pack Saddles furnifhed by him for an Expedition againft the *Shawanefe* Indians, in the Year 1756, which was referred from a former Seffion to the Confideration of this Seffion of Affembly, is reafonable, and that the faid *Richard Pearis* ought to be allowed the Sum of £81.18 for the faid Horfes and Pack Saddles, to be paid by the Publick.

The *firft* Refolution being read a fecond Time, and the Queftion put that the Houfe agree thereto,

It paffed in the Negative.

Refolved, That the faid Petitions are reafonable.

The *laft* Refolution being alfo read a fecond Time, and the Queftion thereupon put that the Houfe agree thereto,

Refolved in the Affirmative.

Ordered, That the faid Committee do prepare and bring in a Bill purfuant to the Refolution of the Houfe.

Ordered, That it be an Inftruction to the Committee of Claims to make the Allowance in the Book of Claims purfuant to the laft Refolution.

Ordered, That Mr *Fitzhugh* be added to the Committee of Propofitions and Grievances, and Mr *William Wager* to the Committee of Courts of Juftice.

Mr *Attorney,* from the Committee of the whole Houfe reported, according to Order, that the Committee had had under their Confideration the State of the Colony, and the feveral Letters to them referred, and had come to feveral Refolutions thereon; which he read in his Place, and then delivered in at the Table, where they were again twice read, and agreed to, with fome Amendments, and are as follow:

Refolved, That a moft humble and dutiful Addrefs be prefented to his Majefty, imploring his Royal Protection of his faithful Subjects, the People of this Colony, in the Enjoyment of all their natural and civil Rights, as Men, and as Defcendents of *Britons;* which Rights muft be violated, if Laws refpecting the internal Government, and Taxation of themfelves, are impofed upon them by any other Power than that derived from their own Confent, by and with the Approbation of their Sovereign, or his Subftitute: And profeffing, that as thefe People have at all Times been forward and zealous to demonftrate their Loyalty and Affection to his Majefty, and efpecially by a ready Compliance with the Requifitions of the Crown to bear their Part in the late War, which they engaged to do with the more Alacrity, from a Confidence that the Royal Benignity would never fuffer them to be deprived of their Freedom (that facred Birthright and ineftimable Bleffing) fo they would be willing to contribute their Proportion of any Expenfes neceffary for the Defence and Security of *America,* as far as Circumftances of the People, already diftreffed with Taxes, would admit of, provided it were left to themfelves to raife it, by Modes leaft grievous.

Refolved, That a Memorial be prepared to be laid before the Right Hon. the Lords Spiritual and Temporal in Parliament affembled, intreating their Lordfhips, by a proper and reafonable Interpofition and Exertion of their Power, not to fuffer the People of this Colony to be enflaved or oppreffed by Laws refpecting their internal Polity, and Taxes

Taxes impofed on them in a Manner that is unconftitutional; and declaring our Hopes that the Prefervation of the Rights of any of his Majefty's faithful Subjects will be thought by their Lordfhips as an Object worthy the Attention of thofe hereditary Guardians and Protectors of *Britifh* Liberty and Property, and efpecially as the Subverfion of thofe Rights, in the Inftance of taxing the People of *Virginia,* at this Time, when they are moft grievoufly burthened by the Expenfes of the late War, muft diminifh that Confumption of Manufactures furnifhed to them by their Mother Country, by which her wealth is very greatly augmented, and her Profperity continued.

Refolved, That a Memorial be prepared to be laid before the Honourable the Houfe of Commons, to affert, with decent Freedom, the Rights and Liberties of the People of this Colony as *Britifh* Subjects, to remonftrate that Laws for their internal Government, or Taxation, ought not to be impofed by any Power but what is delegated to their Reprefentatives, chofen by themfelves, and to reprefent that the People are already taxed, for feveral Years to come, fo heavily, for Expenfes incurred in the late War, amounting to near Half a Million, that an Increafe of that Burthen by the Parliament, at this Time, would be not only a Violation of the moft facred and valuable Principle of the Conftitution, but fuch an Oppreffion as would probably draw after it a Defolation in many Parts of the Country, and muft divert thofe of the Inhabitants, who could not remove from it, to manufacture what Articles they have hitherto been fupplied with from the Mother Country, and confequently one grand Source of Wealth and Profperity will be ftopped up.

Refolved, That the Committee appointed to correfpond with the Agent of this Colony in *Great Britain* purfuant to an Act of Affembly For appointing an agent, be directed to anfwer the Letter of the 25th of *June* laft from the Committee of the Houfe of Reprefentatives of the Province of *Maffachufetts* Bay to the Honourable the Speaker of the Houfe of Reprefentatives for the Province of *Virginia,* and to affure that Committe that the Affembly of *Virginia* are highly fenfible of the very great Importance it is, as well to the Colony of *Virginia,* as to *America* in general, that the Subjects of *Great Britain* in this Part of its Dominions fhould continue in Poffeffion of their ancient and moft valuable Right of being taxed only by Confent of their Reprefentatives, and that the Affembly here will omit no Meafures in their Power to prevent fuch effential Injury from being done to the Rights and Liberties of the People.

Ordered, That a Committee be appointed to draw up the Addrefs, and Memorials, in the faid Report mentioned; and it is referred to Mr *Attorney,* Mr *Richard Henry Lee,* Mr *Landon Carter,* Mr *Wythe,* Mr *Edmund Pendleton,* Mr *Benjamin Harrifon,* Mr *Cary,* and Mr *Fleming,* to prepare and bring in the fame.

And the Houfe adjourned until To-morrow Morning 11 *o'Clock.*

Thursday. the 15th of November. 5 Geo. III. 1764.

A *Petition* of the Truftees of the Town of *Falmouth,* in the County of *King George,* fetting forth that the main Street of the faid Town is at prefent 150 Feet wide, which is more than neceffary, and that it would be a very confiderable Improvement to the faid Town if 50 feet in Breadth of the faid Street was laid off into Lots, and they empowered to fell them, and lay out the Money in other Improvements, agreeable to the Directions of the Act for eftablifhing the faid Town; and that Purchafers of Lots in the faid Town may be left at Liberty to build according to their Circumftances and Convenience, without Reftraint; and that the Inhabitants thereof may be prevented from building wooden Chimnies to their Houfes, and from fuffering Hogs to run at large therein; and praying that an Act may pafs for that Purpofe, was prefented to the Houfe and read.

Ordered

his generation, Adams insisted that Providence had never intended white Americans "for Negroes … and therefore never intended us for slaves…. I say we are as handsome as old English folks, and so should be as free."[7] James Otis, Jr., another Massachusetts lawyer, asked, "Are the inhabitants of British America all a parcel of transported thieves, robbers, and rebels, or descended from such? Are the colonists blasted lepers, whose company would infect the whole House of Commons?"[8] Like the anonymous author of an article that appeared on 8 August 1765 in the *Maryland Gazette*, colonists throughout America found themselves asking an embarrassing question of immense and cultural consequence: "Are not the People of *America*, BRITISH Subjects? Are they not *Englishmen*?"[9]

During the initial stages of the imperial controversy, educated spokesmen such as James Otis, John Dickinson, and Daniel Dulany developed a coherent defense of legislative rights. Although they did not advocate independence, they situated the American protest within an interpretive framework inspired by the Italian Renaissance and the English Civil Wars of the seventeenth century. In these societies, *liberty* had been hounded by *power*, its perpetual adversary. Liberty always seemed horribly overmatched. Power conspired against liberty, employing standing armies, press censorship, and corrupt officials to reduce free people to slavery. Within this ongoing battle, only popular *virtue* could secure liberty. For the colonial gentry republican virtue expressed itself through self-control, particularly the ability to sacrifice the pleasures of the consumer marketplace in the name of the common good. The people themselves bore the responsibility to reject the baubles of Britain—the many imported manufactured goods flowing into the colonies from England—since self-indulgence of this sort eroded liberty and encouraged tyrants to crush popular freedom.[10]

Learned colonial writers thought that Americans still possessed enough virtue to preserve their liberty. About the mother country colonial pamphleteers were less certain. The English appeared to have sold out their freedom to a venal parliament, the very body now passing arbitrary colonial taxes. How much this abstract argument ordinary Americans absorbed is impossible to measure. Highly intellectual discussions of the imperial crisis no doubt helped the members of the colonial elites to make sense of the imperial crisis. At the end of the day, however, this explanation lacked the emotional energy required to mobilize a people in a common cause.[11]

Before 1773 unhappiness about parliamentary taxation need not have sparked a genuine revolution. If British rulers had had sufficient imagination, they might have established an American

OPPOSITE *Journal of Virginia House of Burgesses,* November 14, 1764. Special Collections, University of Virginia Library, Journals of the House of Burgesses of Virginia, 1761–1765, J87. V6. 1761/1765.

parliament, which while subservient to the British parliament would have given the colonial gentry power and prestige within the imperial structure. They might, for example, have created a framework like the Dominion of Canada, which in the nineteenth century helped resolve problems of shared sovereignty. During the 1760s, accommodation would not have been difficult. Ambitious Americans eagerly chased the honors of empire. George Washington longed for a genuine commission in the British Army and rejection mortified the proud Virginian. Benjamin Franklin loved cosmopolitan London. Eager for preferment, he came late and reluctantly to the patriot movement.[12]

Like other revolutionaries in colonial societies, these American leaders found themselves between a rock and a hard place. Feeling abandoned by the empire, they were forced increasingly to speak *for* the ordinary people. However alienated from the mother country they became, they found it hard to show enthusiasm for participatory forms of republican government. In 1774, for example, Gouverneur Morris, a dashing figure in colonial society, commented on a large protest meeting in New York City at which the local gentry were trying to convince the middling and lower sorts obediently to follow patrician leadership. Morris thought it a losing proposition. "The mob begin to think and reason," he observed. "Poor reptiles! It is with them a vernal morning; they are struggling to cast off their winter's slough, they bask in the sunshine, and ere noon they will bite, depend upon it." He feared—as did other colonial gentlemen—"that if the disputes with Great Britain continue, we shall be under the worst of all possible dominions; we shall be under the dominion of a riotous mob."[13]

The drowning of the tea in Boston Harbor on December 16, 1773 radically transformed the American political landscape.[14] Before this moment the ordinary people had shown remarkable indifference to the imperial controversy. To be sure, from time to time urban artisans took to the streets to protest what they regarded as arbitrary forms of taxation. In 1765 a Boston mob registered its contempt for the Stamp Act by tearing down houses owned by crown officials. But throughout the countryside few Americans joined the resistance. The records of New England town meetings occasionally voiced support for boycotts of British imported goods, but they seldom expressed support for the more violent activities encountered in colonial cities. In fact, during the early 1770s Samuel Adams became despondent over the apparent willingness of the American people to accept taxation without representation. Politics seem to have given way to personal pleasures, and people throughout the colonies flocked to stores to purchase imported English goods, including tea, in record amounts, apparently happy that the tensions of the previous decade had dissipated like a passing summer storm.

The Tea Party forced king and parliament to take a tough stance. They really had no choice. The brazen destruction of so much private property could not go unpunished. Most Americans expected some form of chastisement. What shocked them—and what triggered an unprecedented popular mobilization—was the severity of the reprisal. During the early months of 1774 the House of Commons passed a series of statutes known collectively as the Coercive Acts (in the colonies as the Intolerable Acts).[15] They gave the Crown authority to select members of the Upper House or Council of Massachusetts, a privilege previously held by the colony's elected assembly. The Acts closed the port of Boston to all commerce. Until the people of Boston paid for the lost tea, Parliament declared that all imported goods had to land first in cities such as Salem and then hauled overland to Boston at great additional expense. The law caused massive unemployment among dockworkers. The punitive acts also prohibited all town meetings in Massachusetts except for the annual election of local officials.

The legislation struck Americans as grossly unfair. How, they asked, could Parliament punish the entire population of a colony for the alleged crimes of a few criminals who in fact had never been identified? Enforcement appeared in the form of an army of occupation. Several thousand British regulars camped out on Boston Commons, a provocative reminder that in the future, colonial resistance would involve more than gentry petitions and pamphlets. Anger replaced closely reasoned argument in the public sphere. People spoke of suffering and humiliation, and they contemplated retaliation and revenge. As one writer in the Salem newspaper announced, the mother country no longer deserved that name. Great Britain had revealed itself "more cruel than Sea-Monsters toward their young ones! Her Measures tend not only to dissolve our political union to her as a branch of the British Empire, but destroy our affection to her as the Mother State. We have petitioned, prayed, pleaded, argued &c. with her, but all in vain; she is like the deaf Adder that stops her ears, she won't hear!—What must be done?" [16]

George III and his supporters in Parliament had no doubt about how best to proceed. Like so many imperial rulers over the centuries who fear they are losing control over distant colonial subjects, British leaders decided that only a major show of force would bring Americans to their senses. One Member of Parliament informed his colleagues that he was "of opinion that the town of

ABOVE *The Colonies Reduced & Its Companion.* Etching from the *Political Register*, no. 21 (December, 1768), page size 8 × 4 ¾ in (20.3 × 12 cm). Print and Photographs Division, Library of Congress, Washington D.C., PC 1-4183 [P&P].

RIGHT *An Act for granting and applying certain Stamp Duties, and other Duties, in the British Colonies and Plantations in America*, 1765. Parliamentary Archives, London, HL/PO/PU/1/1765/5G3nii.

An Act for granting Stamp Duties and other ... Plantations in America ... the expences of defending pr... same and for amending su... Parliament relating to the ... said Colonies and Plantation... determining and recovering ... therein mentioned.

Anno 5.° Georgii 3.tii

nd applying certain ~~~?
...ies in the British Colonies
...wards further defraying~
...cting and securing the~
...Parts of the several Acts of
...ade and Revenues of the~
...as direct the manner, of ~
...he Penalties and Forfeitures

THE
FEMALE COMBATANTS

I'll force you to Obedience You Rebellious Slut

Liberty Liberty for ever Mother while I exist

FOR OBEDIENCE

FOR LIBERTY

OR WHO SHALL

Boston ought to be knocked about their ears, and destroyed." [17] The majority echoed appeals for toughness, insisting in speech after speech that the Americans had to be taught a lesson about the need to obey orders from London.

Even as the militant rhetoric grew shriller, a few skeptics who were members of Parliament asked whether an army was the best tool for dealing effectively with a political crisis. William Dowdeswell, a member of an opposition group, warned that a policy of punishment will "soon inflame all America, and stir up a contention you will not be able to pacify." George Johnstone, a former governor of West Florida and presumably a person who understood what was happening on the ground in the colonies, warned Parliament, "I must venture to predict to this House, that the effect of the present Bill must be productive of a General Confederacy, to resist the power of this country." [18] From Johnstone's perspective, an army of occupation would make matters worse by transforming ordinary Americans into insurgents.

In this belligerent atmosphere, neither the king nor his chief minister Lord North was willing to retreat. On February 4, 1774, George spoke privately with General Thomas Gage, the officer being considered to lead the British troops in America. Gage made a good impression. He told the king precisely what he wanted to hear. The general declared that the Americans "will be Lions, whilst we are Lambs, but if we take the resolute part they will undoubtedly prove very meek." [19]

Those critics who had warned that a show of military force would energize a massive insurgency were right on the mark.[20] During the summer of 1774 ordinary people throughout Massachusetts made it clear that they would no longer tolerate British oppression. In their families, churches, and town meetings they openly registered opposition to imperial rule. They expressed their anger in different ways, some of which did not initially involve violence. Many ordinary men and women came to revolution in small steps. They boycotted British goods; they refused to serve on juries. They ignored orders from militia officers who had accepted commissions from the royal governor. They sent food and money to the unemployed workers in Boston. And they gathered in town meetings to discuss the looming crisis.

Although none of these acts threatened the viability of British authority in the colony, they served to erode the bonds of loyalty that had held the empire together for a very long time. The king and his advisers ignored the fact that empires are held together as much by consent as by force—or more so. Ordinary Americans were

OPPOSITE Artist unknown. *The Female Combatants*, 1776. Etching on paper, 8⅗ × 6 in. (21.8 × 15.2 cm). The John Carter Brown Library at Brown University, 31576.

reaching out to each other in new ways. They began to develop a feeling of political solidarity. Communication through newspapers was an essential aspect of building trust. As the *Essex Gazette* reported, "The News-Papers from all Quarters, in every British American Colony, so far as we have yet received Intelligence, are chiefly filled with Accounts of Meetings and Resolutions of Towns and Counties, all to the same Purpose—complaining of Oppression, proposing a Congress, a Cessation of Intercourse with Great-Britain, and a Contribution for the Relief of the Poor of Boston."[21] Widespread literacy made it easier to mobilize the people. As Silas Deane of Connecticut explained, almost all free colonists had "some Education," and even "the very poorest" examined "Gazettes & political publications, which they read, observe upon and debate in a Circle of their Neighbors."[22]

Soon Americans resorted to violence. Throughout the Massachusetts countryside—almost two years before the Continental Congress officially declared independence—ordinary farmers forced crown officials to seek safety in Boston. Insurgents cut off the occupied port from the rest of New England. General Gage's determination to behave like a military lion in America had failed utterly to pacify the colonists. He seemed unable to comprehend the full dimensions of the popular mobilization. The Americans, he explained to his superiors in England, "deriving confidence from impunity, have added insult to outrage, have repeatedly fired upon the King's ships and subjects, with cannon and small arms, have possessed the roads, and other communications by which the town of Boston was supplied with provisions." On the distant frontier of empire, Gage confronted a rising of the people. The colonists "make daily and indiscriminate invasions upon private property, and with a wantonness of cruelty … carry depredation and distress wherever they turn their steps."[23] Lord North did not want to hear such intelligence. Even as the insurgency spread, he and the king's friends insisted that the Americans would not stand up to regular British troops.

In early September 1774, an incident occurred which demonstrated the full dimensions of popular mobilization. A series of accidents triggered a rumor that the British navy had destroyed Boston. Troops had shot innocent Americans in the streets. Within hours the story had been carried by fast riders south to Connecticut and Rhode Island and north to New Hampshire and Vermont. Without a second thought, thousands of armed men marched toward Boston determined to take their revenge on the British murderers. Everywhere one encountered "armed Men rushing forward, some on foot, some on horseback, at every house Women & Children making Cartridges, running Bullets, making Wallets, baking Biscuits, crying & bemoaning & at the same time animating their Husbands & Sons to fight for their Liberties, tho' not knowing whether they should ever see them again."[24] No one knows how many colonists responded, but contemporary records suggest the number may have been as high as 30,000. Even taking exaggeration into account, this force was the largest land army ever assembled in the New World.[25]

Of course, the insurgents soon discovered that the British had not burned Boston. Not a single colonist had been killed. But instead of showing embarrassment for having accepted a rumor as truth, ordinary Americans expressed pride in their accomplishment. "The unshaken fortitude and determined resolution to conquer or die, which appeared in all ranks on the arrival of the news, would do honor to veteran troops," concluded a witness from New London.[26] More to the point, the ordinary people had taken charge of their own revolution. They received no orders from the Continental Congress. Indeed, the popular response to a false alarm forced Congressional delegates to take a more radical uncompromising stance toward Great Britain than they would have done in other circumstances.

Within a few months a protest against parliamentary taxation without representation led initially by elite gentlemen had evolved into a popular insurgency. In this highly charged political environment, leaders of the colonial gentry found that they could no longer take the ordinary people for granted. Just how much the character of resistance had shifted became apparent when on October 20, 1774, Congress endorsed the Continental Association, which by early 1775 included a dozen colonies committed to a boycott of British goods.[27] What made this document one of the more significant acts in American history—what made it a truly radical declaration—was Article Eleven. It transferred the power to oversee the enforcement of a boycott of English manufactures to local people actually able to police the movement of imports and exports. The Association marked the establishment of an effective revolutionary infrastructure. Congress ordered "that a committee be chosen in every county, city, and town, by those who are qualified to vote for representatives in the legislature, whose business it shall be attentively to observe the conduct of all persons touching this association."[28] Not surprisingly, in the vacuum created by the collapse of imperial authority outside the occupied port cities, the committees quickly took on new responsibilities. They punished ideological enemies, and often outmaneuvered the loyalists before the king's American supporters could organize a serious counterthreat.[29]

Within only a few months—roughly from the autumn of 1774 to the spring of 1775—communities throughout America had elected committees of safety. Some groups were small, containing no more than a dozen members. But others were huge. A few committees listed over one hundred names. But however the localities defined the selection process, they brought many thousands of new men into politics. The committees served as schools of revolution, where ordinary people who had not held office during the colonial regime nor thought it their right to do so now accepted responsibility for exposing those whom the Congress labeled "the enemies of American liberty." The call to elect committees of safety generated excitement. As one newspaper reported, "It appears the inhabitants of Maryland are all in Motion, forming County Meetings, choosing *Committees of Observation* to carry into effectual Execution, without Fear, Favor or Partiality, the Measures recommended by the Grand Continental Congress."[30]

These committees—often ignored in histories of the American Revolution that focus entirely on the lives of the founding fathers—remind us of the popular foundations of our own political culture. These local groups acquired legitimacy from the Continental Congress, while at the same time boldly experimenting with participatory forms of government at the local level. More than a year before the Declaration of Independence, they served as laboratories for republican rule. Although no one at the time envisioned the development in precisely these terms, the Association effectively became a working constitution, a revolutionary framework in which a central governing body interacted productively with local units. The insurgents never questioned the need for central government. What they condemned were the policies of a corrupt Parliament. Perhaps even more important for devising a comparative analytic framework for discussing late eighteenth-century revolutions throughout the Atlantic world, the committees managed to balance the challenge of ferreting out ideological opponents against the threat that political denunciations would spark wanton bloodshed.[31]

Many Americans elected to serve on these committees probably had not read Locke or Montesquieu. But while they may not have interpreted resistance to Great Britain in highly intellectual terms, they infused abstract notions about rights and liberty with passion. They brought fear, anger, a desire for revenge, and a sense of betrayal to the revolutionary cause. Without this emotional catalyst, it is hard to understand why so many colonists sacrificed so

COMMON SENSE,

ADDRESSED TO THE

INHABITANTS

OF

AMERICA,

On the following interesting

SUBJECTS.

I. Of the Origin and Design of Government in general, with concise Remarks on the English Constitution.

II. Of Monarchy and Hereditary Succession.

III. Thoughts on the present State of American Affairs.

IV. Of the present Ability of America, with some miscellaneous Reflections.

Man knows no Master save creating HEAVEN,
Or those whom choice and common good ordain.
THOMSON.

PHILADELPHIA Printed:

NEW-YORK, Reprinted and Sold, by JOHN ANDERSON, the Corner of Beekman's-Slip.

RIGHT Thomas Paine, *Le Sens Commun: adressé aux habitans de l'Amérique*. Rotterdam: 1776. Repr. Paris: 1793. William L. Clements Library, University of Michigan, #PA 2 Co. Published in the Netherlands to evade French censorship, this translation still softened Paine's criticism of monarchy.

OPPOSITE Thomas Paine, *Gesunde Vernunft an die Einwohner von America, über folgende wichtiger Gegenstände*, Philadelphia: 1776. William L. Clements Library, University of Michigan, C1776.PA. The German translation was directed at Pennsylvania's large population of German readers.

LE SENS COMMUN,
ADDRESSÉ
AUX HABITANTS DE
L'AMÉRIQUE,
SUR LES SUJETS INTÉRESSANTS QUI
SUIVENT.

I. De l'origine & de la fin du Gouvernement en général, avec de courtes remarques sur la Constitution Angloise.
II. De la Monarchie & de la succession héréditaire.
III. Pensées sur l'état présent des affaires de l'Amérique.
IV. De la Puissance actuelle de l'Amérique; avec quelques réflexions diverses.

NOUVELLE ÉDITION,
Avec plusieurs additions dans le corps de l'ouvrage, auquel on a ajouté un
APPENDIX,
Et une Lettre au peuple Appellé QUAKERS.

NB. Cette nouvelle édition augmente l'ouvrage d'environ un tiers.

Man Knows no Master save creating heaven,
Or those whom choice and common good ordain.
THOMSON.

TRADUIT DE L'ANGLOIS.
Sur la nouvelle édition, imprimée à Philadelphie & réimprimée à Londres.

À ROTTERDAM,
CHEZ J. HOFHOUT ET E. WOLFSBERGEN,
Libraires, sur le Visscherdyk. 1776.

much resisting imperial rule. Most of these people viewed politics through the lens of evangelical Protestantism. They were children of the Great Awakening, a religious revival that swept through colonial society at mid-century.[32] It empowered ordinary people, giving them a sense of control over their own lives. God, they believed, had given people certain inalienable rights. With this gift came the responsibility to defend universal rights against tyrants.

Gesunde Vernunft

an die

Einwohner von America,

über folgende wichtige Gegenstände :

I. Von dem Ursprung und der Absicht der Regierung überhaupt, mit kurzen Anmerkungen über die Englische Landsverfassung.

II. Von Monarchie und Erbfolge.

III. Gedanken über den gegenwärtigen Zustand Americanischer Angelegenheiten.

IV. Von der jetzigen Stärke von America, mit einigen vermischten Betrachtungen.

Nebst

Einem Anhang, und einer Zuschrift an die Repräsentanten des Volks, das den Namen Quäker führet.

Der Mensch kennt keinen Herrn, als Den, der ihn erschuf,
Und die, die er sich selbst, zum Wohl des Staates, gab.

Thomson.

Aus dem Englischen übersetzt.

Philadelphia,

Gedruckt bey Melchior Steiner und Carl Cist, in der Zweyten-strasse. 1776.

Those who stood silent in the face of despotism not only suffered enslavement, but also insulted the Lord. As the Reverend Samuel Lockwood, a staunch supporter of American rights, explained: "No one can pretend that civil government, as an ordinance of GOD, was ever designed to advance men to seats of dignity and rule, to plume themselves with gilded feathers of state; in order to indulge sloth—luxury—and avarice, at publick expense, much less wantonly to exercise the power with which they are invested, in acting the tyrant."[33]

More than any other defender of American rights, Thomas Paine captured the sentiments of the ordinary people. Whatever his talents, he does not enjoy the same standing in the story of independence as do Washington, Adams, and Jefferson.[34] Paine certainly won no friends among the elite planters by criticizing the enslavement of African Americans. But he knew that successful resistance required personal courage and emotional commitment as well as intellectual justification. In *Common Sense* he asked Americans "Hath your house been burnt? Hath your property been destroyed before your face? Are your wife and children destitute of a bed to lie on, or bread to live on? Have you lost a parent or a child by their hands, and yourself the ruined and wretched survivor?" If an American could experience such atrocities and still accept the king and Parliament as legitimate symbols of political authority, "then, you are unworthy the name husband, father, friend, or lover, and whatever may be your rank or title in life, you have the heart of a coward."[35]

Like the ordinary colonists who responded so enthusiastically to such rhetoric, Paine knew that the people were fighting not simply for their own freedom. They sensed—and we should remember—that "the sun never shined on a cause of greater worth.... 'Tis not the concern of a day, a year, or an age; posterity are virtually involved in the contest, and will be more or less affected, even to the end of time, by the proceedings now."[36]

Notes

1   Among the many works that helped me develop a broader perspective on the coming of national independence are Hermann Wellenreuther, *The Revolution of the People: Thoughts and Documents on the Revolutionary Process in North America, 1774–1776* (Göttingen, Ger.: Göttingen Univ. Press, 2006); Gary B. Nash, *The Unknown American Revolution: The Unruly Birth of Democracy and the Struggle to Create America* (New York: Penguin Press, 2006); Alfred F. Young, *The Shoemaker and the Tea Party: Memory and the American Revolution* (Boston: Beacon Press, 1999); Woody Holton, *Forced Founders: Indians, Debtors, Slaves, and the Making of the American Revolution in Virginia* (Chapel Hill: Univ. of North Carolina Press, 1999); and Ray Raphael, *A People's History of the American Revolution: How Common People Shaped the Fight for Independence* (New York: W.W. Norton, 2001).

2   The most provocative comparative history of late eighteenth-century revolutions remains R. R. Palmer, *Age of the Democratic Revolutions: A Political History of Europe and America, 1760–1800*, 2 vols. (Princeton: Princeton Univ. Press, 1959–1964). On the language of rights, see Jeffrey N. Wasserstrom, Lynn Hunt, and Marilyn B. Young, eds., *Human Rights and Revolutions* (Lanham, Md.: Rowman and Littlefield, 2000); and T. H. Breen, *The Lockean Moment: The Language of Rights on the Eve of the American Revolution* (Oxford, Eng.: Oxford Univ. Press, 2001).

3   Jack P. Greene, *Quest for Power: The Lower Houses of Assembly in the Southern Royal Colonies, 1689–1776* (Chapel Hill: Univ. of North Carolina Press, 1963); James A. Henretta, *"Salutary Neglect": Colonial Administration under the Duke of Newcastle* (Princeton: Princeton Univ. Press, 1972); John A. Schutz, *William Shirley, King's Governor of Massachusetts* (Chapel Hill: Univ. of North Carolina Press, 1961); and Stanley N. Katz, *Newcastle's New York: Anglo-American Politics, 1732–1753* (Cambridge: Harvard Univ. Press, 1968).

4   See Fred Anderson, *People's Army: Massachusetts Soldiers and Society in the Seven Years' War* (Chapel Hill: Univ. of North Carolina Press, 1984); Linda Colley, *Forging the Nation 1777–1837* (New Haven: Yale Univ. Press, 1992); and T. H. Breen, "Interpreting New World Nationalism," in Don H. Doyle and Marco Antonio Pamplona, eds., *Nationalism in the New World* (Athens, Ga.: Univ. of Georgia Press, 2006), 41–60.

5   *New-Hampshire Gazette*, July 13, 1764.

6   T. H. Breen, "Ideology and Nationalism on the Eve of the American Revolution: Revisions *Once More* in Need of Revising," *Journal of American History* 84 (1997): 13–39. Also, see Frantz Fanon, *The Wretched of the Earth*, trans. Constance Farrinton (New York: Ballantine Books, 1963).

7   *Boston Gazette*, October 15, 1765.

8   James Otis, Jr., *A Vindication of the British Colonies* [1765], in *Pamphlets of the American Revolution*, ed. Bernard Bailyn (Cambridge: Harvard Univ. Press, 1965), 1:568.

9   *Maryland Gazette*, August 8, 1765.

10   Bernard Bailyn, *Ideological Origins of the American Revolution* (Cambridge: Harvard Univ. Press, 1965); and Gordon S. Wood, *Radicalism of the American Revolution* (New York: Knopf, 1992).

11   T. H. Breen, *American Insurgents, American Patriots: The Revolution of the People* (New York: Hill and Wang, 2010), Intro. (3–20) and chap. 9 (241–74).

12   Paul K. Longmore, *The Invention of George Washington* (Charlottesville: Univ. of Virginia Press, 1999), 21–48; and Gordon S. Wood, *Americanization of Benjamin Franklin* (New York: Penguin, 2004).

13   Peter Force, ed., *American Archives: Consisting of a Collection of Authentik* [sic] *Records, State Papers, Debates and Letters…*, 4th Series, 6 vols. (Washington. D.C.: 1837–53), 1:343.

14   David Ammerman, *In the Common Cause: American Response to the Coercive Acts of 1774* (Charlottesville: Univ. of Virginia Press, 1974); and Breen, *American Insurgents*, chaps. 2–5 (76–159).

15   Merrill Jensen, *The Founding of a Nation: A History of the American Revolution 1763–1776* (Indianapolis: Hackett Publishing, 2004), chap. 17; and P. D. G. Thomas, *Tea Party to*

Independence: The Third Phase of the American Revolution, 1773–1776 (New York: Oxford Univ. Press, 1991); and Thomas, *Lord North* (New York: St. Martin's Press, 1976).

16 *Essex Gazette* [Massachusetts], May 31, 1774.

17 Force, ed., *American Archives*, 1:42–46. Also, Thomas, *Lord North*, 32–76; Bernard Donoughue, *British Politics and the American Revolution: The Path to War, 1773–1775* (London: St. Martin's Press, 1964), 63–86.

18 Force, ed., *American Archives*, 1:40–41, 49, 54.

19 Cited in Donoughue, *British Politics*, 49.

20 Breen, *American Insurgents*, chaps. 2–5.

21 July 5–12, 1774.

22 Cited in Robert M. Wier, "The Role of the Newspaper Press in the Southern Colonies on the Eve of the Revolution: An Interpretation," in *The Press and the American Revolution*, ed. Bernard Bailyn and John B. Hench (Worcester, Mass.: American Antiquarian Society, 1980), 100.

23 *Massachusetts Spy*, June 21, 1775.

24 *The Literary Diary of Ezra Stiles*, ed. Franklin Bowditch Dexter, 4 vols. (New York: Charles Scribner's, 1901), 1:476–84.

25 The entire story of the destruction of Boston can be found in Breen, *American Insurgents*, Chapter 5.

26 *Essex Gazette*, September 13–20, 1774; *Boston Gazette*, October 10, 1774.

27 On the use of the consumer boycott as a political weapon during this period, see T. H. Breen, *The Marketplace of Revolution: How Consumer Politics Shaped American Independence* (New York: Oxford Univ. Press, 2004).

28 The full text of the Association can be found in Merrill Jensen, ed., *English Historical Documents: American Colonial Documents to 1776*, 12 vols. (New York: Oxford Univ. Press, 1969), 9:813–16.

29 Ammerman, *In the Common Cause*; Hermann Wellenreuther, "Associations, the People, Committees of Observation and the Culture of Rights, 1774–1776," paper presented at a conference on the Languages of Rights During the Age of the American Revolution, Northwestern University, Evanston, Ill., 14 May 2004; and Breen, *American Insurgents*, chaps. 5–7.

30 *Connecticut Gazette and Universal Intelligencer* [New London], February 17, 1775.

31 The contrast between the American and French committees of safety is striking. See, for example, David Andress, *The Terror: The Merciless War for Freedom in Revolutionary France* (London: Little, Brown, 2005).

32 See, Frank Lambert, *Inventing the "Great Awakening"* (Princeton: Princeton Univ. Press, 1999); Patricia Bonomi, *Under the Cope of Heaven: Religion, Society, and Politics in Colonial America* (New York: Oxford Univ. Press, 1986); Stephen A. Marini, *Radical Sects of Revolutionary New England* (Cambridge: Harvard Univ. Press, 1982); and Christine Leigh Heyrman, *Southern Cross: The Beginnings of the Bible Belt* (New York: Knopf, 1997)

33 Samuel Lockwood, *Civil Rulers an Ordinance of God, for Good to Mankind …* [Election Sermon for Connecticut] (New London, Conn., 1774), 15–16.

34 See, Harvey J. Kaye, *Thomas Paine and the Promise of America* (New York: Hill & Wang, 2006).

35 Thomas Paine, *Common Sense*, ed. Isaac Kramnick (New York: Penguin, 1976), 89.

36 Ibid., 82.

A Port in the Storm:
Philadelphia's Commerce
during the Atlantic
Revolutionary Era

Cathy Matson

Front of Walnut Street Prison

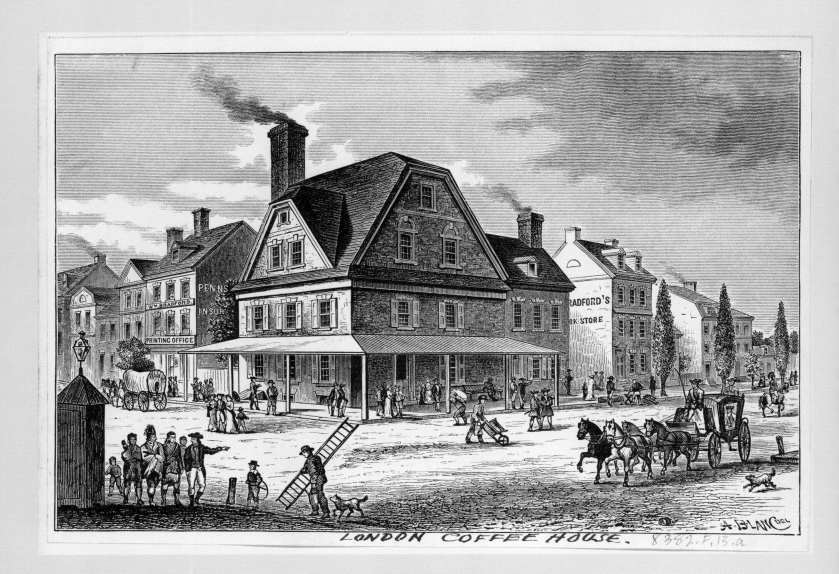

LONDON COFFEE HOUSE.

OPPOSITE A. Blanc, *Old London Coffee House*, ca. 1853. Library Company of Philadelphia.

 oung Samuel Coates hustled through the busy streets of Philadelphia from the store and warehouse kept by his senior partner, John Reynell, to the London Coffee House on Front and Market Streets. Coates had left the company account books open and a barrel lid askew; it was nearly noon and he had only the midday lunch time to accomplish two things Reynell demanded of him. One was to secure the signatures of as many fellow merchants as possible on Reynell's just-penned petition, "Address of the Merchants of Philadelphia to the People of the Colonies, Against the Stamp Act," a Parliamentary measure in 1765 that threatened to stifle city merchants' lucrative smuggling from the French and Spanish Caribbean. Since at least the 1720s, ports of all nations in the Caribbean had been vital markets for British North America's exports of flour, timber products, and various agricultural goods; in turn, the islands—British and foreign alike—were essential sources of "wet goods" such as sugar and molasses, as well as bills of exchange and silver that were essential for balancing North American debts to Europeans. News of the recent Stamp Act had touched off a raucous discussion at the London Coffee House every day for nearly a month, and Reynell was determined to bring an end to the "injustices of so selfish an interference with colonial habits of trade" by calling for repeal of the act.

Since 1754 when it was built, the coffee house had been the unofficial gathering place for all manner of political, economic, and cultural networking, including auctions of goods, sales of slaves, and gentlemen's agreements to form partnerships for foreign trade. Now, as the imperial crisis within the British empire heated up, Coates knew this was where he could find the "best dissenting minds" of the city enjoying large platters of cold beef and bowls of Bohea tea, and within days, over two hundred merchants, tradesmen, and retailers had signed the angry protest against Parliament. As signers waited to hear a transatlantic reply, their impatience grew, and when a captain arrived from Martinique with a newspaper from Barbados bearing a stamp according to the new law, the assembled men burned it in front of the venerable London Coffee House. In May 1766, Captain Wise of the brig *Minerva*, from Poole, England, burst into the coffee house with news that Parliament had repealed the Stamp Act, initiating a two-day celebration.

The second task entrusted to Coates that morning in 1765 was to secure insurance for a shipload of flour he and Reynell wished to send from Philadelphia to Bordeaux. After making his case for Reynell's petition, and as he waited for the insurance broker, Coates also purchased shares in a chartered vessel leaving for Saint-Domingue the next day, chatted with city merchants about subscriptions being raised for a new hospital, placed a few letters in the mailbag, and caught up on newspaper reports of arriving and departing vessels. Coates chose a seat in the more furnished and secluded section of the coffee house, away from the raucous shouts of sailors and tradesmen betting at billiards, as well as the cry of the slave auctioneer just outside the front door. "I sat in quietude," he wrote later, "planning just how I should increase my good fortune among the French." [1]

For decades, Philadelphia's ships had stopped regularly at French ports in Europe and the Caribbean, making multilateral voyages to pick up sugar, coffee, indigo, and dyewoods, and to drop off flour, construction materials, leather goods, and textiles. And despite the official boundaries of war between the British and French empires during the Seven Years' War, North American merchants declared that their commerce reached unheard-of levels; Philadelphia privateers and smugglers captured scores of French vessels with "prize coffee" and fine silk fabric. By the onset of the American Revolution, the long years of trading outside the British empire, coupled with the more recent perceived injustices of new Parliamentary taxes and commercial limitations, provided a heady brew for Philadelphia merchants. They began cultivating expectations about an expansive, open commerce with foreign trading partners, and the 1778 Treaty of Amity and Commerce with France, which provided most favored nation status for both sides,

RIGHT William Dickinson, *The Coffee-House Patriots, or News, from St. Eustatia.* Engraving, 1781. Library of Congress, Prints and Photographs Division, LC-USZ62-20401.

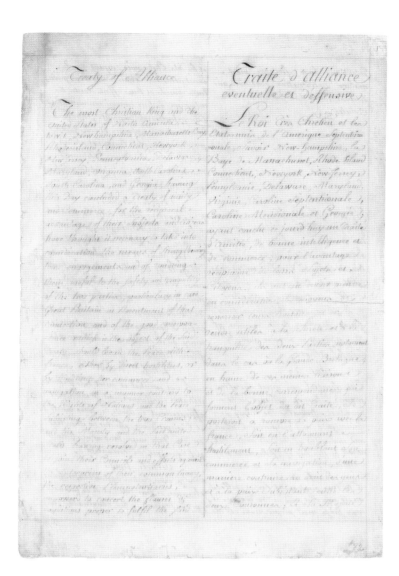
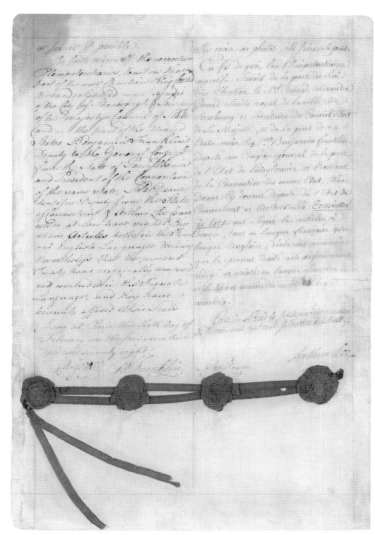

ABOVE *Treaty of Alliance with France,* February 6, 1778. National Archives, Washington D.C. International Treaties & Related records, group #11.

seemed to make great strides toward reciprocal commercial freedoms throughout the Atlantic world. As some Philadelphians projected, Europeans might now, at long last, recognize the commerce and culture of North America as equal to the greatest ports of Europe.[2]

Reynell and Coates had waited eagerly along with dozens of other Philadelphia traders for this "French trade" to flourish. So had Stephen Girard. A native of Bordeaux, transplanted to Philadelphia, Girard had clerked as a commission agent for his brother, Jean Girard, at Le Cap and for his father's friends at Port-au-Prince, where he learned English, met arriving North American captains, and eventually secured a position in New York with Thomas Randall & Son. Girard rose quickly in Randall's favor because the shipments of flour and leather goods he assembled for merchants at Le Cap, Port-au-Prince, or Môle Saint-Nicolas (the Mole) sold rapidly and

Front of Walnut Street Prison

To Counterfeit is DEATH

Printed by HALL and SELLERS.

Two Pounds Ten Shillings.

Randall's schooners returned full of cheap sugar. Randall and Girard teamed up in ventures to Saint-Domingue through the American Revolutionary years, but the restless Girard yearned to "venture on my own account."[3]

In an era when banking, brokerage, credit bureaus, limited liability, and bankruptcy statutes provided only scant protection, the risks taken by merchants during revolutionary turmoil seem quite remarkable. While some of them had extensive networks of family to cover the losses of failed ventures, many sent their cargoes to distant places underinsured and without reliable correspondents at destination points. The deceit of other traders or absconding partners, the violence of privateers and pirates, and the deep disappointments of leaky ships, moldy goods, or torrential rains were regular features of eighteenth-century commerce. So in order to compensate for their vulnerability, many merchants had developed intricate networks of private credit among trusted friends, skills in accounting and letter writing, and formalized methods of correspondence. Girard went even further. While many other North American merchants retreated from commerce during the Revolutionary difficulties, Girard seemed to thrive on the belief that if he kept ships outfitted and launched toward the Caribbean, he might reap an occasional windfall "should just one great venture reach its mark." Although he confided with his Revolutionary-era correspondents that he "grew frantic with concern for news" of safe arrivals and good sales, he re-outfitted every vessel that returned to Philadelphia as quickly as he could. When questioned by a merchant neighbor about his many losses, Girard retorted "I shall always take the gamble."[4]

During the American Revolution, he stored bags of coffee and barrels of sugar in scattered city warehouses until prices were favorable, and he smuggled regularly in the "Le Cap trade" when French decrees forbade the entry of North American flour at island ports, for the risk of seizure was "worth it." He also paid cash for goods at West Indies islands or ordered his captains to barter directly with island merchants, exchanging goods for goods right on the shoreline. He sent captains to Havana or New Orleans, expecting them to befriend expatriate Philadelphians who could recommend Girard to French and Spanish networks. On other occasions, when captains could not directly exchange provisions for sugar or coffee at Le Cap, they set off without delay to Sint Eustatius, a neutral Dutch island, to sell their cargoes for silver coin. Although reports reached Philadelphia in 1779 that "a swarm of men, from all parts of the world" docked at Sint Eustatius waiting for auspicious markets

OPPOSITE *Two Pounds Ten Shillings*, currency with image of Walnut Street Prison, in *Watson's Annals Ms*. Philadelphia: Hall and Sellers, 1775. Library Company of Philadelphia.

before selling their goods, Girard ordered his captains to "sell our flower at first contact in that place and take nothing but silver." To Girard's "mystified Chagrin," the result was "heavy losses" that year, for "none but those who take a promise of payment in the future are permitted to land goodes." By 1780 Saint-Domingue markets were "dead" and Martinique was "a guess." Girard's captains squeezed through British blockades in the Delaware Bay, only to encounter British privateers in the Caribbean. Occasionally captains successfully landed their bags and barrels of French coffee at Delaware's inlets "under cover of night," but when the American Continental Army began moving south for its final campaigns, patriot officers seized the small vessels that Girard and Randall used to collect flour and wheat along the Delaware coastline, producing "the most alarming agitations" in Girard. Insurance underwriters delivered a further blow in 1780 when they announced that rates would rise steeply. At war's end, Girard was only a little better off than he had been at its start.[5]

Nevertheless, in 1782, Girard announced to his brother in Le Cap that he had caught the "recovery fever." "Many houses and shops [in Philadelphia] are as yet abandoned, but I see now that all my zeal of recent years was but practice for what is to come." He moved from the boarding house where he had stayed at the end of the Revolution and rented a store on Water Street, the back of which abutted the city docks; in time, he bought the building and added a counting house, where he lived in the vital center of Philadelphia's commerce for the next nearly forty years. Though not in the fashionable upscale part of the city where "the best sort" resided, his commercial complex was nestled among neighbors of "steady reputation and reasonable comfort."[6]

From this location, Girard kept a steady, if anxious, eye on the tangle of Atlantic events following the American Revolution. At first, a number of other optimistic Philadelphia merchants took a heady plunge into commerce with the French empire. The city docks, "presented a din to the ears" of shipbuilding and new dock construction, while carters and apprentices stuffed warehouses with goods waiting to be sold to war-weary consumers. These expectations of commercial abundance also seemed to be rhetorically linked to the creation of new states during the Revolution and the creation of a brilliantly negotiated federal structure of American government in 1787, one that would tame the commercial warfare that continued after Americans won independence and provide other nations with a model of republican liberty that was far more compelling than European monarchies.[7]

Drawn Engraved & Published by W. Birch & Son.   Sold by R. Campbell & Cº Nº 30. Chesnut Street Philadª 1799.

South East *CORNER* of *THIRD*, and *MARKET* Streets.

PHILADELPHIA.

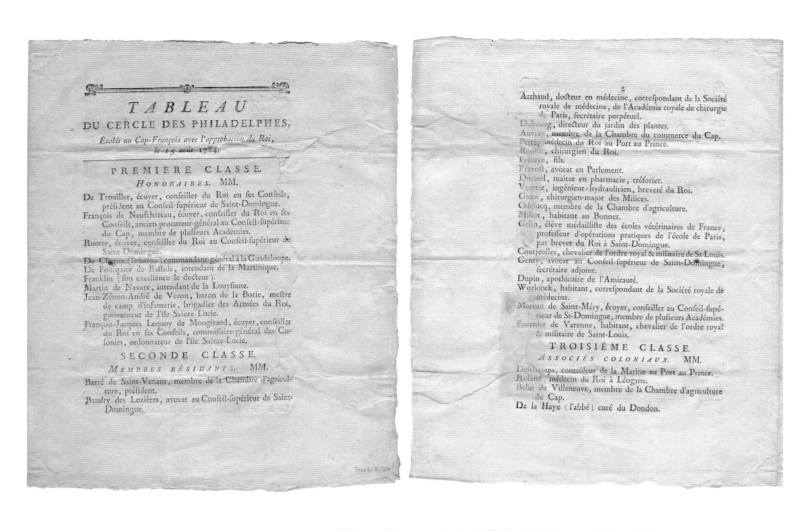

Many of these optimistic Philadelphians anticipated that French, not British, ports in Europe and the Caribbean would be their best post-Revolutionary trading partners. So they outfitted more cargoes for trade with Le Cap and Port-au-Prince, in some years more ships than were sent to any other West Indian locations, on the assumption that all would be calm in the Caribbean. Though Le Cap was a relatively small city of some eighteen thousand people in the 1780s, less than half the size of Philadelphia, it was home to a remarkable melting pot of slaves, free colored residents, soldiers and bureaucrats, a small white minority, and a waterfront crowded with transnational peoples. Philadelphians prided themselves in living in the most cosmopolitan North American city, the "Pearl of the Atlantic," but Le Cap's spectrum of class and racial identities was more intricate and this French colonial city was a multicultural gateway to the tropical riches produced on the great plantations of the interior. The two ports, thought many Philadelphia merchants, were most "congenially suited to each other."[8]

Gauché, administrateur des eaux de Boînes.
Tanguy de la Boissière, habitant aux Cayes.
Mozard, auteur & rédacteur des Affiches américaines.
Monier, médecin du Roi à Saint-Marc.
Thimotée (le père) curé au Port-de-Paix.
De Saint-Bris, maître en chirurgie à l'Acul.
Mouchet, habitant à l'Artibonite.
Louis Dumenil, arpenteur du Roi à Plaisance.
Decout, maître en chirurgie à Acquin.
D'Aussigné (le marquis) habitant au Gros-Morne.
Vantage, maître en chirurgie au quartier Dauphin.
Genton de Barssac, habitant.
Du Puget (le marquis) mestre de camp d'artillerie, chevalier de l'ordre royal & militaire de Saint-Louis, sous gouverneur de Monseigneur le Dauphin.
Blain du Verger, chevalier de Saint-Louis.
Mallet de la Brossière, médecin du Roi, correspondant de la Société royale de médecine.
De la Corbière, à la Guadeloupe.
Baron, arpenteur du Roi au Cap.
De Villars, habitant aux Fonds.
Farribauld, habitant aux Piments.
Charet, maître en chirurgie au Terrier-rouge.
Milon, démonstrateur de physique.
De Larche, habitant à l'Artibonite.
Regnaudot, docteur en médecine à la Guadeloupe.
Muz, à la Martinique.
Prat, docteur en médecine au Cap.
Vergnier, médecin du Roi à la Guadeloupe.
Tinglek, vétérinaire breveté du Roi à la Guadeloupe.
Quenet du Hamel, habitant à la Mine.
Milscent de Mussé, habitant à la Grande-Rivière.
Adam List, arpenteur du Roi au Môle.
Berger, maître en chirurgie au Port au Prince.
Genton, habitant au Môle.

Robert Coël, habitant à l'Azile.
Bayard père, habitant à Jérémie.

QUATRIÈME CLASSE.
ASSOCIÉS NATIONNAUX ET ÉTRANGERS. MM.

Dutrone, docteur en médecine.
Maerter, botaniste de Sa Majesté l'Empereur.
Le Masson le Golft (mademoiselle) demeurante au Havre.
Huzard, vétérinaire breveté du Roi, à Paris.
Grente de Grecourt, avocat-général au Parlement de Normandie.
Dicquemare (l'abbé) au Havre.
Eriau, greffier de la Juridiction consulaire à Rouen.
Baré de Saint-Leu, de la société militaire de Cincinnatus.
Raimon de Narbonne-Pelet (le comte) secrétaire du Musée de Paris.
De Goussier (le marquis) président du Musée de Paris.
Gaucher, des Académies & Sociétés royales de Londres, Caen, Orléans.
Dubois de Faussu, secrétaire de l'Académie d'Arras.
Le Brigant, avocat, membre du Musée de Paris.
Ponce, membre du Musée de Paris.
Le Brasseur, ordonnateur-général des Colonies.
Dazile, médecin pensionné du Roi.
Ceuret de Villeneuve, de la Société royale d'Orléans.
Chabanon, de l'Académie françoise, &c.
Thibaud, conseiller, médecin du Roi à Dunkerque.
Oriot, ancien chirurgien-major & maître en chirurgie à Dunkerque.
Rolland, démonstrateur & professeur de physique à Paris.
Baumes, docteur en médecine à Nîmes, membre de plusieurs Académies.
Benjamin Rush, docteur en médecine, professeur de chimie en l'Université de Philadelphie.

AU CAP-FRANÇOIS, DE L'IMPRIMERIE ROYALE, 1787.

However, a dizzying array of transnational affairs and insecure Atlantic markets seriously qualified Philadelphians' post-Revolutionary optimism. By 1784, city neighborhoods were overcrowded with returning loyalist refugees, public markets and shops reported shortages of necessities, and farmers brought scanty loads of exportable commodities to city wharves. Despite a flurry of efforts along the city's waterfront to send out ships, no more than a handful of city merchants posted the profits they anticipated that year. A crush of imported dry goods entered the city but few would-be customers could pay. As a depression set in, merchants in Philadelphia lamented "the forlorn appearance of the shops" along streets. Girard complained in early 1785 that "business is execrable." Even when exporters could fill the holds of their ships with flour, horses, and wood products, Caribbean prices for these goods fluctuated "to madness," and only a few of the best-placed merchants had good connections in the Gulf Coast, Latin American, or northern European markets at this time.[9]

ABOVE *Vue du Cap François, Isle de Saint Domingue*, in *Recueil de Vues des Lieux Principaux de la Colonie Françoise de Saint-Domingue*, by Nicolas Ponce. Paris: Chez M. Moreau de Saint-Méry, Rue Caumartin, no. 31. Paris: M. Moreau de Saint-Méry, M. Ponce, M. Phelipeau, 1791. William L. Clements Library, University of Michigan, FF1791.

Compounding these problems, new British regulations severely restricted American trade in the Caribbean during the 1780s, and French merchants regularly violated the 1778 treaty between America and France guaranteeing reciprocal and open trade by trying to keep Americans away from their islands. Word spread through Philadelphia that merchants in Bordeaux and Nantes also sent only high-priced inferior silk and brandy that had gone unsold in French markets for months. To make matters worse, French consumers did not yet have a great sweet tooth for Caribbean sugar; nearly three-quarters of French imported sugar was re-exported in foreign (mainly German) vessels to northern Europe during the 1780s, which added to French fears that Philadelphians like Girard and Dorey would seize France's re-export trade. Captains often returned to Philadelphia with unspectacular cargoes of coffee and sugar through the 1780s. Moreover, periodic rumors filtered through Baltimore and Philadelphia about a "plague" (perhaps a virulent strain of flu) in the French Caribbean, which forced some of Girard's vessels into quarantine at Le Cap and the Mole. As the ships sat offshore, his captains watched flour prices fall or water seep into their barrels, "render[ing] the whole lot suitable only for the [live]stock." In short, Philadelphia's real post-Revolutionary commerce took place in a huge terrain of permeable and uncertain international markets. Fortunes rose and fell at an alarming rate during the 1780s; some traders vanished from the high seas after one season of trading, while others reconstructed their investments, only to fail again.

Breaking through these difficulties was not easy, but Girard and a few other Philadelphians experimented with pragmatic solutions. To circumvent obstacles at Le Cap and Port-au-Prince, northern captains regularly bribed French island officials and supplemented "just half full" cargoes of Brandywine flour with Carolina rice. "It seems necessary to me to run some risks or to remain always poor," wrote Girard, for only "prudence will risk nothing." Anxious for a quick turnaround, Girard instructed captains to write false passes for Jamaica in order to break out of quarantines at Le Cap. Once released, however, his captains "missed the Jamaica markets" and learned that the Havana markets also were glutted. Imagine, then, Girard's jubilance when France opened five of its Caribbean ports to "free trade" in 1784; he redoubled efforts to race against his competitors "to make a good market" at Saint-Domingue. He informed captains to sail to any other ports if they must, but "at all odds, you must land my goods" and "offer them [merchants at Saint-Domingue] the usual discounts of direct sales."[10]

A few years later, a new flurry of commercial hopefulness washed over Philadelphia as the French Revolution began. Newspapers predicted during 1789–90 that Americans soon would supply hungry French republican revolutionaries with

BELOW Top portion of a page from Insuring Records of Shoemaker & Berrett, from Shoemaker, Shoemaker and Berrett, Marine insurance records, 1796–1797. The Historical Society of Pennsylvania, Miscellaneous Professional and Personal Business Papers, 1732–1945.

necessary food as they achieved their independence from monarchy.
Many expectations were dashed when flour shipments failed to make
it through hostile port systems at Bordeaux and Nantes. Marine
insurance premiums—including those of Samuel Shoemaker—rose
steeply, and royalists who fled from France warned Philadelphians
that even if ships could get through pirate-infested waters, many
French merchants were buried in bankruptcy proceedings.

In contrast, when French Revolutionary events severed a
lifeline of supply to the French Caribbean, Philadelphia exporters
once again sent more vessels to Saint-Domingue than any other
port in the Atlantic world. Overall, northern American merchants

sent over half of their exportable cargoes of flour, beef, pork, fish, and wood products to the West Indies in 1789, mostly to French ports, and over one-fifth of Philadelphia's returning trade came from Saint-Domingue during the first three years of the French Revolution.[11] Girard stood out once again as one of Philadelphia's most ambitious Saint-Domingue traders, spending hours each day overseeing the preparation of "my philosophers," the ships *Rousseau*, *Voltaire*, *Helvetius*, *Diderot*, and *Montesquieu*, for their voyages to Le Cap and the Mole, as well as Sint Eustatius, Jamaica, and Cuba. As a consignment agent for a few French Caribbean correspondents, he also sold sugar in Philadelphia at a 200 percent markup during spring 1791. In a similar vein, when Peter Dorey asked Samuel Shoemaker to underwrite insurance for a voyage to Bordeaux, Shoemaker could "not recommend the risk of such a venture." Instead, he suggested a gamble on the market at Le Cap, where "[you] will surely find buyers for all manner of our produce at the highest prices," "for the ships of France, England, and all nations arrive daily to carry away [from Le Cap] whatever sugar they may." Dorey accepted Shoemaker's reasoning, completely unaware of the revolutionary storm brewing in Saint-Domingue.[12]

If Dorey had waited a few weeks longer for letters arriving from Saint-Domingue, he might have jettisoned French Caribbean trading altogether. In August 1791, the *Grand Blancs* of Saint-Domingue initiated protests over their status in the French empire that rippled back to revolutionary France and then across many imperial borders. By early fall, an "ocean of slaves on land" rose up in violence against crops and masters on the island. As the revolution spread through wide swathes of Saint-Domingue, port merchants wrote about outbreaks of "ship fever" at Le Cap, as well as rotting cargoes in the harbors. For a while, planters and merchants, now unable to import French goods, encouraged Americans to keep bringing all the flour, leather, and timber goods they could, promising duty-free exports of sugar and coffee as an incentive.

Enticed by such offers, a few Philadelphians happily announced to their correspondents at Saint-Domingue that they could have large vessels of high-quality flour readied quickly. But by the time these cargoes entered the Caribbean, Port-au-Prince was being torched by revolutionaries, and soon the island's rising civil war brought an end to almost all sugar production on the northern plantations. Planters and merchants who had not yet fled Saint-Domingue clamored for—and temporarily won—sterner regulations of international trade, including a warehousing system for imports and restrictions governing where Americans could land their goods, which troubled

Philadelphians' traffic to no end. In January 1792, *Pennsylvania Gazette* readers learned that "only four merchants' houses have escaped the conflagration" of slave uprisings at Port-au-Prince.[13]

Girard held out some hope of "making a market" when he heard about opportunities to provision the French troops arriving at Saint-Domingue to stifle the slave rebellion. After all, he reasoned, they would bring silver coin to pay directly for provisions. But the French revolutionary government was no better at paying its commissions to suppliers than the American Congress had been ten years earlier. Depreciation of French *assignats* was about as steep in the early 1790s as Continental currency had been in the 1770s, and drove Philadelphia traders away from French government contractors into the arms of island merchants again. Navigating all the dangers of the spreading international conflicts at Saint-Domingue, a few mid-Atlantic captains tried to land their flour deceptively with bribes or night landings near Le Cap, and by using false clearances to depart for other Caribbean islands in order to fill the holds of their ships.

On the books, Girard sent well over forty-five thousand barrels of flour to Saint-Domingue during 1792; but in reality, much of his flour never found acceptable markets and eight vessels were captured or capsized, while seven came into Philadelphia with cargoes too small to cover his debts.[14] By September 1792, Jacob Broom of Wilmington, Delaware, wrote to his commission agent at Saint-Domingue that "the troubles on your Island are so great and affairs with you so Gloomy that we do not know if it will be prudent…to sett the Cargoe at the Cape" as they had for many previous seasons. Sending cargoes to Martinique (via Saint Thomas), Guadeloupe, and Sint Eustatius proved equally disappointing, and word spread quickly in Philadelphia that "the islands are now but dead markets."[15]

By the time France declared war on England in February 1793, residents of Saint-Domingue had become desperate for food imports. Declarations of French and English conditional neutrality in March 1793, as well as the French National Convention's agreement to open all French West Indian possessions to American trade, also initially buoyed the hopes of Philadelphia's merchants that their ships might be able to navigate hostile waters. But in the coming months neutrality withered. The French "continental system," which prohibited importation of British manufactured goods, was matched with Britain's blockades of French coastal ports, effectively ending credit and silver payments to Americans. Privateering and piracy also heightened dangers for Americans, and by late 1793, French and British privateers were seizing neutral vessels that carried enemy property (in the form of exports from the Caribbean islands), regardless of the ship's registration or destination. Philadelphia traders responded that their only hope of protection from the seizures was to supply every captain with two sets of papers vouching simultaneously for the British or French origins of their cargoes and the neutral intentions of the shippers. But even armed with these paper protections, captains encountered British scouts hovering near Le Cap who grabbed vessels during 1793, on the (often justified) suspicion that Americans carried French goods. More than one of Girard's captains wrote that scores of ships from North America were being detained at Sint Eustatius, Bermuda, Basseterre, Martinique, Montserrat, St. Kitts, and other islands, where flour "rotted along the beaches."[16]

In the terrible logic of both the Napoleonic Wars and the revolution in Saint-Domingue, commercial conditions deteriorated rapidly during 1793. British patrols seized two of Girard's ships carrying hundreds of barrels of flour that fall, and even when a vessel or two got to Le Cap, the only viable return cargoes were refugee planters and their household slaves. A handful of other city merchants joined in these refugee transports to Baltimore and Philadelphia as the exodus from Saint-Domingue reached a zenith late that year. Meanwhile, as the Terror began in France, Girard's agents living there were guillotined or fled from the country, so that although his ships had not carried sugar and flour to France for some time, he feared he would never collect long overdue debts.

That same fall 1793 a "Malignant fever [was] raging" in Philadelphia and Wilmington, believed (but never proven) to have been introduced by Caribbean refugees, forcing massive evacuations.[17] As Girard played an active role in tending to the sick and dying in Philadelphia, his letters note the "dire failures" of dozens of British, Scottish, and French agents at Saint-Domingue, Martinique, and Sint Eustatius, as well as dozens of merchants in Philadelphia who could not fill export orders. Thousands of residents evacuated the city, and in the ghost town they left behind Girard and a few other merchants somehow secured loans for ships and goods to send to Le Cap, Aux Cayes, and Jeremie—some by way of Sint Eustatius and Curaçao—in September and October.

In November, when England tightened its commercial restrictions and ordered the detention of any ship entering or clearing a French colony, regardless of its cargo, Girard hedged his risks not by halting his trade to the French islands, but by sharing ownership in vessels and sending them on circuitous routes.[18] The *Polly*, *Kitty*, and *Nancy* were detained and ransacked near Le Cap, "in the same manner as if they had been taken by the Algerines," and vessels returned to Philadelphia "molested" and empty, "everything lost." But Girard meticulously noted the captains' details of voyages while loading up his "philosophers" once again. Finally, the *Nancy* smashed against rocks at Mogane Island during a storm, permitting Girard the luxury of applying to his insurance underwriters for compensation.[19]

Events in 1794 and early 1795 nearly halted Philadelphia's commerce with France and its Caribbean ports. In March, a group of city traders who identified closely with the French republicans, blamed commercial problems on British policy makers. The "hoped for reciprocal display of impartiality" between England and the newly independent Americans, they argued, which might have "obliterate[d] the remembrance of the wrongs" before the American Revolution, had deteriorated into "an ambitious and vindictive policy … [that] denied the rights, attacked the interests, interrupted the pursuits, and insulted the dignity, of the United States." "Britain has violently seized and sequestered the vessels and property of the citizens of the U.S. to the value of several millions of dollars." As Girard paced the Philadelphia wharf restlessly, news reached the city about British troops landing on Saint-Domingue to crush the revolution there, followed by the British seizure of Martinique and the brutal suppression of a large uprising on Jamaica of runaway slaves and maroons in the hill country. But then in early 1795, British reinforcements succumbed to a new outbreak of yellow fever, Spain handed over Santo Domingo to the French, and Toussaint Louverture soon became the head of the slave and free black majority on Saint-Domingue, rendering Philadelphia's exporting to the Caribbean "a ruinous business."[20]

Nevertheless, when news of abundant exportable surpluses in the Delaware Valley reached his warehouse in fall, 1795, and agents at Le Cap assured Girard that flour was selling at extraordinarily high prices, Girard prepared for "a gambling venture" to Saint-Barthélémy and Saint Thomas with huge loads of flour, hoping to get them to Le Cap indirectly. Most of it, however, was captured by French privateers or spoiled sitting in harbors before it could be offloaded and sold at Caribbean ports. Meanwhile, the French government had demonetized silver in 1795 and prohibited its export, prompting Girard to lament to his remaining French correspondent, Horquebie & Cie, that he now faced the "Calamity" of never collecting debts in Bordeaux. Worse still, Philadelphians were reportedly "in the greatest confusion so far as business was concerned" because of rumors about a possible war with two

Freight list of the Brig Betsey Capt R.ᵈ George bound to Martinique & elsewhere — being on her 3.ᵈ voyage —

by whom shipped	articles & freight	Am.ᵗ Dollars	
Pearson Hunt & C.º	35 barrels flour – 25 barrels Pork 19 tierces gammons. 32 kegs lard.	429	67
Nathaniel Lewis	150 barrels flour	150	0
William Nichols	100 do . . do	100	0
Phillips & Crosby	112 bbl. flour, 42 half bbl. flour, 32 bbls beef, 25 bbl. Pork, 4 tierces Gammon 3 tierces cheese, 5 bbl. vinegar, 44 kegs lard, 15 boxes candles, 12 boxes soap, 12 bbl. potatoes, 29 bbl. beer –	292	
E. E.		Doll. 971	67

Philad.ª Decem.ʳ 26. 1793 —

William Phillips

The Brig with the above freight & cargo was captured by the English at Martinique for which I have made application . . .

ABOVE Bottom portion of William Phillips's account for Brig *Betsy*, bound from Philadelphia to Martinique, December 26, 1793, and subsequently captured by English privateers, Phillips Family Business Records, 1793–1838, Hagley Museum and Library, Soda House Manuscripts, Wilmington, DE.

powerful European nations. Marine insurance companies closed, many ships were auctioned off, and dozens of Girard's fellow merchants in Philadelphia failed.[21]

In 1795, the trading giants Robert Morris and John Nicholson failed to pay debts for western land and city real estate, largely because the flow of silver and sugar from the French Caribbean had slowed enormously. In the wake of their tarnished reputations, some 150 more commercial houses were tumbling down in Philadelphia, and flour prices fell precipitously during 1796 when French and Saint-Domingue merchants defaulted on their debts. One Philadelphia observer was convinced that there was "an auction sale of French sugar or mouldy Flower on every corner."[22] By then, slave trading to Saint-Domingue had come to a virtual halt, severing

A SHORT

ACCOUNT

OF THE

MALIGNANT FEVER,

LATELY PREVALENT IN

PHILADELPHIA:

WITH A STATEMENT OF THE

PROCEEDINGS

THAT TOOK PLACE ON THE SUBJECT IN DIFFERENT
PARTS OF THE

UNITED STATES.

———

TO WHICH ARE ADDED,

ACCOUNTS

OF THE

Plague in London and Marseilles;

AND A LIST OF THE DEAD,

From August 1, to the middle of December, 1793.

———

BY MATHEW CAREY.

———

FOURTH EDITION, IMPROVED.

———

PHILADELPHIA:

PRINTED BY THE AUTHOR.

January 16, 1794.

an additional limb from Philadelphia's international commercial body. In 1797 France retracted its neutrality position, and its customs agents at Saint-Domingue indicted over three hundred American vessels. Now made vulnerable as enemies of France, doing its best to defeat the Haitian Revolution, trade out of Philadelphia to that part of the Caribbean crumbled. Thomas P. Cope estimated that "We have men among us, who owe millions...now that our neutral trade is closed."[23] The Quasi War of 1798 and 1799 only deepened the existing problems in Philadelphia. When the French government closed its West Indies possessions to Americans and authorized its privateers to seize American vessels with impunity, Philadelphia trade felt the disastrous consequences immediately. In response, the American government granted permission to its Caribbean-bound ships to capture any French vessels interfering with their trade. When this brought little relief to American shippers, Congress cut off trade with all French islands in mid-1798.[24]

By the close of the century, Philadelphia merchants faced important choices, each of which underscored how their transnational commerce had become intertwined with the destinies of three Atlantic revolutions in America, France, and Saint-Domingue. As before, some merchants succumbed to the informal belligerency and diplomatic constrictions by withdrawing from trade altogether. Many of those who remained active in commerce turned away from ports in France and its colonies; the problem, however, was that few other ports in the Caribbean offered the lucrative commerce that French ones had in recent years. As Philadelphians rediscovered, British West Indies markets at Jamaica and Barbados rarely had sufficient tropical exports or cash to pay for American imports. And Cuba was just beginning its rise to becoming the preeminent Caribbean sugar producer. So adventurous Philadelphians adopted a policy of multilateral trade, or stopping at numerous islands to get small loads of coffee and sugar before returning home, though they complained that this made their voyages longer and more costly.[25] Trade from Philadelphia to Nantes and Bordeaux was "perplexed" by privateers during the Quasi War, by piracy during the early 1800s, and rarely on stable footing during the remainder of the Napoleonic Wars.[26]

Together, the Haitian Revolution and long era of Napoleonic Wars provoked many Philadelphia merchants—though by no means all of them—to search for non-French markets by 1800. Philadelphia ships went more frequently to Amsterdam and Hamburg, and occasionally to St. Petersburg, Copenhagen, and Riga. From 1801 to 1807 about one quarter of American exports were sent to these

OPPOSITE Mathew Carey, *A short account of the malignant fever, lately prevalent in Philadelphia: with a statement of the proceedings that took place on the subject in different parts of the United States.* Philadelphia, January 16, 1794. Massachusetts Historical Society, Boston.

European destinations. During these years, Girard, now over fifty years old, drew funds from his savings in Amsterdam and London to outfit voyages of the *Voltaire* and *Montesquieu* to "Bengal or China."[27] But after a few good years of stretching into new spheres of commerce, three problematic years followed: the Jeffersonian embargoes during 1807–09, the depredations of Algerian pirates, and the rising wave of Latin American revolutions reminded Philadelphia merchants again that their commercial republic remained fragile.

Philadelphians' most significant commercial adjustment resulting from the Haitian and French Revolutions involved sending more food and slave labor to Cuba, where Spanish officials temporarily opened a neutral trade with Americans in early 1797. Mid-Atlantic merchants already had entrenched habits of smuggling goods into Havana, and they built legalized binational partnerships during the early 1780s. In 1797, then, they easily grasped the opportunity to create strong international business enterprises in Cuba just as the turmoil on Saint-Domingue shut out almost all North American importation. By 1802, a consortium of some thirty mid-Atlantic merchants hailed the "sugar revolution" and "abundance of silver coin" in Cuba as they took large amounts of Spanish wine and American flour to the island's consumers. Still stinging from the "derangements" of the revolution at Saint-Domingue, Girard wrote that "the gambles upon the [French] republic and its colonies will soon be put aside when we see returns from this other [Spanish] nation."[28] Indeed, the French empire continued to decline in the western hemisphere when Napoleon's sale of the Louisiana territory doubled America's size, and when revolutionary slaves in Saint-Domingue finally were able to declare the independent republic of Haiti.

Notes

1 The first three paragraphs are reconstructed from *Samuel Coates Journal, 1767–1776*, Library Company of Philadelphia; John Reynell Papers, Historical Society of Pennsylvania; Shoemaker, Shoemaker, and Barrett, Insurance Records, Historical Society of Pennsylvania; Thomas Westcott, *The Historic Mansions and Buildings of Philadelphia* (Philadelphia: Porter and Coates, 1867), 67–78; and *Proceedings of the American Philosophical Society*, VII for 1859–1861 (Philadelphia, 1861): 159–60. The London Coffee House was turned into a general store during late 1791, to be eclipsed by the elite City Tavern and numerous new neighborhood inns and taverns near the waterfront by the mid-1790s.

2 For example, Willing & Morris to Lawrence Reade, August 22, 1757, Charles Willing & Son, Letterbook, 1754–1761, Historical Society of Pennsylvania.

3 This, and the next paragraphs draw from the Papers of Stephen Girard (GP), Series II, Reels 121–123, American Philosophical Society (APS), a collection of over 600 reels of microfilm. For Girard's early career, see Cathy Matson, "Accounting for War and Revolution: Philadelphia Merchants and Commercial Risk, 1774–1811," in Margaret C. Jacob and Catherine Secretan, eds., *The Self-Perception of Early Modern Capitalists* (New York: Palgrave-Macmillan, 2008), 183–204. Until the onset of the War of 1812, Girard sank most of his capital into commerce; thereafter, banking, philanthropy, and entrepreneurial projects absorbed much of his attention and capital.

4 GP, Series II, Reels 123, 127, APS; William Duer Papers, New-York Historical Society (N-YHS); Willing and Morris Papers, Historical Society of Pennsylvania (HSP); Cathy Matson, *Merchants and Empire: Trading in Colonial New York* (Baltimore: Johns Hopkins Univ. Press, 1998), chaps. 6, 8; Peggy Liss, *Atlantic Empires: The Network of Trade and Revolution, 1713–1826* (Baltimore: Johns Hopkins Univ. Press, 1983), 108–91, 283–84 n.37; Franklin Knight, "The Origins of Wealth and the Sugar Revolution in Cuba, 1750–1850," *Hispanic American Historical Review* 57 (1977): 231–53, at 242, 244; Chaloner & White advertisements during the 1760s in *Pennsylvania Gazette;* and Linda Salvucci, "Development and Decline: The Port of Philadelphia and Spanish Imperial Markets, 1783–1823" (Ph.D. diss., Princeton University, 1985), esp. 85–86.

5 GP, Series II, Reels 121–123; Brooke Hunter, "Rage for Grain: Flour Milling in the Mid-Atlantic, 1750–1815" (Ph.D diss., University of Delaware, 2001); Sherry Johnson, *The Social Transformation of Eighteenth-Century Cuba* (Gainesville: Univ. Press of Florida, 2001), chap. 8; and Knight, "Origins of Wealth," 249.

6 GP, Series II, Reel 121; Clifford Family Papers, 1722–1832, HSP; Jones & Clarke, Papers, 1784–1816, HSP; Philadelphia City Directory, 1791; and Lewden Family Papers, Delaware Historical Society (DHS).

7 Cathy Matson, ed. & intro., "The Atlantic Economy in an Era of Revolutions," Special Forum, *William and Mary Quarterly*, 3rd ser., 62 (July, 2005) (*WMQ*); D. A. Farnie, "The Commercial Empire of the Atlantic, 1607–1783," *Economic History Review*, 2nd ser. (1962): 205–18; Ralph Davis, *The Rise of the Atlantic Economies* (Ithaca, N.Y.: Cornell Univ. Press, 1973); Liss, *Atlantic Empires*; David Hancock, *Citizens of the World: London Merchants and the Integration of the British Atlantic World, 1735–1785* (Cambridge, Eng.: Cambridge Univ. Press, 1995); Thomas Doerflinger, *A Vigorous Sprit of Enterprise*, (Chapel Hill: Univ. of North Carolina Press, 1986), esp. 77–126; Jacob Price and Paul G. E. Clemens, "A Revolution of Scale in Overseas Trade: British Firms in the Chesapeake Trade, 1675–1775," *Journal of Economic History* 47 (1987): 1–43; Cathy Matson and Peter Onuf, *A Union of Interests, Political and Economic Thought in Revolutionary America* (Kansas City: Univ. of Kansas Press, 1990). For historians' arguments that the political Revolution and economic growth were intertwined, see e.g., E. James Ferguson, *The Power of the Purse: A History of American Public Finance, 1776–1790* (Chapel Hill: Univ. of North Carolina Press, 1961). For rapid commercial recovery, see, e.g., Joyce Appleby, *Inheriting the Revolution: The First Generation of Americans* (Cambridge, Mass.: Harvard Univ. Press, 2001); Doerflinger, *A Vigorous Spirit*, chap. 5, 222–45; and Geoffrey Gilbert, "The Role of Breadstuffs in American Trade, 1770–1790," *Explorations in Economic History* 14 (1977): 378–84.

8   For Le Cap and other French colonial ports, see, e.g., Matson, *Merchants and Empire*, 135–50, 260–69; Shipping Records, 1708–1892 (mostly 1790–1820), 5 boxes, Winterthur Library, Del.; Willing and Morris Papers, HSP; William Walton Papers, New-York Historical Society (hereafter, N-YHS); John H. Coatsworth, "American Trade with European Colonies in the Caribbean and South America, 1790–1812," *WMQ* 24 (April 1967); Liss, *Atlantic Empires*, 29–30; A. P. Whitaker, "The Commerce of Louisiana and the Floridas at the End of the Eighteenth Century," *Hispanic American Historical Review* 8 (1928): 190–203; and Knight, "Origins of Wealth," 231–53.

9   For post-war failures and ship seizures in this and the next paragraph, see, e.g., Stephen Girard to Jean Girard, May 28 and November 28, 1783, March 28, 1784, and April 15, 1785, and records of the ship *Les Deux Amis*, 1785, GP, Series II, Reel 121; Chaloner & White Papers; John Ball Family Papers; John Nixon Papers, 1707–1845; Willing and Morris Papers; and John Brown Account Book, 1774–1777, 1783–1787, all at HSP; Amos Brinton, Account Book, Hagley; and *Delaware Gazette*, June 27, 1789. For "forlorn appearance," William Constable to Daniel McCormick, February 9, 1784, Constable Papers, N-YHS; for "execrable," Stephen Girard to Balthazar Ortt, Amsterdam, March 31, 1785, and for "ready money," Stephen Girard to Byrne & Von Dorsten, New York, September 22, 1783, GP, Series II, Reel 121. For the 1780s downturn, see *American Museum* (Philadelphia: Carey, Stewart, and Co., 1787), 5:381; The Duke of La Rochefoucault Liancourt, *Travels Through the U. S. of N. A.* (London: R. Phillips, 1800), 3:493–99, 562, 694; Levi Hollingsworth Papers and Coates & Reynell Letters, HSP; Thomas Canby Papers, Lea Ledger A, 1784–1804, and George Latimer Letters, DHS; Thomas Lea Account Book, 1775–1783, and Lea & Sons, Account Book, 1773–1787, Hagley; Arthur H. Cole, *Wholesale Commodity Prices in the U.S., 1700–1861* (Philadelphia: Univ. of Pennsylvania Press, 1938; repr. 1969), 120, 143; Matson and Onuf, *Union of Interests*, chaps. 3–4, 7–8; Lance Davis and Stanley Engerman, "The Economy of British North America: Miles Traveled and Miles Still to Go," *WMQ*, 3rd ser., 56 (1999): 21; Drew McCoy, *The Elusive Republic: Political Economy in Jeffersonian America* (Chapel Hill: Univ. of North Carolina Press, 1980); and John E. Crowley, *The Privileges of Independence: Neomercantilism and the American Revolution* (Baltimore: Johns Hopkins Univ. Press, 1993).

10   For "just half full" and "prudence," Stephen Girard to Jean Girard, January 26, 1785, GP, Series III, Reel 113; and for other merchants' experiences, Anon., Account Book, 1781–1797, Hagley; Hollingsworth Family Records, John Ashmead Papers, and Jonathan Lawrence Papers, HSP; William and Jacob Walton, Book of Insurance, Jan. 1773–Mar. 1781, New York Municipal Archives; Russell Family Papers, 1783–1823, and William Smith, Letter & Record of Vendue, 1786, 1791, Winterthur; and Joseph Waln, Jr., Letters, 1787–1799, Richard Waln Collection, HSP. For the French West Indies generally in the mid-1780s, see, GP, Series III, Reels 44, 48, 113; William Stevenson Papers, HSP; William Hemphill Papers, DHS; Robert Ralston Letters, HSP; and Lewden Papers, Joseph Shallcross Papers, and John Morton Papers, DHS. For Sint Eustatius, see Jacob Clarkson Papers, HSP; and for Guadeloupe, see Levi Hollingsworth Papers, HSP.

11   Shoemaker, Shoemaker, and Barrett, Insurance Records, HSP; Anne C. Clauder, *American Commerce as Affected by the Wars of the French Revolution and Napoleon, 1793–1812* (Philadelphia: Univ. of Pennsylvania Press, 1932); Jean Meyer, "Les difficultés du commerce franco-americain vues de Nantes, 1776–1790," *French Historical Studies* 11 (1979): 159–83; Paul Butel, *Les negociants bordelaise* (Paris, 1974; repr. 1996); Francois Crouzet, "Wars, Blockade, and Economic Change in Europe, 1792–1815," *Journal of Economic History* 24 (1964): 131; and Silvia Marzagalli, "The Establishment of a Transatlantic Trade Network: Bordeaux and the U.S., 1783–1815," Working Paper No. 03-06, International Seminar on the History of the Atlantic, Harvard, 2003. Gary Walton and James Shepherd show effectively that in 1790–92, Philadelphia's exports levels had finally recovered to their pre-Revolutionary levels; *The Economic Rise of Early America* (Cambridge, Eng.: Cambridge Univ. Press, 1979), 186–97.

12   For Girard's 1789–91 accounts of ships *Polly*, *Ann*, *Active*, *Virginie*, *Exua*, *Bernardo*, *Deux Freres*, and his "philosopher vessels," see GP, Series III, Reel 113, APS; and for comments on flush times, GP, Series III, Letter Book II, and Invoices for 1783-1800, Reel 132. For other merchants, see papers of Dutilh & Wachsmuth, HSP; Andrew

Pettit, Andrew Bayard, Henry Pratt, William Gallathea, Harvey & Daves Papers, all at Hagley; Bjork, "Weaning," 550–53; NARA, Record Group 36, Entry 1059B, Boxes 2–15; *New American State Papers-Commerce & Navigation*, ed. Thomas Cochran, 47 volumes (Wilmington, Del., 1973) 1:72, 226, 275; *Pennsylvania.Gazette*, February 10, 1790; and Alec Dun, "'What avenues of commerce, will you, Americans, not explore!': Philadelphia's Commercial Vantage on St. Domingue, 1789–1793," *WMQ* 62 (July 2005): 473–504. Girard dissolved his partnership with brother Jean in 1790, leaving Stephen with two ships and $30,000, which he used to repay creditors.

13   For 1791–92, see e.g., Peter Dorey Letterbook, Hagley; Warner, Stockton & Craig Papers, 1791–1804, HSP; William Hemphill, Letterbook, 1792–1802; and Broom, Hendrickson & Summerl, Letterbook, 1792–1794, DHS; and papers of Etienne Dutilh, Manuel Eyre, Charles Massey, John Brown, and John Churman, all at Hagley. For the importance of imported food on Caribbean islands, see Richard B. Sheridan, "The Crisis of Slave Subsistence and the British West Indies during and after the American Revolution," *WMQ*, 3rd ser., 33 (1976): 618–24. In 1792, flour represented about 45.5 percent of Philadelphia's exports to the West Indies and southern Europe, and 19 percent of New York's exports; *American State Papers*, 7:148–62.

14   GP, Series III, Letter Book II, Reel 113; and papers of Rumford and Abijah Dawes (HSP), Peter Dorey (Hagley), Broom, Hendrickson, and Summerl (DHS), and Samuel Gilford, Joseph Hallett & Co, Ebenezer Stevens, and Isaac Roosevelt (N-YHS).

15   Broom, Hendrickson, and Summerl Papers, 1792–1793, DHS.

16   For news of the 1793 measures, e.g., *General Advertiser*, February 20 and May 10, 1793; *American Daily Advertiser*, February 20, 1793; *Federal Gazette*, June 6, 1793; NARA, Record Group 36, Entries 1057 and 1059; and Girard to L. Trinquart, St. Marc, June 23, 1793, GP, Series III, Letter Book IV, 399. For an example of a Philadelphia ship captured by British privateers near Martinique, condemned by the British consul there, and the subsequent suit for recovery of the ship, its cargo, and the insurance premium, see the record of Brig *Betsy*, December 1793, William Phillips Account Book, Hagley Museum and Library. For a ship taken and released, see the *Isabella and Ann*, in James Hemphill, Letterbook, 1793, DHS. For ships seized and not recovered from British privateers, see the *Pratt* and the *Sally* of Isaac Hendrickson, in Hendrickson Mss., 1795, DHS.

17   For Saint-Domingue in 1793, see GP, Series III, Letter Book II, Reel 113; Lewden Family Papers, DHS; Chaloner & White Papers, HSP; Joseph Donath & Co. Papers, HSP; BHS Papers, DHS; and Eli Mendenhall Folders, 1800–1801, DHS. For the yellow fever, see J. H. Powell, *Bring Out Your Dead: The Great Plague of Yellow Fever in Philadelphia in 1793* (Philadelphia: Univ. of Pennsylvania Press, 1949; repr. 1993); and for the refugees, see Frances S. Childs, *French Refugee Life in the United States, 1793–1800* (Baltimore: Johns Hopkins Univ. Press, 1940).

18   For failures, see, e.g., Hendrickson & Summerl to William Stevenson of Philadelphia, October 5, 1793; to Joseph Hallett of New York, December 4, 1793, BHS Correspondence; William Hemphill Correspondence, DHS; Thomas Canby Papers, DHS; George Latimer Correspondence, DHS; BHS Letterbook, DHS; William Hemphill Log Book, 1793, DHS; and Thomas P. Cope, Letterbooks, 1796–1798, Hagley. For new routes in 1793–94, see papers of James & Shoemaker, Offley & Paxon, Jonathan Ogden, Hayman Levy; James Willink, William Deas, Wall & Flower; and Byrnes, Sweetman & Rudolph, all at HSP.

19   GP, Journals and Letter Book V, 1794, Series III, APS, esp. Girard to Capt. John Cochran, Kingston, June 18, 1794; to Edmund Randolph, Philadelphia, June 6, 1794; to Jean Girard, New London, April 20, 1795; to Jean Girard, New London, May 21, 1795; and to Paul Bentalou, Baltimore, January 6, 1796. The quotes are in the letter to Randolph.

20   *Pennsylvania Gazette*, March 26, 1794; and for the French republican circle, Andrew Shankman, *Crucible of American Democracy* (Lawrence: Univ. Press of Kansas, 2004), 99, 143.

21   Girard to Paul Bentalou, Baltimore, December 14, 1796, GP, Series III, Letter Book VI, 135, APS; records of Girard's vessels the *Good Friends, Polly, Kitty, Nancy, Liberty*, and *Sally*, GP, Series III, APS.

22   *Pennsylvania Gazette*, November 19, 1794, and July 29, 1795. For failures in Philadelphia, 1795–97, see papers of Robert Ralston, Samuel Hopkins, and Henry Bell, HSP; GP, Series III, APS; and Thomas Shallcross Correspondence, DHS.

23   Cole, *Wholesale Commodity Prices*, 109–12; T. Cope to J&J Pim, August 10, 1797, Cope Letterbooks, Hagley.

24   Coatsworth, "American Trade with European Colonies;" and, for comparative prices at French and Spanish islands, *American State Papers*, I:passim.

25   On turning to the British West Indies, see, e.g., Masters & Markoe Accounts, Box 9, 1800–1806, Hagley.

26   For trade to Bordeaux and Nantes during the 1790s, see Girard's voyages of the *Liberty*, *Good Friends*, *Sally*, and correspondence with French merchants Bonnaffe, Fenwick & Mason, and Horquebie, as well as Hamburg merchants Berenger, Gossler & Co. in GP, Series III, Letters, 1796–1799, APS; and records of Jonathan Jones, John Bernard, John Gernon, Justin Foussat, John Bousquet, and Bousquet & Odier, all at HSP.

27   For Amsterdam and Hamburg, see, e.g., Warner, Stockton & Craig Papers, HSP; William Hemphill Letters, 1794, DHS; and GP, Journal, 1786–1790, Reel 113, APS. There is little evidence that mid-Atlantic American exporters *preferred* Europe *over* the West Indies until 1798; for evidence of reticence about Europe, see, e.g., Thomas P. Cope, Letterbooks, 1792–1798, Hagley. For redirecting cargoes from the West Indies to Europe *after* 1797, see, e.g., Manuel Eyre Papers, 1777–1845, and Masters & Markoe Papers, 1788–1814, both at Hagley; the papers of Savage & Murgatoyd; Francis Breuil; Abraham Piesch; Augustin Bousquet; Louis Crousillat; and John W. Foussat, all at HSP; and Sam Mustafa, *Merchants and Migrations: Germans and Americans in Connection, 1776–1835* (Burlington, Vt.: Ashgate, 2001). For China, see GP, Series III, Reel 125, #335; and Coatsworth, "American Trade," 254–55.

28   Girard to Sebastian de Lasa, Havana, March 31, 1798, Letter Book, VII, 75; to Paul Bentalou, Baltimore, December 29, 1798, Letter Book, VI, 447; to William Douglas, Petersburg, January 22, 1798, Letter Book, VII, 22; Captains' Reports on the ships *Liberty*, *Modesty*, and *Sally*, GP, Series III, 1797–1799, APS; Robert Morris Papers, and John and George Morton Letterbook, both at HSP; Liss, *Atlantic Empires*, 200, 210; Salvucci, "Development and Decline; Javier Cuenca Esteban, "Trends and Cycles in U.S. Trade with Spain and the Spanish Empire, 1790–1819," *Journal of Economic History* 44 (June 1984): 521–43, at 541–43; Knight, "Origins of Wealth," 241. A few merchants in Philadelphia began to transfer Cuban silver into the China trade, making stops at Argentina and Peru for beef and hides sold at Havana on their return, though this route was regularized only in 1805. For Girard's economic makeover after 1800, see Matson, "Accounting for War and Revolution," in Donald Adams, *Finance and Enterprise in Early America: A Study of Stephen Girard's Bank, 1812–1831* (Philadelphia: Univ. of Pennsylvania Press, 1978); Ralph Hidy, *The House of Baring in American Trade and Finance: English Merchant Bankers, 1763–1861* (Cambridge, Mass.: Harvard University Press, 1970); and GP, Series II, Reels 127, 184, 477.

Atlantic Revolutions and the Age of Abolitionism

David Brion Davis
and Peter P. Hinks

PLAN AND SECTIONS OF A SLAVE SHIP.

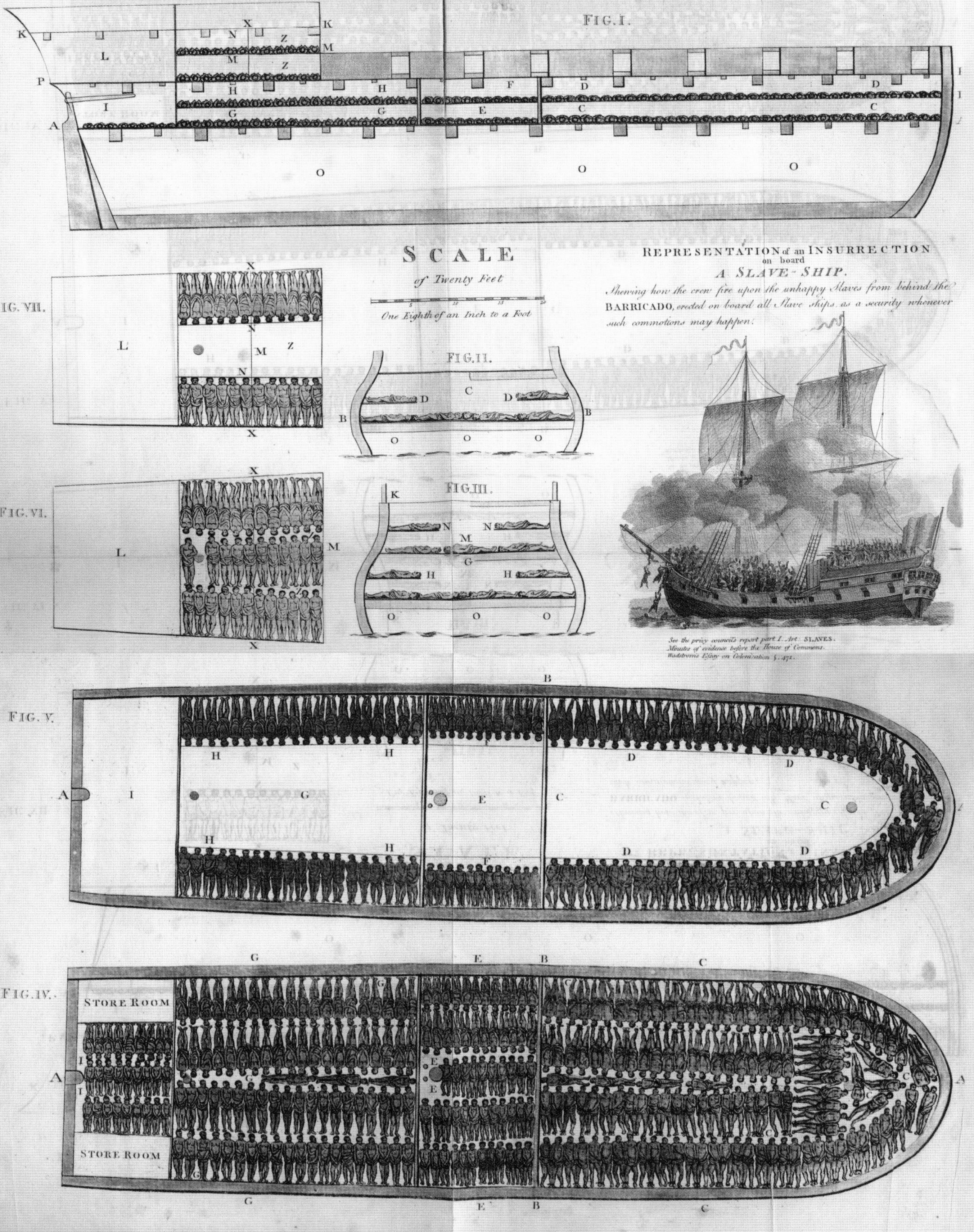

FIG. I.

FIG. VII.

FIG. VI.

SCALE
of Twenty Feet

One Eighth of an Inch to a Foot

FIG. II.

FIG. III.

REPRESENTATION of an INSURRECTION
on board
A SLAVE-SHIP.

Shewing how the crew fire upon the unhappy Slaves from behind the BARRICADO, erected on board all Slave ships, as a security whenever such commotions may happen.

See the privy council's report part I. Art. SLAVES.
Minutes of evidence before the House of Commons.
Waldstrom's Essay on Colonisation §. 171.

FIG. V.

FIG. IV.

STORE ROOM

STORE ROOM

apoleon's secret restoration of slavery in the French West Indies in late 1801 heralded a resurgence of slavery and the Atlantic slave trade in the Americas after a quarter century of signal challenges to its dominion. The slave insurgencies of the 1790s in the Caribbean, most notably in Saint-Domingue (later Haiti), along with the warfare between Britain and France, had wrought the greatest opposition and disturbance.[1] During the early Haitian Revolution, Saint-Domingue's black rebels first gave flesh to emancipation, a fact on the ground that France's National Convention acknowledged and endorsed with its abolition of colonial slavery in 1794. Against such challenges to the century's predominating sense of order, Napoleon now plotted. Dispatching his brother-in-law, General Victor-Emmanuel Leclerc, with a vast fleet and an expeditionary force of 50,000 troops in late fall 1801, Napoleon sought once and for all to re-immure and kill the ghost of abolition in revolutionary Saint-Domingue. Louisiana, secretly returned to French control in 1800, would become a vast granary for West Indian slavery while simultaneously checking America—in the throes of its own paradoxical grappling with slavery—at its indispensable western mouth. Once secured, France would "restock" its Caribbean colonies infected by "the contagion of liberty" with tens of thousands of Africans carried across the Atlantic. Great Britain, soon signatory to the Treaty of Amiens, allowed this transit after Napoleon sought its approval. Between the January 1802 arrival of Leclerc's army off Cap Français and the following December, close to 100,000 more kidnapped Africans would have arrived in Saint-Domingue and the Americas if Napoleon had had his way. As 1803 dawned, planters and merchants alike anticipated a renewed smooth sailing for Atlantic slavery. Indeed, by the end of the year, South Carolina reopened its ports to the slave trade and imported some 38,000 Africans.

Yet, a mere six years later, Britain, indisputably the Atlantic's single greatest vendor of humans, would voluntarily remove itself from any further participation in the lucrative traffic and pivot the institution in its own colonies towards dissolution. This remarkable reversal had a great deal to do with the vast French army off Le Cap in January 1801, whose monumental defeat in Saint-Domingue and abandonment of Louisiana were all sealed by the end of 1803. Over the ensuing years, Britain would counter Napoleon's vision of a resurgent militaristic Roman-like imperium with its own distinctive re-visioning of empire, one gestating since the 1760s as the British

OPPOSITE *Plan and Sections of a Slave Ship*, in *An Essay on Colonization … by* C. B. Wadström. 1789, reprinted London, 1794. Engraving, 20$\frac{7}{10}$ × 14$\frac{1}{2}$ in. (52.58 × 36.83 cm). Library Company of Philadelphia, *U Afr Wads, accession #728.Q.

gained vast new territories from France and then lost their own most valuable colony to American revolutionaries.[2] In the enormous revolutionary and imperial turbulence of the Atlantic in the late eighteenth and the early nineteenth centuries, Britain stumbled towards re-framing empire around freedom and Christian mission, nailed together with the more traditional beams of national interest and glory. Nothing illustrated this reconstruction more dramatically than Britain's voluntary, startling, and wholesale removal of itself from participation in the Atlantic slave trade in 1807. An enactment that would have seemed only a ludicrous paradox in 1775 emerged by 1807 as a new paradigm of Christian and moral orderliness, energizing the nation's own breathtaking imperial expansion over the next century. The mass upendings that resulted from the American, French, and Haitian revolutions made such an unexpected renovation possible. To summarize how is our object here.

First, however, it is crucial to stress that the New World slave system was not in any kind of economic decline. In recent decades historians have come to agree that the Atlantic slave trade and slave colonies were extraordinarily productive and profitable, and that Britain's abolition of the trade in 1807 was not only counterproductive, in economic terms, but a form of "econocide" that would lead to the decline and stagnation of the nation's most valuable New World colonies.[3] The movement against the slave system was the result of a major and complex public transformation of moral perception, aided by the fortuitous events of the American, French, and Haitian revolutions.

Two intercoiled but wholly different narratives launched by 1763 undergird the story: the dramatic expansion of the British empire with the Treaty of Paris in 1763 and the publication of the American Quaker Anthony Benezet's highly influential *A Short Account of that part of Africa Inhabited by the Negroes* (1762), which for the first time comprehended the whole of Atlantic slavery in a major antislavery work.

With the conclusion of the 1763 Treaty, Great Britain acquired vast new territory in North America and predominated in the emerging colonial giant of India.[4] On the seas, Britain's maritime and naval fleets mastered the Atlantic while they strengthened its sea lanes beyond and expanded exploration into the Pacific. Moreover, the vanquishing of absolutist France heightened Britain's heralding of itself as the guardian of liberty and mixed government. Yet, while having greatly reduced France's threat, this First British Empire was newly saddled with huge administrative and military outlays to control its imperium, only compounding the national debt it inherited from the preceding war. In America, these imperial imperatives led immediately to bloody and expensive battles with Native Americans in the northwest and escalating confrontations with colonists over taxes and jurisdictions of governance that compromised its assumption of the shield of guardian. Ensnared in a web of competing claims and escalating force from which it could not disentangle itself, Britain looked more and more the absolutist tyrant itself, ready to squelch and drain the vital liberty of the subjects it claimed to safeguard. As 1775 approached, the Patriots had sharpened their representation of Britain as a brutal overseer deadset on enslaving its subjects if they did not heel totally to its coercion.

Simultaneously, Anthony Benezet had comprehensively indicted a more vivid and concrete slavery that corrupted the empire. Between 1762 and 1771 Benezet published three major works of antislavery that moved beyond the limited focus of his Quaker predecessors to condemn the several Atlantic powers that despoiled Africa in selfish pursuit of power and wealth.[5] Perhaps Benezet's greatest contribution to the emerging matrix of Atlantic antislavery was to include West African peoples themselves and their interactions with Europeans in a representation of a horrible commerce spanning the whole of the Atlantic world. Benezet portrayed Africans, however skewed historically, as a peaceable, agriculturally productive, and naturally virtuous people whom Europeans corrupted through violence and debauchery in order to induce them to seize and sell countless other Africans to the Europeans. Not only did the Europeans despoil an innocent continent; they defamed the Christianity they professed. Their transportation of the enslaved to the Americas, where they were forced to produce goods and wealth carried back to Europe, indicted the whole of the Atlantic in the crime. Benezet's innovative and extensive reliance on the actual accounts of French and English slave traders in West Africa substantiated these characterizations while situating all the details more graphically in the machinations of an Atlantic slave system. The Abbé Raynal's *Philosophical and Political History of the European Settlements and Commerce in the Two Indies* (1770) elaborated upon Benezet's core assertion that Atlantic slavery was a vast European violation of human freedom and dignity. He forecast the rise of a Black Spartacus in the West Indies to avenge these vast wrongs against an unoffending people.[6]

In 1767, Benezet argued in *A Caution and Warning to Great Britain and her Colonies* that England in particular led in this oceanic commerce to its peril before God. This first extensive fusing of the nation and empire to the profound sin of slavery wielded enormous

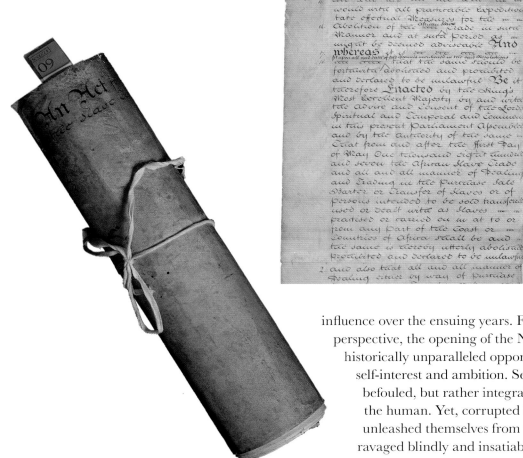

influence over the ensuing years. From Benezet's abolitionist perspective, the opening of the New World had created historically unparalleled opportunities for the pursuit of self-interest and ambition. Self-interest was not inherently befouled, but rather integral to God's animation of the human. Yet, corrupted by the Fall, free humans unleashed themselves from their grounding in God and ravaged blindly and insatiably instead in the transient ground of Earth. With the opening of the New World, Europeans used it to amplify avarice, appetite, and pride to scales previously unwitnessed. This near total collapse of Christianity in the Atlantic world imperiled everyone, a plight demanding urgent regeneration. This rebirth, soon sought by other British and American abolitionists, must be premised upon a renunciation of slavery and an assertion of universal human fellowship. For leaders like William Wilberforce, for example, the goals of abolitionism went beyond the elimination of a particular evil. The movement would revive and regenerate Christianity and put humanity on a wholly new track of moral progress.[7]

In England, Benezet's urgent mandate moved Granville Sharp to help lead a first institutional disruption of slavery in the British Empire. By the mid-1760s, slavery and the routine debasement of people of African descent troubled Sharp, a devout Anglican, more and more. As black numbers expanded in London after 1763, he had ample opportunity to witness these abuses. Since early in the century, West Indian planters had brought their enslaved domestics to attend them in their London residences, comfortable in the security of their title to the slaves within England. By mid-century, their numbers in London and elsewhere mounted, some estimating them at 10,000 or more by 1770.[8] Compounding these numbers were the black mariners and transients of uncertain status who debarked in England after the peace of 1763. By the 1760s, increasing numbers of the enslaved ran away, some assuming lives of quasi-freedom in the extensive and impoverished inter-racial underworld of London. Many, however, were recaptured by owners, brutally punished, and often forced to return to Caribbean cane fields. Yet William Blackstone's recently published *Commentaries on the Laws of England* raised serious issue with the security of the title of slave in England, where the law in fact was supposed to consider the individual not as a slave, but as a freeman whom the law protected "in the enjoyment of his person, his liberty, and his property."

Granville Sharp had been very familiar with Blackstone and with the plight of grossly abused slaves ever since Jonathan Strong had sought his protection in 1765.[9] Sharp's response to these encounters was animated by his reading of Benezet and his own growing conviction that righteousness and justice must prevail in Britain and its colonies over national glory, dominion, and wealth. In 1769, his *A Representation of the Injustice and Dangerous Tendency of Tolerating Slavery in England* first articulated those principles and the unusual threat that slavery posed to their preservation in Britain. As Sharp's advocacy of a fledgling antislavery became more widely known and as his encounters not only with aggrieved blacks but with learned ones, such as Ignatius Sancho, expanded, he mobilized to challenge slavery institutionally. In 1772, the crucial opportunity arose after a master had seized a runaway, James Somerset, and sought to return him to Jamaica for sale. Through an artful orchestration of Somerset's defense, which included guidance and supportive publications from Benezet, the defense was enabled to gain the King's Bench assent to their position that any contract surrendering one's body to another is by definition void and that the laws of England recognize no civil dominion such as Somerset's master claimed over him. While this decision did not instantly free the slaves in England, as many British and Americans later thought, it upset fundamental assumptions about the legality of the ownership of humans in England, paving the way for an onset of individual challenges to their enslavement. More broadly, it raised significant issue with the legitimacy of slavery existing *anywhere* within English territories. The *Somerset* case and the writings of Blackstone, Benezet, and Sharp, were all associating Great Britain with ideals of liberty and justice.

After 1772, Granville Sharp turned his attention to the distressed American colonies. His work and the *Somerset* decision coincided with the excitement for liberty growing throughout the American colonies by the early 1770s. In Philadelphia, Sharp's correspondence with Benezet established an Anglo-American antislavery nexus that British and American Quakers and more secular advocates would advance over the decades.[10] The scope of Benezet's influence upon early antislavery advocates in Great Britain is breathtaking—he was their principal informant upon the crimes of the slave trade up through Thomas Clarkson's 1786 *An Essay on the Slavery and Commerce of the Human Species*. Moreover, Benezet would spearhead the conclusion of the effort by Quakers, begun in the 1760s, to require all members to remove themselves totally from the slave trade and slaveholding. In 1775, he joined with other local Quakers to create the Atlantic's first antislavery organization, the Society for the Relief of Free Negroes Unlawfully Held in Bondage.

Yet the *Somerset* decision and Sharp's work early returned the favor to Benezet's America, providing positive affirmation to the mounting efforts of Benezet and Benjamin Rush in Philadelphia and the Congregationalists Samuel Hopkins, Ezra Stiles, and Jonathan Edwards, Jr., in New England to separate the emerging American movement for independence from a damning tolerance of slavery.[11] While by no means the only influence, the efforts of these early abolitionists contributed importantly to the enactment of gradual abolition laws throughout the North, commencing with Pennsylvania in 1780. At the beginning of the American Revolution, racial slavery was legal throughout America's North and South. In 1777 Vermont's constitution outlawed the institution and within a few years Massachusetts courts achieved the same objective. By 1804 New Jersey concluded the North's enactment of gradual abolition.

Nevertheless, loyalists and many Britons castigated the hypocrisy of slaveholding American rebels. "How is it," the great Samuel Johnson famously asked, "that we hear the loudest *yelps* for liberty among the drivers of negroes?" But though skeptical, even derisive, as late as 1769 of American professions of liberty while upholding slavery, Sharp increasingly favored American independence as colonial assemblies and the Continental Congress sought to ban further importations of Africans despite British vetoes. Indeed, by late 1774, Sharp had transformed so thoroughly as to pronounce that "the horrid guilt of persisting in that monstrous Wickedness must reside on this side [i.e. England] of the Atlantic!"[12] Patriot forces deftly deployed their ban of the Atlantic trade to assert the Confederation's freedom from British commercial tyranny *and* America's moral superiority.

Despite these various laudable measures, America would remain deeply mired in slavery and evidently vulnerable to attack for such when proclaiming its fidelity to liberty. Fledgling American antislavery would never deprive Great Britain of its claim to be guardian of liberty and justice, especially as Britain itself had experimented with emancipation under Lord Dunmore and General Henry Clinton, giving provisional freedom to blacks who escaped behind British lines, and then evacuating in 1782–83 with many thousands of these "black loyalists" in tow (some of whom, however, were sold as slaves in the West Indies). To cast aside slavery's umbrage, even for a time, required the brilliance of the Declaration of Independence, a revealed script of liberty and national independence for which Patriots readily sacrificed their security and lives to defend. In 1776 and for many years after, Great Britain could produce nothing to challenge its luster in a revolutionary era. With the Declaration, revolutionary America proclaimed itself the foremost guardian of liberty against the pretensions of a tyrannical Britain, which had betrayed the promise of the 1688 Constitution and thrived in the slave trade. America embodied civic liberty and national independence, which would seize the political imaginations of the Atlantic's peoples for decades. The apparent paradox of slavery and freedom could be reasonably set aside, even after 1783 when America appeared to many to be steering towards a general—if very gradual emancipation. This belief seemed to be confirmed when Congress, responding to an appeal from President Jefferson, outlawed American participation in the Atlantic slave trade beginning January 1, 1808, the earliest date allowed by the U.S. Constitution.[13]

After 1783 a besmirched and defeated Britain settled into a painful reevaluation of the governance and premises of its empire.

The nation had suffered an ignominious defeat in its apparent struggle to crush the spirit of liberty. Britons could no longer be assured they possessed "the freest and most representative government in the world." [14] The war, managed by a coalition around Lord North and appointed by the King, revealed again the pitfalls of oligarchy: it had left behind only the loss of the colonies and a shocking expansion of the national debt. Demands for Parliamentary reform, blunted during the war, sharpened after it. Reformers throughout Britain began scrutinizing a contracting and perhaps superannuated empire.

Such renewed reckonings created breaches for Britain to question its own relationship with liberty, justice, and slavery. Some focused on imperial aggrandizement and oppression on the other side of the globe, indicting Warren Hastings, the East India Company's governor of Bengal, who was guilty of vast abuse of office in India, for rendering British rule synonymous with despotism and pillage. [15] But the African commerce and the rule of the British West Indies, the heart of the British Empire for the balance of the century, centered the scrutiny. Granville Sharp signaled this new inquiry after 1763 and his presence remained central after 1783. His impact on James Ramsay, an Anglican cleric from Saint Christopher in the West Indies, was enormous. Familiar with Sharp's earliest work and with his proposals in the late 1770s on liberalizing manumission laws (influenced by such actions in the new American states), Ramsay submitted a plan to the bishop of London in 1778 "for the education and gradual emancipation of the slaves in the West Indies." His 1784 work, *An Essay on the Treatment and Conversion of the African Slaves* had far broader circulation and significance. The association of Britain with slavery—now presented as a heinous institution that bestialized Africans and denied them access to the word of God and salvation— was deeply disturbing to Ramsay and he sought to disrupt the bond, but only over time. Despite the American Revolution, Ramsay located the proliferation of slavery and its excesses in colonial autonomy. His recalibrating of the empire demanded a greater, more deliberate focus of imperial power on its colonial possessions to check the colonists' predilection to wander into an unregulated liberty. A liberty "thriving in godlessness," in fact, was the very centerpiece of imperial corruption in the New World. Thus the state should ensure limits to planters' dominion over their slaves and ensure that those in bondage received adequate care, a rudimentary education, and full access to Christian clergy and catechism. While not reducing imperial power—in fact welcoming it because it would protect the enslaved—Ramsay helped shift the focus of empire from

CLARKSON'S WEST AFRICAN COLLECTION.

dominion towards a humanitarian stewardship. His work seeded the Caribbean for the so-called amelioration movement of the early nineteenth century, which would propel the British antislavery movement toward emancipation after 1823.[16]

In the 1780s and 1790s religious sensibility spurred broad transformations in the popular understanding of slavery and the empire's association with it. Dissenting Methodists such as John Wesley had railed against slavery since the 1770s and their intensely emotional preaching rapidly expanded their popular appeal. Evangelical Anglicans such as the Reverend George Whitefield, who shared emotional enthusiasm with the Methodists, also struck a popular resonance while nurturing a more moderate doubting of slavery that attracted the financial sustenance of Selina Hastings, Countess of Huntingdon. The era's broadening evangelical enthusiasm helped prompt the religious conversion of William Wilberforce, a Minister of Parliament from the West Riding and a close associate of the Prime Minister, William Pitt, as well as Thomas Clarkson, a brilliant recent graduate of Cambridge. Integral to their spiritual rebirth was their painful recognition of the horrible sin of slavery and the slave trade and the nation's abominable complicity with both. While their conversion experience served for decades as the paradigm for bringing the wayward to a godly antislavery movement, Wilberforce's position of power and privilege in particular afforded the opportunity for national action against slavery. Over the coming years, Wilberforce came to embody the essence of the reformed empire, one founded on liberty, humanitarianism, stewardship, and the multifarious benefits of British rule and civilization.[17]

A powerful amalgam of individual regeneration and imperial re-framing energized Wilberforce, Clarkson, Quakers, and numerous other reformers for the daunting task of bringing Britain to a similar awakening: they would lead a popular movement thunderous enough to bring a recalcitrant Parliament to end the nation's involvement in the Atlantic slave trade. The organization in 1787 of the Society for Effecting the Abolition of the Slave Trade launched the drive. Clarkson visited key ports in the English slave trade, gathering damning evidence to reinforce his recently published *An Essay on the Slavery and Commerce of the Human Species* (1786) as well as the bedrock work of Benezet. At the same time, an anti-slave trade petition campaign had been commenced in Manchester where over ten thousand signatures were soon secured. The petition campaign spread rapidly, especially among other towns in the north poorly represented in Parliament, asserting pressure on Parliament as it

OPPOSITE, ABOVE Clarkson's Africa box, with assorted objects, ca. 1780. Wisbech & Fenland Museum, 1870.3.

Within the image:

My Eyes Jack our Girls at Wapping are never flogged for their modesty

Dam me if I like it I have a good mind to let go

By G—d thats too bad if he had taken her to bed to him it would be well enough. Split me I'm allmost sick of this Black Business.

Pub. April 10 1792 by S W Fores N 3 Picca.

The ABOLITION of the SLAVE TRADE.
Or the Inhumanity of Dealers in human flesh exemplified in the Cruel treatment of a young Negro Girl of 15 for her Virgin Modesty

ABOVE Isaac Cruikshank (ca. 1756–ca. 1811). *Abolition of the Slave Trade*, 1792. Etching with hand coloring on paper, 8 ¾ × 13 ¼ in. (22.23 × 33.66 cm). Lewis Walpole Library, Yale University, 792.04.10.03.

opened committees to inquire into the slave trade. Granville Sharp's simultaneous publicizing of 125 Africans thrown overboard as "jetsam" on the slave-ship *Zong* and other horrifying accounts of the Middle Passage aroused popular sentiment to the nightmare of the slave trade.[18] Meanwhile, Wilberforce introduced resolutions against the traffic in the House of Commons and argued eloquently against the wrongs of the commerce. Yet this first wave of opposition finally failed to secure abolition: the strength of the West Indian lobby and its warm reception in the House of Lords, the radicalizing of the French Revolution by 1792, the outbreak of war between France and Great Britain in 1793, and Pitt's campaign against Jacobinism and domestic dissent forestalled abolition in Parliament. Yet the key arguments were laid out and knowledge of how to mobilize the ever-deepening popular support for reform had been grasped.

The simultaneous outbreak of a vast slave rebellion in the French colony of Saint-Domingue, the world's major source of sugar and coffee and the wealthiest and most productive of the plantation colonies, rapidly forged a whole new trajectory against slavery and forced the issue of colonial slavery with an even greater urgency. In 1789, the outbreak of the French Revolution and the creation of a National Assembly enabled the leaders of the *Amis des Noirs*, a fledgling French antislavery group closely associated with Thomas Clarkson, to argue for the right of free people of color from Saint-Domingue, many of whom owned slaves and coffee plantations, to address the Assembly, to be seated in it, and to participate fully as citizens in their island's colonial assemblies. But the *Amis* lacked the influence and the budding infrastructure of the anti-slave trade movement in Britain and faced the might of the pro-planter lobby at the Massiac Club and a government committed to maintaining stability in the treasured island. Back in the island, an uprising of the free colored in the north was crushed while white royalists and republicans, both deeply averse to any expansion of the rights of the island's colored, were themselves embroiled in a bitter struggle for control of the island.

BELOW James Gillray (1756–1815). *Barbarities in the West Indies*, 1791. Etching with hand coloring on paper, 9¾ × 13¼ in. (24.8 × 33.7 cm). Lewis Walpole Library, Yale University, 791.04.23.01.

AN

HISTORICAL SURVEY

OF THE

FRENCH COLONY

IN THE

ISLAND OF ST. DOMINGO:

COMPREHENDING

A SHORT ACCOUNT OF ITS ANCIENT GOVERNMENT,
POLITICAL STATE, POPULATION,
PRODUCTIONS, AND EXPORTS;

A NARRATIVE OF THE CALAMITIES WHICH HAVE DESOLATED
THE COUNTRY EVER SINCE THE YEAR 1789,

*WITH SOME REFLECTIONS ON THEIR CAUSES AND
PROBABLE CONSEQUENCES;*

AND

A DETAIL OF THE MILITARY TRANSACTIONS
OF THE BRITISH ARMY IN THAT ISLAND TO THE END OF 1794.

By *BRYAN EDWARDS*, Esq. M.P. F.R.S. &c.
AUTHOR OF THE HISTORY OF THE BRITISH COLONIES IN THE WEST INDIES.

LONDON:
PRINTED FOR JOHN STOCKDALE, PICCADILLY.

1797.

Observing all this tumult carefully and patiently was Saint-Domingue's vast majority—the hundreds of thousands of slaves. In August 1791, both touched by the Revolution and Ogé's free colored uprising and acting independently of them, a mass slave insurrection broke out in the north which quickly pushed aside the white and free colored actors and seized the political stage. The insurgency bypassed parliamentary reform altogether: it single-handedly shut down by armed force a slave trade that in 1790 alone brought 50,000 coerced Africans to the island. By the summer of 1793, the insurgents and their handful of white republican allies expelled the royalist planters who then encouraged Britain to seize the island and reinstate slavery. Yet emancipation only expanded. By August 1793, Léger-Félicité Sonthonax, the intrepid republican civil commissioner from France, acknowledged provisionally what the tens of thousands of black insurgents north and south had already well established on the ground—that slavery was all but abolished in Saint-Domingue. In a flurry of colonial self-interest and revolutionary idealism, the French National Convention, formalizing Sonthonax's field measure, enacted abolition in all its colonies in February 1794. Yet, finally, neither commissioners nor the Convention—and certainly not the enervated *Amis des Noirs*, despite charges from planter advocates that they had conspired to achieve it—had much to do with forging emancipation. The French simply grabbed nimbly a hold of the banners of the insurgents charging before them, hoping not to lose control altogether of the Pearl of the Antilles.

Nevertheless, the act of February 1794 burnished France's revolutionary heraldry of liberty and equality, uniting them and the nation with emancipation—and at the convenient expense of English puffery. Georges Jacques Danton promptly proclaimed before the Convention:

> Representatives of the French people, until now we have decreed liberty as egotists for ourselves. But today we proclaim universal liberty.... Today the Englishman is dead. Pitt and his plots are done for! France, until now cheated of her glory, repossesses it before the eyes of an astonished Europe and assumes the preponderance which must be assured her by her principles, her energy, her land, and her population![19]

England had wasted no time in caricaturing France's revolution as it turned Jacobin and more radical by 1792. The engravings of Cruikshank, Gillray, and Rowlandson abound with ragged French

OPPOSITE Bryan Edwards, *An historical survey of the French colony in the island of St. Domingo.* London: Printed for J. Stockdale, 1797. New-York Historical Society, F1923 .E26 1797.

delighting in the severed heads of royals and a liberty to "national & private ruin."[20] Now the French responded to English pretenses as they sanctioned emancipation while the British sought to stunt it by occupying a Saint-Domingue in tumult and reinstating slavery.

However the National Convention might strive to seize it for France, abolition in Saint-Domingue was an extra-parliamentary endeavor and this was precisely what worried abolitionists back in England. Failure to address a crime as enormous as slavery promptly and judiciously would only provide occasion for the horrible and understandable frustrations of the Africans to burst through in the sweeping interracial violence gripping Saint-Domingue. Thomas Clarkson warned in 1792 of carnage in the British Caribbean if the current momentum towards abolition was not sustained. Jonathan Edwards, Jr., and Theodore Dwight would make similar arguments in New England in 1793 and 1794, when Raynal's "Black Spartacus" was much more alive than when first imagined in 1770.

Despite these critical efforts to interpret popularly the meaning of the insurrection in Saint-Domingue and infuse its example with abolitionist urgency, Bryan Edwards established a dominant interpretation by 1797 which, reinforced by three later slave insurrections in the British Caribbean, would profoundly influence American debates over slavery and abolition extending down to the Civil War.[21] Edwards, a British West Indian planter and Member of Parliament, wrote as an eyewitness of the Haitian Revolution. He argued that the *Amis des Noirs* was entirely responsible for the insurrection in Saint-Domingue, and advanced the highly influential thesis that slaves were in general docile and content but that when alerted to antislavery agitation and legislative debates over their status, they were likely to rise in rebellion.

Edwards's graphic descriptions of the slaughter and torture of whites and the raping of white women also represented Saint-Domingue through a wholly different lens—as an emblem of the savagery into which bestial Africans would inherently plunge if the presiding colonial power failed to regulate them properly. Along with the earlier deeply anti-black work of Edward Long, Edwards raised troubling questions about the fitness of people of African descent for any unsupervised liberty.[22] Unlike Ramsay, Edwards located the threat from excess liberty within the enslaved population itself. This interpretation of the Haitian Revolution wielded much popular influence and undermined support in England for abolition by the second half of the 1790s. And the Edwards thesis gained momentum when later British parliamentary debates seemed to promote the large Barbadian slave revolt of 1816.

The Mode of exterminating the Black Army, as practised by the French.

The British intended their occupation of 1793–97 to save the island for slavery and plantation culture, which it did only temporarily and then only in a sharply curtailed south-central region of the colony.[23] What the occupation accomplished more substantively was to weaken French rule much further while unintentionally promoting the rise of the black general, Toussaint Louverture. Indeed, after the departure of the British in 1797, the British General Thomas Maitland actually worked in concert with the administration of President John Adams to secure Louverture in power within the island and to supply his growing forces with food and arms in their struggle in the south against the mulatto general, André Rigaud, who remained much more deferential to France. Thanks in part to Louverture, the British and the American Federalists exhibited at least some strategic willingness to envision and allow a semi-autonomous black realm, however restricted and insular, to emerge in the Caribbean. In 1799, Alexander Hamilton even wrote a draft constitution for the island![24] By early 1801, after Louverture, the British, and the Americans had largely chased the French from the West Indies, Louverture moved decisively towards independence, outlawing slavery, writing a constitution, imposing a draconian labor policy, and declaring himself governor for life. Perhaps, contrary to Bryan Edwards, Saint-Domingue could settle down and in fact become again another plantation economy of the Caribbean, but, most significantly, not as a colony.

But this was something Napoleon could never abide, and as we have seen, he proceeded ahead to his colonial doom. A whole year before their collapse at Vertieres in November 1803, however, the dying Leclerc and his fierce replacement, Donatien Rochambeau, initiated a policy of total extermination of all Africans, male and female, above the age of twelve on the island, an act of unspeakable horror, and one that is often overlooked in accounts of the last year of the French invasion.[25] With an unbridled license to murder, the French, in a frenzy for slavery, plummeted every bit as low as Bryan Edwards's depiction of blacks in the 1790s. The extermination was not overlooked, however, at the time. In his popular *An Historical Account of the Black Empire of Hayti* (1805), Marcus Rainsford summarized the French invasion in devastating depictions of the atrocities they routinely perpetrated.[26] With such titles as "The Mode of exterminating the Black Army as Practised by the French," Rainsford's images inseparably joined Napoleon and the French imperial army with an insatiable savor for savagery. This was empire fundamentally premised on slavery and the most brutal tyranny, neatly packaged and illustrated for popular consumption. And

Rainsford, never denying the violence of the blacks, had nonetheless transformed it into an avenging reaction that looked much more like that characterized by Clarkson and Dwight. Revealing the spectrum and intensity of convictions regarding the meaning of the upheaval in Saint-Domingue, Rainsford significantly countered his countryman, Bryan Edwards.

As Britain crushed the combined Spanish and French fleets at Trafalgar soon after Napoleon's defeat in Saint-Domingue, Britain in effect gained mastery of the Atlantic for its vessels. A vast barricade shuttered England from Europe as Napoleon installed the Continental System after 1805. Britain, facing the enmity of not only France, but of the rest of Europe and Russia, required banners and narratives rallying it to the demanding work ahead and clarifying what exactly distinguished it from a violently ambitious

ABOVE Richard Newton (1777–1798). *Cruelty and Oppression Abroad*, 1792. Etching with hand coloring on paper, 15 × 20½ in. (38.1 × 52.07 cm). © The Trustees of The British Museum, 2007, 7058.2.

France. Much was brought to bear, especially an innovative focus upon promoting national patriotism. But reinforcing and deepening the meaning of that patriotism after 1805 would be the nation's unassailable attachment to Christianity and humanitarianism as it voluntarily removed itself from the Atlantic slave trade. Dominating the vulnerable colonies of the Caribbean, and moved by Denmark's recent renunciation of the trade, Parliament by 1805 returned to a dormant antislavery that, despite persisting powerful opposition from the planters' lobby, effloresced into abolition in 1807. Wilberforce, allied with the powerful George Fox and William Grenville, convinced Parliament that acting now against the slave trade served both to forward sound policy in the national interest and to elevate the British Empire before the world to universal principles of benevolence and justice. While debate has persisted among historians over the degree to which the secular or the sacred predominated in British motivations, this dramatic promulgation transformed the meaning of the empire for the British and the world. However imperfect and human, it gave witness to a profound moral transformation and irreversibly steered the Atlantic and then the world towards the epochal emancipations of the nineteenth century.[27]

Notes

1   Numerous works, especially recently, have admirably treated the Haitian Revolution. Among the finest are C. L. R. James, *The Black Jacobins: Toussaint L'Ouverture and the San Domingo Revolution*, 2nd ed. (New York: Random House, 1963); Laurent Dubois, *Avengers of the New World: The Story of the Haitian Revolution* (Cambridge: Harvard Univ. Press, 2004); David Geggus, *Haitian Revolutionary Studies* (Bloomington: Indiana Univ. Press, 2002); and Carolyn Fick, *The Making of Haiti: The Saint-Domingue Revolution from Below* (Knoxville: Univ. of Tennessee Press, 1990).

2   For a broadly related discussion, see David Brion Davis, *The Problem of Slavery in the Age of Revolution, 1770–1823* (New York: Oxford Univ. Press, 1999); Christopher Brown, *Moral Capital: Foundations of British Abolitionism* (Chapel Hill: Univ. of North Carolina Press, 2006); Robin Blackburn, *The Overthrow of Colonial Slavery, 1776–1848* (London: Verso, 1988); Roger Anstey, *The Atlantic Slave Trade and British Abolition, 1760–1810* (Atlantic Highlands, N.J.: Humanities Press, 1975).

3   See especially Seymour Drescher, *Econocide: British Slavery in the Era of Abolition*, 2nd ed. (Chapel Hill: Univ. of North Carolina Press, 2010).

4   See, for example, Colin G. Calloway, *The Scratch of a Pen: 1763 and the Transformation of North America* (New York: Oxford Univ. Press, 2006) and Fred Anderson, *The Crucible of War: The Seven Years' War and the Fate of Empire in British North America, 1754-1766* (New York: Knopf, 2000).

5   Anthony Benezet, *A Short Account of that Part of Africa Inhabited by the Negroes…* (Philadelphia, 1762); *A Caution and Warning to Great Britain and Her Colonies in a Short Representation of the Calamitous State of the Enslaved Negroes in the British Dominions* (Philadelphia, 1767); *Some Historical Account of Guinea … An Inquiry into the Rise and Progress of the Slave Trade, Its Nature, and lamentable Effects* (Philadelphia, 1771).

6   Abbé Raynal, *Histoire philosophique et politique des etablissemens et du commerce des Europeens dans les Deux Indes*, 6 vols. (Amsterdam, 1770).

7   For a broad discussion of this renovation, see David Brion Davis, *Slavery and Human Progress* (New York: Oxford Univ. Press, 1984).

8   For further discussion see Edward Scobie, *Black Britannia: A History of Blacks in Britain* (Chicago: Johnson Publishing, 1972), especially 5–117; Paul Edwards and James Walvin, *Black Personalities in the Era of the Slave Trade* (Baton Rouge: Louisiana State Univ. Press, 1983); Gretchen Gerzina, *Black England: Life before Emancipation* (London: John Murray, 1995).

9   For a recent treatment of the case, see Steven Wise, *Though the Heavens May Fall: The Landmark Trial that Led to the End of Human Slavery* (Cambridge, Mass.: Harvard Univ. Press, 2005).

10 See the particularly insightful discussions of these inter-connections in Brown, *Moral Capital*, 98–153, and Davis, *The Problem of Slavery in the Age of Revolution*, 213–54. See also Betty Fladeland, *Men and Brothers: Anglo-American Anti-Slavery Cooperation* (Urbana: Univ. of Illinois Press, 1972).

11 Regarding Hopkins, Stiles, Edwards, and the neo-Edwardsian New Divinity, see Brown, *Moral Capital*, 167–69, and Davis, *The Problem of Slavery in the Age of Revolution*, 285–99. See also Joseph Conforti, *Samuel Hopkins and the New Divinity Movement: Calvinism, the Congregational Ministry, and Reform in New England between the Great Awakenings* (Grand Rapids, Mich.: Christian Univ. Press, 1981).

12 David Brion Davis, *The Problem of Slavery in Western Culture* (Ithaca, N.Y.: Cornell Univ. Press, 1966), 3; Brown, *Moral Capital*, 167–69.

13 In striking contrast to Brazil and the Caribbean colonies, the slave population in North America had long had a strong positive growth rate, thus reducing or even eliminating the need for any further importation of slaves from Africa.

14 Blackburn, *The Overthrow of Colonial Slavery*, 135.

15 Brown, *Moral Capital*, 203–06.

16   James Ramsay, *An Essay on the Treatment and Conversion of African Slaves in the British Sugar Colonies* (London, 1784). See also, Brown, *Moral Capital,* 228–58, 346–77.

17   On the role of evangelicalism in late eighteenth-century antislavery, see Davis, *The Problem of Slavery in the Age of Revolution,* 285–99, 523–56; *Slavery and Human Progress,* 107–226; and Brown, *Moral Capital.*

18   The subject of the *Zong* is to be covered by James Walvin (New Haven: Yale Univ. Press, forthcoming).

19   As cited in Blackburn, *The Overthrow of Colonial Slavery,* 225.

20   See Rowlandson, "The Contrast" (1792), The Lewis Walpole Library, Digital Call #: 792.12.0.3.1.

21   Edward Bartlett Rugemer, *The Problem of Emancipation: The Caribbean Roots of the American Civil War* (Baton Rouge: Louisiana State Univ. Press, 2008), 43–52, and passim.

22   Edward Long, *Candid Reflections upon the judgment lately awarded by the court of the King's bench in Westminster Hall on what is commonly called 'the negro case'* (London, 1772) and *History of Jamaica,* 3 vols. (London, 1774).

23   David Geggus, *Slavery, War, and Revolution: The British Occupation of Saint-Domingue, 1793–1798* (New York: Oxford Univ. Press, 1982).

24   Daniel G. Lang, "Hamilton and Haiti" in Douglas Ambrose and Robert W. T. Martin, eds., *The Many Faces of Alexander Hamilton: The Life and Legacy of America's Most Elusive Founding Father* (New York: New York Univ. Press, 2006), 239–44.

25   See Paul Roussier, *Lettres du Général Leclerc: Commandant en Chef de l'Armée de Saint-Domingue en 1802* (Paris: Société de l'histoire des Colonies françaises, 1937), 237–39, 253–59.

26   Marcus Rainsford, *An Historical Account of the Black Empire of Hayti* (London, 1805).

27   Blackburn, *The Overthrow of Colonial Slavery,* 295–329.

The Achievement of the Haitian Revolution, 1791–1804

Robin Blackburn

I n the sequence of revolutions that remade the Atlantic world between 1776 and 1825, the Haitian Revolution is rarely given its due, yet without it there is much that cannot be accounted for. The revolutions—American, French, Haitian, and Spanish-American— should be seen as interconnected, with each helping to radicalize the next. The American Revolution launched an idea of popular sovereignty, which, together with the cost of the war, helped to bring about the downfall of the French monarchy. The French Revolution, dramatic as was its impact on the Old World, also became a fundamental event in the New, since it eventually challenged slavery as well as royal power. The French Assembly's resounding "Declaration of the Rights of Man and the Citizen" in 1789 was not, however, the trigger for the abolition of slavery. That came, instead, from events taking place in the French Caribbean colonies themselves.

OPPOSITE (DETAIL) Agostino Brunias (1728–1796). *Linen Market, Dominica*, ca. 1780. Oil on canvas, 19⅝ × 27 in. (49.8 × 68.6 cm). Yale Center for British Art, Paul Mellon Collection, B1981.25.76. The Bridgeman Art Library International.

SLAVERY AND THE FRENCH REVOLUTION

By the mid-eighteenth century, the toil of over three million slaves in the Americas yielded a booming commerce in plantation produce. Slaves were a form of property, a component of patriarchy. As Africans or descendants of Africans, they were not members of the polity but simply parts of their owners' households. But for the first time slavery also had become the object of public controversy and criticism among sections of "enlightened" and "awakened" opinion. On both sides of the Atlantic the new patriotism celebrated liberty and denounced despotism. The patriots were inspired by Roman republicanism, but some were not entirely comfortable with slavery or the African presence. The American War of Independence and its immediate aftermath had helped to put the issue of the slave trade, and even slavery itself, on the political agenda, but both protagonists had shied away from decisive action. By the early 1790s, plantation slavery had recovered from a quarter-century of turmoil. The Atlantic trade in slave produce and slaves had never been larger.

French colonial slavery had been initially sponsored by royal absolutism but had evolved into a major component of French capitalist and bourgeois development. About a tenth of the members of the National Assembly formed in 1789, both nobles and members of the Third Estate, were colonial proprietors. Bordeaux and Nantes, the two Atlantic ports that virtually monopolized the colonial trade, were the hubs of the Jacobin and Girondin network of revolutionary clubs. The Massiac Club, a lobby by colonial proprietors, inclined towards a moderate but constitutional royalism but above all focused tenaciously on the defense of white slaveholders.[1]

The French Revolution at first presented barriers to slave emancipation as strong as those present in North America. The discourse of 1789–92 made liberty conditional on public utility, property, and membership in the community. Only propertied French men could be "active citizens"; French women and children were "passive" citizens. The enslaved were treated as both minors and aliens. The first clause of the Declaration of the Rights of Man stated: "Men are born, and always continue, free and equal in respect of their rights. Civil distinctions, therefore, can be founded only on public utility." The last clause reinforced "public utility" as a potential qualification of freedom by insisting: "The right to property being inviolable and sacred, no one ought to be deprived of it, except in cases of evident public necessity, legally ascertained, and on condition of a previous just indemnity."[2] Since slaves were unquestionably a sort of property, as well as arguably a prop of public utility, the qualification of natural liberty seemed robust enough to reassure the many colonial proprietors in the Assembly. The Duc de la Rochefoucault proposed freedom for slaves during the famous session that made a bonfire of feudal privileges, but his proposal was not accepted.

Encouraged by British abolitionists, and patronized by prominent philosophers, financiers, and political leaders, a French abolitionist society was formed in 1788. The *Amis des Noirs* opposed the slave trade but focused mainly on defending the civic rights of the free men of color. When the slaves of Saint-Domingue launched their historic uprising in August 1791 the *Amis des Noirs* had yet to propose the dissolution of slavery.

HAITI AND HUMAN RIGHTS

At what point did the revolutionary challenge to slavery emerge? Was it with the first large-scale slave uprisings in 1791? Or the proclamations against slavery made by Sonthonax, the Jacobin Commissioner, and Toussaint Louverture, the black general, on August 29, 1793? Or the eventual decree of February 4, 1794 (16 Pluviose An II) declaring the end of slavery in the French colonies? Or the French defeat in Saint-Domingue, and the proclamation of the Republic of Haiti on January 1, 1804? Each of these were certainly important interrelated stepping stones. Their connection explains why the leaders of the Revolution took so long to rally to emancipationism, as well as why they eventually did so. It also weighs the respective contributions of metropolitan abolitionists and black revolutionaries.

Saint-Domingue was already in turmoil on the eve of the great slave uprising of August 1791. The colony was gripped by intense battles between supporters and opponents of the metropolitan Revolutionary authorities. The latter had announced modest concessions to the free people of color, sparking intense opposition from many of the resident *petits blancs* and *grands blancs.* The slave uprisings were seen by many Jacobins as the result of a royalist provocation and plot, and the rebels as dupes of Counter Revolution. While the mass of rebels were certainly motivated by their desire to throw off enslavement, some leaders may indeed have been encouraged by royalists or Spanish agents. Within a week or two of the slave uprising, some thirty thousand rebels had fanned out across the Northern plain, burning plantations and urging slaves to join them. The French Revolutionary garrison and militia were just strong enough to venture outside the provincial capital, Le Cap, and restore a very fragile control over some of the devastated estates.

Yves Benot, surveying contemporary accounts of the great uprising, highlights a significant phrase used by the rebel leaders, one that echoes revolts in other parts of the colony. The leaders proclaimed that their intention was to "seize the country."[3] A somewhat similar idea was conveyed to a French soldier in this description, in a letter home, of the outlook of slave rebels in the south: "They come and treat us as if we were the brigands and tell us '*nous après tandé zaute,*' which is to say, 'we had expected you, and we will cut off your heads to the last man; and that this land is not for you it is for us'."[4] Documents relating to the slave uprisings occasionally described their goal as "liberté," a word and concept much in play but not the same as general emancipation or "liberté général." The leaders of the northern revolt negotiated for the liberty of their immediate followers, and for a three-day workweek, or a ban on the whip, rather than for general emancipation.[5]

The slave community included both literate creoles and newly arrived Africans. Kreyòl was far more widely spoken than French, and varieties of African culture still had great importance. A famous Kreyòl saying insisted that *tou moun se moun,* or "everyone is a person." If this was already current in the Kreyòl of the early 1790s, then the philosophical premises of a doctrine favorable to general liberty were already active. Another approach was a direct reworking of the French discourse of liberty, as in a letter reputed to have been sent by three rebel leaders in July 1792 to the colonial assembly in which they

PROCLAMATION

NOUS, ÉTIENNE *POLVEREL* & *LÉGER-FÉLICITÉ SONTHONAX*, *Commissaires Civils*, que nation Française voyé dans pays-ci, pour mettre l'ordre et la tranquillité tout par-tout.

A vla yo donc yon foi démasqués cila la yo toi hélé z'amis pays cila la, qui livré la ville du Cap dans difé et dans pillage, z'amis de France la yo qui gagné pour cri ralliement *vive le roi*, qui hélé Pagnols sur terre à nous, qui groffi z'armée à yo, qui livré yo poftes que nous té confié yo, qui ofé faire complots pour prend pays-ci baye Pagnols; z'amis de la loi la yo et tout cila yo qui gagné pouvoirs de commiffaires et qui chargé exécuter z'ordre à yo; à vla nous voir yo marcher fous z'ordres à Galbaud, Galbaud li même qui té connait la loi défende li commandé dans pays-ci; Galbaud qui té dit li pas vlé obéir à z'ordres à c mmiffaires la yo.

Au Cap yo tiré en haut nous pendant deux jours, avec canons et fufils; cila yo qui pas té gagné quior paraitre in mitend les autres, yo caché la case à yo, yo tiré par fenêtre, yo faziné monde qui batte pour la république et yo fini par bourler Cap.

A Jérémie, Cayemittes, z'Abricots, yo femblé négres en pile, yo retranché dans camp, yo pas vlé recevoir commiffaires que nous té voyé avec foldats pour bayo la paix et fuivre la loi; yo batte avec l'armée la république la.

Marmelade yo cherché cordé avec Pagnols pour yo vivre avec yo.

Mouchier Nully, qui té commandé cordon de l'Ouest, voyé z'ordre tout côté pour rêter nous; après li déferté pofte à li, li paffé dans partie pagnole avec trois officiers 84eme. régiment.

Mouchier Lafeuillée qui té commandé Ouanaminthe, place qui forte, et qui té gagné yon bon garnison, Lafeuillée livré li à Pagnols la fur yon fimple demande.

Qui complot ça donc qui formé contre république française la? Qui cila yo qui fait complot là côté li, et qui qui chofe çà qui fait yo cordé fi ben ensemble?

Cila yo qui fait complot là, c'eft prefque toutes blancs qui té à Saint-Domingue, cila yo qui té gagné dettes en pile, quoique yo té gagné l'air riche, cila yo qui té vlé pillage parce que yo té pas gagné à rien.

Tout plein grand Mouchier qui forti en France, et qui pitôt pays-ci pacé pays outi z'ennemis à nous yès, parce que yo té cré mieux réuffi dans pays-ci pour faire faire z'affaires là vini comme li té yès l'autre fois.

Yo toute vlé monde mouvé corps; yo toute vlé grands malheurs, les uns pour faire monde laffe pour pays-ci pas dépende encore ia France, et pour yo pas payé dettes à yo.

Non, cila la pas lé mourir: li pas lé jamais quine à roi encore, ni quine à maitres qui méchans; li va fortir de cendres à li, et li va plus brillante que jamais; li va femblé en France, qui aftor terre à liberté et terre à l'égalité, et république française là va trouver encore petites à li qui va fervi li ben.

Citoyens 4 avril 1792 layo, cila yo du 20 juin 1793, cila yo qui va mériter encore yo libres, yo pas té jamais blié que de toutes nations dans monde, république française la, li yone qui fait refpecter droits de l'homme et q'yo pas lé capable conferver droits à li cordé yo, qu'autant yo vas vini battre zennemis à république la, fous z'ordres à commiffaires civils la yo, et que pays Pagnol comme pays-ci, va gagner pavillon national.

Nous vlé et nous dire:

ART. PREMIER. Nous déclaré traitres à la nation mouchier Nully, qui té lieutenant-colonel dans 84e. régiment qui té forti en France, mouchier Lafeuillée, capitaine au régiment du Cap, mouchier St.-Simon qui té capitaine dans même régiment, mouchier St.-Simon et mouchier Defbouville, lieutenans tous deux dans même régiment, et toutes z'officiers layo, caporals, fergens, foldats qui té dans confeil guerre io té quinbé Ouanaminthe pour baye Pagnols quartier Ouanaminthe.

ART. II. Commandans volontaires Cap à pied et à choual, nous déclaré io traitres auffi, parce qu'au lieu io vini prendre z'ordre à commiffaires civils la io, comme io té ordonné io, io armé foldats à io, io faire io marcher fous z'ordres à Galbaud contre commiffaires civils.

ART. III. Nous déclaré auffi traitres à la nation z'officiers municipalités quartier Jérémie, quartier Cayemittes, quartier z'Abricots, parce que io femblé en pile nègres z'efclaves io armé io, io faire camps pour repouffer monde que commiffaires civils té voyé pour la paix.

ART. IV. Nous déclaré auffi traitre à la nation Mouchier Dupérier, capitaine général troupes io té dire patriotes, dans quartier Cayemittes et Jérémie, parce que li té batte contre l'armée la république la au camp Riveau.

ART. V. Nous déclaré traitres à la nation auffi Mouchier Sage, qui té z'abitant Marmelade et qui aftor dans Pagnols, parce que li té engagé z'abitans à baye quartier Marmelade à Pagnols.

ART. VI. Nos déclaré traitre auffi à la nation Mouchier Capet, qui té chef la municipalité et z'officiers municipalité, parce que io té hélé toute z'abitans pour baye confentement à io d'après confeils à Mouchier Sage, pour livrer quartier la à Pagnols.

ART. VII. Toute monde-nous forti nommé, nous ôté commandement dans main à io tout, parce que io pas bon pour commandé encore; io traitres à la nation.

ART. VIII. Nous ordonné à toute monde qui commandé, et à toutes citoyens de courir la fus fi io contré io, & prend io mort ou vivant pour mené baye commiffaires.

ART. IX. Nous déclaré hors la loi tout cila io nous forti nommé; io pas capable faire aucun z'affaires en juftice; nous défende à toutes perfonnes libres, comme z'efclaves recevoir io la cafe à io ni rende io aucun fervice, ni couté io fi io parlé io qui chofe, fous peine io va cré io dans complots à io va puni io tant comme grands criminels.

ART. X. Nous pardonné toutes z'officiers, foldats qui té dans camp Ouanaminthe et pas té dans l'affemblée la io té faire, pour baye Pagnols Ouanaminthe et Maribaroux; nous engagé io vini plus vite que io capable, prendre pofte à io dans fervice république la, et pour défende pays-ci.

ART. XI. Toutes z'efclaves qui té dans brigands, et qui vlé profiter pardon commiffaires laio qui vlé libres, comme nous déjà parlé dans premier billet à nous, du 21 juin, io obligé vini dans huit jours fans faute, compté jour io va publié billet cilala.

Cilaio qui au Cap, haut di Cap, morne di Cap, io doit vini baie nom aio l'affemblée termédiaire qui quinbé au Cap.

Cila io qui dans plaine ou dans mornes, chacun va lé trouvé commandant quartier à io pour baye nom à io, foit dans camps ou ben la cafe à io, fans craindre io pas lé faire io à rien, pour engager io dans troupes que nous ordonné.

ART. XII. Papier là, ou ti io va metté nom à chaque n'homme qui va prendre parti la guerre côté Pagnols et z'autres z'ennemis à nous, io va metté nom à z'habitation où ti io forti, ou ben nom à z'ancien maitre à io.

ART. XIII. Commandans là io va voyé copie papier là, qui gagné nom à chaque guerrier, pardevant commiffaires civils, gouverneur général et l'affemblée termédiaire.

ART. XIV. Ci la io qui va enrôlé pour fervice la république, et qui va ben faire devoir à io, tant q'io qui va libres.

ART. XV. Huit jours après qu'io va publié papier cila la, toute cila io qui pas lé enrôlé, et dans mains à qui io va trouvé fufil, trabouck, fpingoles, piftolets, manchettes, flèches, lances, fabres, io va prend io pour brigands, io va reté io et pini io comme criminels.

ART. XVI. Toutes z'efclaves io va trouver dans grand chimin fans billet, malgré io pas gogné z'armes, après huit jours la io paffé, io va guetté io comme z'efclaves marrons et io va pini io.

Nous vlé papier cila là lire, piblier, imprimer, afficher tout par-tout, pour perfonne pas capable dire io pas connaît li, et regiftrer l'affemblée termédiaire et dans toute tribunal et municipalité pays-ci.

Nous vlé gouverner là, li faire li exécuter et li voyé li baye toute commandant qui dans camps et dans poftes.

Fait au Haut-di-Cap, le 2 juillet 1793, l'an 2 de la république.

POLVEREL, SONTHONAX.

Par les Commiffaires civils de la République,

PICQUENARD, Secrétaire adjoint de la Commiffion.

De l'Imprimerie de la Commiffion civile de la République.

pour copie conforme à l'original

Paul

ask: "Have you forgotten that you have formally vowed the Rights of man?" and present as their first demand "general liberty for all men detained in slavery."[6] The appeal, however, was ignored by the assembly.

In France, with the support of the *Amis des Noirs*, a decree extending full civil rights to all free colored men, together with provisions to enlist them in militia battalions, was adopted on April 4, 1792. Those who sent Léger-Félicité Sonthonax, a denouncer of slavery and the white *colons*, to be Commissioner of the Northern province of Saint-Domingue expected him to vigorously promote the Convention's strategy of allying with the free people of color against the treachery of white colonists, many of whom were conspiring with the royalists and the British. The Commissioner for the West was the like-minded Polverel. Sonthonax formed new colored battalions and cracked down on counterrevolutionary conspiracies, causing much anger among the white colonists. This opposition was encouraged in mid-1793 by the arrival of a new military Governor, General Galbaud, whom the white colonists hailed as a savior. Though a Republican, he had both property and family in Saint-Domingue, and was soon persuaded that Sonthonax and Polverel were ruining the colony. The Commissioners had simply pursued the construction of multiracial order in conformity with metropolitan instructions. They appointed colored officers both to a new legion of colored troops and to the white garrison regiments. They freed slaves willing to fight for the Republic and arranged 'republican marriages', whereby a slave woman who married such a republican soldier was also freed. With his mulatto partner Eugenie on his arm, Sonthonax presided over official receptions at which—to the scandal of many white colonists—people of all colors would mingle.[7]

In June 1793 the Commissioners moved to arrest Galbaud but this only emboldened the Governor to seize Le Cap, the capital of the Northern plain. The Governor could count on much of the garrison, the white militia, and the bulk of the white inhabitants. Retreating to the Bréda plantation on the outskirts of Le Cap, Sonthonax took a string of fateful steps. He promoted black Jacobins like Jean-Baptiste Belley and Colonel Pierre Michel to important commands in Le Cap.[8] Some key commanders remained loyal to the Commissioners, notably General Laveaux and the mulatto veteran Jean Villate. Sonthonax also forged an alliance with Louis Pierrot, an African-born commander and insurgent chief who maintained an independent column in the hills flanking the Northern plain. Pierrot descended to the environs of Le Cap and helped to secure it for the Commissioner. Galbaud and a few thousand of his supporters

OPPOSITE Broadside for *Proclamation/Nous, Étienne Polverel & Léger-Félicité Sonthonax, Commissaires Civils, que nation française voyé dans pays-ci, pour mettre l'ordre et la tranquillité tout par-tout*, also known as the *Kreyol Proclamation*, July 2, 1793. The John Carter Brown Library at Brown University, Oversize bEB .S137 1793 9. One of the earliest documents printed in Haitian Kreyòl.

clambered aboard the ships in the harbor and sailed for the United States. In the struggle to regain Le Cap, Sonthonax also offered freedom and citizenship to black insurgents held in the city's prisons if they were willing to join the fight.

The trouncing of Galbaud was celebrated in late July at a Republican military parade outside Le Cap comprising one hundred whites, three hundred mulattoes, and six thousand black soldiers. Pierrot swore an oath of loyalty to the Republic. Sonthonax liked to say that the republic was the needed vessel for equality: "It is the kings who want slaves. It is the kings of Guinea who sell them to the white kings."[9]

The Commune of Le Cap held a mass assembly of fifteen thousand "souls" on August 26, which passed by acclamation a call for the freeing of all slaves. The idea of "general liberty," which had first surfaced a year earlier in the appeal of three rebel leaders to the colonial assembly, was now adopted by a representative institution. Perhaps Sonthonax had arranged this meeting, though we cannot be sure that he directly inspired the sweeping motion it passed.[10] In any case, the commissioner issued a decree of general emancipation throughout the North on August 29.[11] Toussaint Louverture, then the commander of a large black force still serving the Spanish King, declared on the same day that he, too, was fighting to end slavery.

At a desperate moment for the Republic, Sonthonax had gone far beyond his instructions and powers. The Girondins who had sent him were moderate abolitionists who wanted to save the colonies from slave revolt as well as treason and free trade. Indeed the decree of April 1792 had been in part a response to the great revolt of August 1791 as well as to the treachery of the white colonists—it was hoped that the free people of color, who included quite a few slaveowners, would be a source of stability as well as loyalty.[12] But faced with the clash with Galbaud, Sonthonax decided that the best way of saving Saint-Domingue for France was to appeal to the black rebels and commit the Republic to emancipation. Sonthonax and Toussaint were willing, as no abolitionist had been before, to end slavery immediately, without delay, compromise, or compensation. In the rush of events both men had exceeded their powers.

The French Commissioners were, however, concerned to ensure the continuation of plantation labor. New labor regulations required former slaves to remain at work for at least another year. The whip was to be banned and the cultivators were promised compensation equivalent to a third of the value of the crop. The cultivators also retained possession of their personal gardens so long as they remained on the plantation. Polverel, who was based in Port

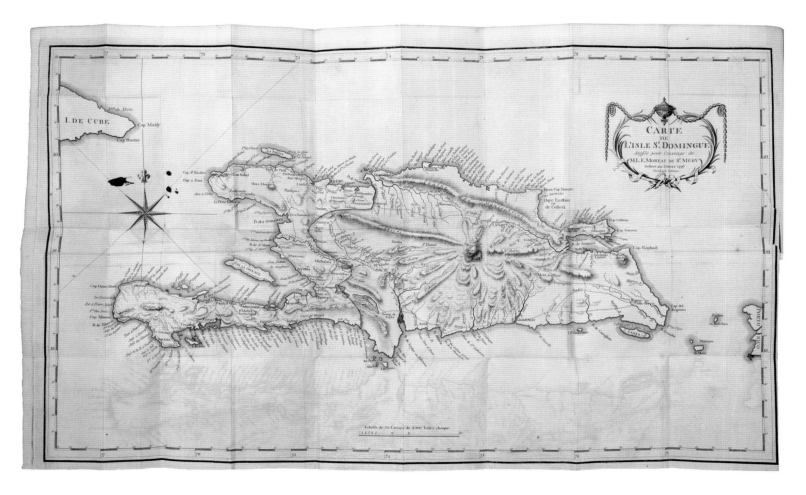

CARTE DE L'ISLE St. DOMINGUE

Republicain (formerly Port-au-Prince), ordered that the property of enemies of the republic was to be confiscated. These estates would now be held in common by the cultivators and warriors, with a codicil that the land might be distributed after order had been restored.[13]

Still, the Convention in Paris had not spoken. As Jeremy Popkin argues, its decision to seat black and brown representatives from Saint-Domingue in February 1794 was momentous.[14] At the time, the election of a black member of the British Parliament or the United States Congress would have been unthinkable. When the delegates arrived from Saint-Domingue, they had actually been arrested as royalist agents. But they were speedily freed, and their seating as deputies was a blow to the friends of slavery and the "aristocracy of the skin." These decisions led directly to the debate and passage of a motion on 16 Pluviôse (February 4, 1794) pronouncing the end of slavery in the French colonies. This was itself a transformative moment.

ABOVE Map from Médéric-Louis-Elie Moreau de Saint-Méry, *Description Topographique, Physique, Civile, Politique et Historique de la partie Francaise de l'Isle Saint Domingue*, 1798. William L. Clements Library, University of Michigan, C2 1797 Mo.

The abolition act was over-determined by the insurgency. But it was also one of those rare occasions when a text can redefine context and subtext by establishing a new horizon. While the Jacobins were in the ascendant at the time the decree was passed, the Girondins must be given credit for having sent Sonthonax to Saint-Domingue and for educating the Convention on the need for antislavery measures.

The motion that was passed read as follows: "The National Convention declares slavery abolished in all the colonies. In consequence it declares that all men, without distinction of color, domiciled in the colonies, are French citizens and will enjoy all the rights assured under the Constitution." The ending of slavery and the extension of citizenship offer a more clear-cut verdict on the institution than any earlier declaration of rights. Still, legalistically, the motion was less radical than it appeared. Since the Constitution was suspended, the precise import of the last promise was not clear, while the phrase "domiciled in the colonies" could be linked, via regulations that had already been reported, to continuing labor obligations laid on the former slaves. But while some colonial proprietors may have comforted themselves with such interpretations, the plain meaning of the motion is what counts, and what counted at the time.[15] Laveaux's promotion of the black general, the dispatch of thirty thousand muskets and much ammunition from France, and the offensive of Victor Hugues's forces in the Eastern Caribbean, all helped to spell out the meaning of 16 Pluviôse. Since the Constitution was suspended, the motion, together with instructions for implementation, had the force of a decree.

There was also an international aspect to emancipation. Although it was partly a response to the large-scale British expedition to seize the French islands, it cannot be dismissed as mere realpolitik. While emancipation corresponded with resistance to Britain, it also posed a great strategic risk—that of antagonizing the "sister republic," the United States. News soon arrived from the U.S., however, that Thomas Jefferson had stepped down as Secretary of State in December 1793, and Washington had chosen to entrust to John Jay the task of negotiating a rapprochement with the British. Reservations concerning the emancipation policy were swept aside and in March and April 1794 the decree of Pluviôse was carried to the New World.

The huge military force dispatched by the British to the Caribbean had seized the French islands of the Eastern Caribbean as well as significant territory in Saint-Domingue. The Hugues expedition soon recaptured Guadeloupe and some smaller islands but Martinique remained in British hands. The Republic's emancipation policy encouraged Toussaint Louverture to turn on the Spanish forces and rally to the Republic. The Revolution's prospects in the Caribbean were transformed. The policy of revolutionary emancipation was maintained after Robespierre's downfall and inflicted heavy losses on the British. It also helped to trigger the "Quasi-War," the undeclared naval conflict between France and the United States of 1796–99.

The French republican antislavery offensive lasted for a relatively brief period, from mid-1794 to late 1799, with a few wobbles. But given its boldness the surprise should be that it lasted so long. The Directory that took charge after Robespierre's overthrow had a reputation for great moderation and for abandoning Jacobin orientations. But as far as the Americas were concerned, this is misleading. The Directory maintained the emancipationist strategy in the Caribbean and reappointed Sonthonax. The Constitution it adopted held that the colonies were an integral part of the republic, governed by the same laws.

The radical antislavery policy gave vital breathing space to Toussaint's republican black power in Saint-Domingue, and helped him to defeat the Spanish, the British, and the royalists. The French Republic of 1794–99 should be given credit for sealing an alliance with black emancipation and giving it a few years to consolidate itself in Saint-Domingue. The Republic's offensive in the Eastern Caribbean tied down forty-five thousand British troops who could otherwise have been deployed in Saint-Domingue, and the British forces committed to the Caribbean exceeded those sent to fight in continental Europe. Toussaint would have found it very difficult, by himself, to build a new black power capable of defeating the Spanish and the British and of uprooting slavery throughout the colony.

Nevertheless, the cause of black emancipation remained fragile so long as it depended on the fluctuating fortunes of the Directory and its "neo-Jacobins." The rise of Napoleon, with his personal ties (via Josephine) to colonial planters, merchants, and bankers boded ill for the emancipationist policy. So did the prospect of peace, since it would give the French authorities an opportunity to restore control over their colonies. Napoleon's decision to destroy black power in Saint-Domingue and attempt to restore slavery followed the Quasi-War and the conclusion of the Peace of Amiens. The freed-people of the French Caribbean needed a state to defend their human rights. If the French state abandoned them, they would need to found one of their own.

The black revolt contained the seeds of independence from the outset. Toussaint's treaty with General Maitland securing British

Pl. 9.

TOUSSAINT L'OUVERTURE

reçoit une Lettre du premier Consul.

Dessiné par Monnet. Tom. I.er *Gravé par David.*

withdrawal in 1798 was an act of sovereignty. Shortly thereafter Toussaint accepted help from American warships when moving forces to crush the mulatto general Rigaud—a rival who was politically closer to France. Finally, he devised and unilaterally proclaimed a constitution for Saint-Domingue in 1801. These were all acts befitting a sovereign power. But it remains significant that Toussaint did not declare a formal breach with the French republic—not even in his last battle with Leclerc. Perhaps he still harbored hopes of an agreement with Napoleon, or a change in Paris; or he may have believed that with the leading powers anxious for peace and fearful of slave revolt no government would recognize an independent, black-led Saint-Domingue.

Toussaint himself had no difficulty in seeing that the Leclerc expedition was Napoleon's bid to crush black power in the Caribbean. His attempt to resist the expedition was soon overwhelmed and he was captured and jailed in France. Most of the remaining black and mulatto generals were at first misled by General Leclerc's assurances and offers of commissions in the French forces. The resistance instead came from more obscure grassroots leaders, many of them African-born. After a few months, Christophe, Pétion, and Dessalines—all of them Creoles—led their own troops into an alliance with these insurgents into the fight against France.

HAITI AND THE IDEA OF LIBERTY

The new Republic of Haiti adopted the trappings of a European state. Its African roots, however, were affirmed by giving a central founding role to the reenactment of the midnight Vodou rites at the Bois Caïman that prepared for the great uprising in August 1791.

The Haitian revolution channeled the mass longing for freedom into a ban on slavery. It also forged new identities and new ideals in a colony with a new language (*Kreyòl*) and a new religion (*Vodou*).[16] Sonthonax's decision in 1793 to issue official decrees in French as well as in *Kreyòl*, the language spoken by the great mass of the slaves, was a highly significant mark of his seriousness and recognition of the new and distinctive society.

The title of C. L. R. James's classic 1938 study, *The Black Jacobins*, unsettled the idea that emancipation had been a gift bestowed by the French, and it implied that "black Jacobins" found something in the discourse of the Revolution that helped them to elevate and generalize their struggle. But the history is more complicated. The Haitian revolutionaries' experiences in a slave society and memories from Africa radicalized the ideas

OPPOSITE Charles Monnet (1732–ca. 1808). *Toussaint Louverture reçoit une Lettre du premier Consul.* Engraving, date unknown. Bibliothèque nationale de France, Qg3. vol I, #75c74090.

they appropriated from France. The travail of Africa's sons and daughters in the New World gave a new scope and meaning to the freedom they claimed. In citing the diversity of black revolutionary inspiration, Laurent Dubois cites the example of one insurgent who was captured in possession of a pamphlet on the Declaration of the Rights of Man along with a packet of tinder, phosphate, and lime, as well as a sack of herbs, bone, and hair, a fetish in the Haitian Vodou religion. Dubois comments: "The law of liberty, ingredients for firing a gun, and a powerful amulet to call on the help of the gods: clearly, a potent combination." [17]

By contrast, both Toussaint and the French commissioners repeatedly sought to substitute obligatory plantation labor for slavery. Military commanders were converted into plantation managers who attempted to confine the "cultivateurs" to a narrow "plantation citizenship." [18] While black soldiers were honored, black laborers were obliged to stay on the plantation and work for the doubtful prospect of a small share of future revenue. That plantation output reached as much as a quarter of prerevolutionary levels around 1800 shows that militarized labor was not entirely unproductive. But coercive labor regimes proved enormously difficult to sustain. Soldiers and cultivateurs did not see themselves as separate species and both had witnessed the breakdown of authority. "Slavery without the whip" proved an empty formula. Toussaint's difficulty in rallying resistance to Leclerc stemmed in part from this failed experiment in unfree labor.

Later rulers of Haiti made the same mistake. Henry Christophe, ruler of the short-lived Northern kingdom, had some limited success with a military mobilization of workers for plantation labor and construction projects, such as his famous Citadel or palace at Sans Souci. His overthrow in 1820 reflected the difficulty of sustaining a forced labor regime amongst a people who had rejected slavery. In 1827 Jean-Pierre Boyer issued a draconian labor code, with provisions against vagrancy similar to those found in most European countries, but he lacked an administrative apparatus capable of implementing it. The peasants of Haiti simply refused to be dragooned, and armed irregulars (*piquets*) sometimes came to their aid. The revolution persisted thanks to their tenacity in the struggle for the control of time, land, and movement, in and through several changes of formal jurisdiction, and whatever the stance of the famous leaders.

The Republic of Haiti presented a façade worthy of recognition by the Atlantic diplomatic world, but the peasants of the interior created their own distinctive culture, with its own language, religious cults, and music.[19] Michel Hector and Laënnec Hurbon argue that the Haitian revolution was not only a triple revolution against "slavery, colonialism and racial oppression," but also a revolution whose social base in the former slaves gave it "a strong orientation towards rejection of the plantation system." This opened the way to diverse interpretations concerning an "ultimately anticapitalist or antifeudal revolution in Saint-Domingue."[20] Over successive decades, and in the course of rivalries within the Haitian elite, the former slaves defeated attempts to press them into plantation labor.

Military conflicts, revolutionary ideology, and nationalism all contributed to the exclusively masculine character of Haiti's political system. There were some female soldiers, however, and the exploits of a few of these, notably Marie Jeanne's heroism in the defense of Crète à Pierrot, were celebrated. Suzanne Simone and Claire Heureuse, Toussaint's and Dessalines's wives, were public figures.[21] But the real changes for women did not occur at the elite level. The overthrow of slavery had brought fundamental changes in women's position. Fewer women than men had obtained privileges under slavery. With the suppression of slavery, women still had to work hard, but were better able to enjoy the fruits of freedom.

The position of women improved a little once a degree of pacification was achieved. Although certainly excluded from all political roles, females were not absent as social and economic agents. While elites aspired to an observance of the family norms preached by the Catholic Church, the family structure practiced by the mass of the population was more flexible. The 1805 Constitution devoted twenty-five pages to the question of divorce and the status of children born out of wedlock. These laws envisaged women having custody of their children and required their former husbands to contribute to their support. Women were not allowed to divorce men who were absent on military service but they could unilaterally divorce men who had emigrated. These laws, if applied, were more liberal than those prevailing in Europe, while remaining broadly patriarchal nonetheless.[22]

The growing population testified to a revival of family life, with considerable responsibility in the hands of women. It was widely observed that women held the purse strings, and in typical West African style dominated local markets. The *revendeuse* bought and sold a vast range of produce while the coffee *speculateurs* were women; they bought the crop from peasants and sold it to the export houses. President Salnave (1867–69) was supported by a march of market women brandishing butcher knives, and appointed two of them as Army generals.[23] Furthermore, women were often respected because

OVERLEAF Agostino Brunias (1728–1796). *Linen Market, Dominica*, ca. 1780. Oil on canvas, 19⅝ × 27 in. (49.8 × 68.6 cm). Yale Center for British Art, Paul Mellon Collection, B1981.25.76. The Bridgeman Art Library International.

of their knowledge of sorcery and the secrets of Vodou. It was thought that the *manbo* or Vodou priestess could cast out a zombie or restore a *petit bon ange*.[24] Some were recognized as the *Reine de la rara*, or Queen of the shrine. While women's spiritual power commanded some respect, it also could be misused or subordinated in various ways. Haiti's civil society was by no means monolithically patriarchal.

HAITI AND THE OUTSIDE WORLD

The Haitian victory over Napoleon encouraged the British Parliament and United States Congress to end British and American participation in the Atlantic slave trade. The saga of black resistance, seen as a warning by some and an inspiration by others, made a deep impact on public opinion throughout the Atlantic world. In the 1780s both New York and New Jersey had rejected emancipation laws which were subsequently passed in 1799 and 1804 respectively. The events in Saint-Domingue had underlined how dangerous as well as valuable the institution of slavery could be.

Abandoning his attempt to restore a French empire based on slavery, Napoleon decided to sell the vast territory of Louisiana to the United States. While the Haitian revolution persuaded some to reduce or end their stake in slavery, the ruin of such an important producer was seen by others as a major opportunity. The sugar economy of Louisiana expanded significantly as a result, often managed by exiled planters fleeing Haiti; Cubans, as well, not only took in Haitian planters but invested heavily in the expansion of sugar plantations cultivated by slaves.

During the period 1804–20 Haiti faced commercial blockade and diplomatic isolation from France and the United States, and even a new attempt to restore French rule. The United States did not recognize Haiti until 1862. For much of this time Haiti was politically fragmented, but by the 1820s the country was reunited and even enjoyed a degree of recovery. While the slave populations of Caribbean plantation colonies, excluding new arrivals, declined each year by one or two percent, Haiti's [free?] population instead roughly doubled in size in the nineteenth century.

In 1825–26 President Boyer undertook an extraordinary negotiation with the French monarchy. Boyer sought to break Haiti's isolation by undertaking to lower the tariffs on French imports and to pay 150 million francs in compensation to the French proprietors of Saint-Domingue, their estates valued at 1789 prices. The Franco-Haitian Treaty embodied formal recognition and allowed Haitian coffee exports to rise to £1 million a year in the 1830s, making Haiti

ABOVE *Tableau des Finances et du Commerce de la partie Francoise de St. Domingue*, 1791. Hand-colored broadside. The John Carter Brown Library at Brown University, 09-146.

one of the world's leading producers. Paying off the debt absorbed much of these earnings.[25]

The first payment of the indemnity was financed by floating a bond on the Paris bourse. In 1838 the debt was restructured to make the payments more manageable. Nevertheless servicing the debt was an onerous drain on Haiti's public finances for many decades and was not wound up until the 1880s. Moreover, the mere existence of this debt prevented Haiti from floating any other bond on the Paris bourse to pay for badly needed investments in roads, bridges, and waterways.[26]

EPILOGUE

In 1811, John Adams almost ruefully observed to Benjamin Rush: "Did not the American Revolution produce the French Revolution? And did not the French Revolution produce all the calamities and desolations of the human race and the whole globe ever since?"[27] Adams's stoic despair and foreboding contrasts with a very different assessment of the revolution in Haiti eight years later in the *Quarterly Review*. The conservative British magazine abhorred Jacobinism, yet declared in 1818:

> The abolition of Negro slavery and the civilization of this long oppressed race of human beings will probably in later ages be considered to date from the era of the French Revolution. In the midst of all the mischief and misery occasioned by the eruption of that volcano of the moral world the first germ of Negro emancipation was unintentionally planted in the island of Santo Domingo…whence it can hardly fail to spread its roots, in the course of no very distant period, through the whole of the…Antilles."[28]

The leaders of Haiti in the first decades of its existence, whether monarchical or republican, went to considerable lengths to adopt the prevailing state forms and styles of the European and American world. Their public buildings, dress, legal arrangements reflected this and French remained the official language. Henry Christophe invited Protestant missionaries and educators while the Catholic Church continued to function, often with official blessing, in the Republic. Writing in 1830 Hegel wrote that the Negroes of Haiti 'had formed a state built on Christian principles'.[29] While this was certainly meant as a tribute, it also pointed to what can also be seen as a defect. If formal state structures typically misrepresent their citizens, the gulf was quite glaring in the case of Haiti..

Laurent Dubois suggests that the soul of Haiti is still found in a religious ceremony, the legend of the Bois Caïman, not in a Declaration of Independence, a Constitution, or a Panthéon. Yet there are secular as well as religious underpinnings for Haitian nationalism. The spirit of the revolution lives on in the people, with their stubborn defense of an autonomous personal realm, but despite the efforts of such nineteenth- and early twentieth-century reformist leaders as Anténor Firmin or Jean Price-Mars, or Jean Dominique, Aristide, and René Préval more recently, it does not yet exist in the formal arrangements of the state. It is only the efforts of the country's own citizens, not foreign intervention, that could mend this absence of a properly functioning and legitimate state. The terrible earthquake of January 2010 has revealed all of this complexity and the challenges still faced by Haiti and those beyond Haiti who recognize the nation's claim on all of us.

Notes

1   The classic study of the powerful colonial lobby is Gabriel Debien, *Les colons de Saint-Domingue et la Révolution* (Paris: Librairie Armand Colin, 1953). But see also M. B. Garrett, *The French Colonial Question, 1789–1791* (Ann Arbor: George Wahr, 1916).

2   "Declaration of the Rights of Man and the Citizen," in Merryn Williams, ed., *Revolutions, 1775–1830* (Harmondsworth, Eng.: Penguin, 1971), 97–99. The limits of the French Revolutionary concept of citizenship are explored in Olivier le Cour Grandmaison, *Les Citoyennetés en révolution 1789–94* (Paris: Presses Universitaires de France, 1992), especially 191–238 so far as slavery is concerned. The idea that men are not only born free and equal but remain so potentially headed off the idea that, though naturally free and equal, men lost these attributes once they entered society. But in the 1789 Declaration this improved formulation was already mortgaged to property and public utility.

3   Yves Benot, *Les Lumières, l'esclavage, la colonisation* (Paris: Editions La Découverte, 2005), 230–41. An English version of this chapter appears in David Geggus and Norman Fiering, eds., *The World of the Haitian Revolution* (Bloomington: Indiana Univ. Press, 2009), 99–110. It was presented as a paper at a conference organized by the John Carter Brown Library in 2004. A number of the references in this section are also to texts that appear in this volume. Sadly Yves Benot was to die in the following year. The French volume I cite contains well-merited tributes to his studies of colonialism, Enlightenment and slavery.

4   Carolyn Fick, *The Making of Haiti: The Saint Domingue Revolution from Below* (Knoxville: Univ. of Tennessee Press, 1990), 156.

5   Fick, *Making of Haiti*, 114–15.

6   Letter to the General Assembly from Biassou, Jean François and Belair (nephew of Toussaint Louverture). For an English translation see Toussaint L'Ouverture, *The Haitian Revolution*, New York: Verso, 2008, 5–8 (7).

7   Elizabeth Colwill, "'Fêtes d'hymen, Fêtes de la liberté': Marriage, Manhood and Emancipation in Revolutionary Saint-Domingue," in Geggus and Fiering, eds., *The World of the Haitian Revolution*, 125–55.

8   Belley, later to be elected to the Convention, has become the iconic "black Jacobin." Attired in his French deputy's uniform he proudly gazes out of Anne-Louis Girodet's 1797 painting, a bust of Raynal by his side. These events are recounted in Laurent Dubois, *Avengers of the New World: The Story of the Haitian Revolution* (Cambridge: Harvard Univ. Press, 2005), 155–65.

9   Quoted in Dubois, *Avengers of the New World*, 159.

10 While Sonthonax may have persuaded the Commune to adopt general liberty—wishing to be seen to be responding to their call—this possibility does not fit well with his preoccupation at this time with promoting marriage as a route to emancipation. If he intended to issue and implement a decree of general liberty why concern himself with partial emancipations via marriage to enlisted men? For the latter see Colwill, "'Fêtes d'hymen, Fêtes de la liberté'", in Geggus and Fiering, *The World of the Haitian Revolution*, 125–55.

11 Dubois, *Avengers of the New World*, 156–63. Florence Gauthier, director, *Périssent les colonies plutôt qu'un principe!: Contribution à l'histoire de l'abolition de l'esclavage, 1789–1804* (Paris: Société des études robespierristes, 2002), 108.

12 A point made by Frédérick Régent, *Esclavage, métissage, liberté: La Révolution française en Guadeloupe, 1789–1802* (Paris: Grasset & Fasquelle, 2004), 437.

13 Dubois, *Avengers of the New World*, 165–70. See also one of the earliest histories of Haiti and its revolution, Gaspard Théodore Mollien, *Haïti ou Saint-Domingue* [before 1830], 2 vols. (Paris: L'Harmattan, 2006), I:81–86. Toussaint, at this point, had not addressed the labor issue. His appeal simply offered an end to slavery.

14 Jeremy D. Popkin, "The French Revolution's Other Island," in Geggus and Fiering, *The World of the Haitian Revolution*, 199–222.

15 The attempt of pro-slavery forces to somehow amend or stymie the motion is explained by Yves Benot, "Comment la Convention à-t-elle voté l'Abolition de l'esclavage en l'An II," in *Les Lumières, l'esclavage, la colonisation*, 252–63. See also Jean-Daniel Piquet, "L'Emancipation des Noirs dans les débats de la Société des Jacobins de Paris (1791–94)," in Marcel Dorigny, ed., *Esclavage, Resistances, et Abolitions* (Paris: Editions du CTHS, 1999), 187–98. In *Mer et Liberté: Haiti, 1492–1794* (Port-au-Prince: FOKAL, 2009), Vertus Saint-Louis points to the key role of the policeman André Amar in seeking to frustrate anti-slavery initiatives. The legal dimensions are stressed by Miranda Frances Spieler, "The Legal Structure of Colonial Rule during the French Revolution," *William and Mary Quarterly* (April 2009): 365–408.

16 Laurent Dubois, *A Colony of Citizens: Revolutions and Slave Emancipation in the French Caribbean* (Chapel Hill: Univ. of North Carolina Press, 2004).

17 Ibid., 103.

18 The concept of plantation citizenship—*citoyenneté d'habitation*—is elaborated by Vertus Saint-Louis, *Mer et Liberté*, 315.

19 A point often made for the revolutionary period by C. L. R. James in *The Black Jacobins: Toussaint L'Ouverture and the San Domingo Revolution* (1938. Repr. ed.: New York: Random House, 1963) and Carolyn Fick in *The Making of Haiti*.

20 Michel Hector and Laënnec Hurbon, eds., "Introduction," *Genèse de l'état haïtien, 1804–1859* (Paris: Editions de la Maison des Sciences de l'Homme, 2009), 11–24 (16–17).

21 Sabine Manigat, "La rôle des femmes," in Hector and Hurbon, eds., *Genèse de l'état haïtien*, 331–37.

22 *Lois et Actes sous le règne de Jean-Jacques Dessalines* (Port-au-Prince: Editions Presses nationales d'Haïti, 2006), 77–105.

23 David Nichols, "Holding the Purse Strings: Women in Haiti," *Haiti in Caribbean Context: Ethnicity, Economy and Revolt* (Basingstoke, Hants., Eng.: 1985), 121–29.

24 Laënnec Hurbon, *Le Barbare imaginaire: Sorciers, zombis et cannibals en Haiti* (Paris: Cerf, 1988), 181.

25 A disciplined labor force was essential to the credibility of the state finances, and the president's 1827 labor code was partly designed to reassure foreign bondholders that Haiti had a disciplined work force and did not tolerate idlers and vagrants.

26 Alex Dupuy, *Haiti in the World Economy: Class, Race and Underdevelopment since 1700* (Boulder, Colo.: Westview Press, 1989), 93–94. Dupuy is careful to put the debt problem in a wider context of neo-colonial dependence on France. When President Aristide requested return of this compensation in 2003 Jacques Chirac, the French president, established a commission headed by Régis Debray, whose report found that even though Haiti had been "impeccable" in its servicing of the debt, the repayment proposed by Aristide was wholly inappropriate. See Peter Hallward, *Damming the Flood: Haiti, Aristide and the Politics of Containment* (London: Verso, 2008), 228–29.

27 John Adams to Benjamin Rush, 28 August 1811, quoted in David Brion Davis, *Revolutions: Reflections on American Equality and Foreign Liberations* (Cambridge: Harvard Univ. Press, 1990), 49.

28 *Quarterly Review* 42 (1819); cited in David Barry Gaspar and David Patrick Geggus, eds., *A Turbulent Time: The French Revolution and the Greater Caribbean* (Bloomington: Indiana Univ. Press, 1997), vii.

29 M. J. Petry, ed., *Hegel's Philosophy of Subjective Spirit* (Dordrecht: Reidel, 1979), 2:55; quoted in Susan Buck-Morss, "Hegel and Haiti," *Critical Inquiry* 26 (Summer 2000): 854.

An African Revolutionary in the Atlantic World

Laurent Dubois and Julius S. Scott

I n late 1793, a ship arrived in Philadelphia carrying a man named Jean-Baptiste Belley. He was on his way to Paris, travelling from the French colony of Saint-Domingue. It was not his first trip across the Atlantic. Born in the 1740s in West Africa, he had traveled, decades before, in the other direction from Africa, as a slave brought via the Middle Passage to the Caribbean. Now he was free, a veteran of the war that had transformed Saint-Domingue since 1791, an officer, and a representative traveling to take up a seat in France's National Convention.[1]

The currents that brought the ship from Saint-Domingue to Philadelphia had, since 1791, and especially in the summer of 1793, brought many refugees from France's colony to North America. These currents, like those that connected the Caribbean to all the major ports in the United States, as well as connecting the Caribbean islands to one another, to Mexico, Central America, and the Northern coast of South America, and of course to Europe and Africa as well, also brought news—lots of it. Indeed, in the Atlantic world information travelled startlingly quickly along informal routes, often more quickly than it did through official channels. People spoke about what they had seen in the places they had come from, and while some of this information made it into print in local newspapers, much more was transmitted from mouth to ear, as rumor or as news—the difference was very often unclear. Depending on who spoke, and who heard, the news from Saint-Domingue took on very different meanings. While slave owners generally were frightened and appalled at the progress of the slave insurrection, slaves themselves likely found hope, or at least satisfaction, in hearing of the ways the tables had been turned by at least some of the enslaved. The currents of communication that tied together the Atlantic world, and in particular linked together Afro-American communities throughout this world, buzzed with discussion about the events in Saint-Domingue, about where they might lead and what they might portend for individual and collective futures.[2]

When Belley arrived in Philadelphia, he was a bearer and a symbol of very dramatic news: slavery had been abolished outright in Saint-Domingue, the slaves transformed into free men and women, and into French citizens. In the wake of emancipation, an election had chosen Belley and four other delegates to leave Saint-Domingue and represent the colony, and its new order, to the National Convention, in order to argue in favor of emancipation.

For white slave-owners exiled in Philadelphia, the arrival of Belley in their midst provided them with an opportunity to strike out directly at a symbol of what many of them considered to be an unacceptable transformation in the social order. The group had barely anchored on the docks, they later recounted, before a number of French sailors shouted that the group should be hung or shot. One of the white delegates, Dufay, entered Philadelphia and was immediately surrounded by a murderous crowd, surviving only thanks to the protection of a woman who led him through the side streets of the city. Another crowd boarded the ship and attacked the other delegates. They were particularly brutal towards Belley. They took his sword, his watch, his money and his papers, and attacked him for "daring" to serve as an officer and "commanding whites." Belley—who had served as an officer in Saint-Domingue, and played a crucial role in defending the Republican commissioners on the island, Sonthonax and Polverel, against an attempt by planters and their allies to get rid of them—responded that if he knew how to "save whites and defend them" there was no reason he could not command them. The crowd demanded he remove his tricolor cockade, shouting that a black man should not be allowed to wear one. When he refused, they tore it off. The crowd then pillaged the quarters of the absent Dufay, declaring that "whites who sided with blacks were the guiltiest of all." One of the five delegates was spirited off the ship by the crowd, and taken hostage, though he managed to escape and rejoin the delegation later in New York. In order to make sure some of them made it to Paris, the five delegates split into two groups. Three of them—Belley, Louis Dufay, and Jean-Baptiste Mills—finally made it to Bordeaux and, after being briefly imprisoned by local authorities, arrived in Paris in mid-February.[3]

The task of the delegates was to explain to the National Convention how, in a colony that until recently had been the heart of France's booming Atlantic economy, the slavery that sustained that economy had been abolished. Of course, news of the slave revolution that began in Saint-Domingue in August 1791 had been arriving steadily in metropolitan France for two years, prompting various reactions and responses, including an April 1792 decree that granted full rights to free people of African descent, in the hopes that by assuring their allegiance to France the nation could still and ultimately crush the slave revolt. Still, the news brought by Belley and his colleagues was stunning indeed. Not only had the slave revolution not been defeated, it had been actively embraced. The demands of the slave revolution had become the policy of the

142 | Revolution! The Atlantic World Reborn

Republic in Saint-Domingue. And now the delegates elected there requested that it become the policy of the Republic throughout its empire.

When Belley, Dufay, and Jean-Baptiste Mills, a free man of color, entered the Convention, a deputy rose and announced that it was a great day. While the "aristocracy" of both nobility and church had been destroyed by the Revolution, the "aristocracy of the skin" had remained strong. All that, however, had just changed. "Equality is consecrated; a black, a yellow [i.e., mulatto], and a white have taken their seat among us, in the name of the free citizens of Saint-Domingue." The Convention erupted with applause, and another deputy asked that particular recognition be given to the two free men of color—Belley and Mills—whose class had been oppressed "for so many years." The next day, Dufay took the stand at the Convention and delivered a powerful speech describing the events that had transformed Saint-Domingue. He recounted how the slaves in Le Cap, and on surrounding plantations, had come to the rescue of the Republican commissioners when they were attacked by the counter-revolutionary Galbaud. "'We are negroes, and French,' they said, … 'we will fight for France, but in return we want our freedom.' They even added: "our *Droits de l'Homme*." Dufay argued that the commissioners had taken the only reasonable course of action in creating "new citizens for the Republic in order to oppose our enemies." Immediately after his speech, a deputy rose and asked that the National Convention declare that slavery was abolished throughout the Republic. There was no opposition, and the law was quickly written and voted: "The National Convention declares that slavery is abolished throughout the territory of the Republic; in consequence, all men, without distinction of color, will enjoy the rights of French citizens."[4]

Belley shouted: "I was a slave during my childhood. Thirty-six years have passed since I became free through my own labor, and purchased myself. Since then, in the course of my life, I have felt worthy of being French." He continued, "It is the tricolor flag that has called us to our liberty," and vowed "on behalf of my brothers," that it would fly on the shores and mountains of Saint-Domingue "as long as there is a drop of blood in our veins." "This is the death of the English!" the famed revolutionary leader Danton proclaimed. The colony would have a powerful army born out of emancipation and ready to die to defend it.[5]

The dramatic decision made by Sonthonax and Polverel in Saint-Domingue had become the law of the French Republic. Throughout this empire, whose prosperity rested on a foundation of

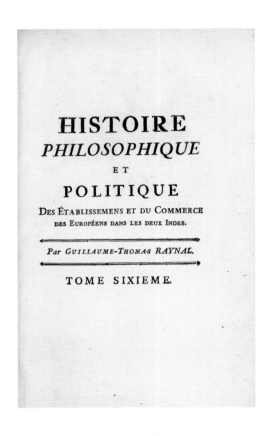

ABOVE Abbé Raynal, title page of *Histoire Philosophique et Politique des Établissemens et du Commerce des Européens dans les deux Indes,* volume 6. Genève: chez Jean-Leonard Pellet, imprimeur de la ville & de l'Académie, 1782. New-York Historical Society, D22. R26 1782.

OPPOSITE Thomas Koning after Charles Nicolas Cochin (1715–1790). *W. Th. Raynal.* Engraving. Emmet Collection, Miriam and Ira D. Wallach Division of Art, Prints and Photographs, The New York Public Library, Astor, Lenox and Tilden Foundations, Image ID: 424008.

slavery, there would be no more masters and no more slaves, only citizens. It was a truly radical change, the most dramatic of the many augured by the French Revolution. It took individuals who had been stripped of all human rights, and made them members of a democratic Republic. Perhaps as importantly, it represented the incorporation of the political project and demands of the slave insurrection, a movement composed to a large extent by men and women born in Africa, like Belley, into the ideological and political future of the French Republic.

***

The arrival of slave insurgents as citizens, symbolized powerfully in Belley's arrival in the National Convention, was seen by some as a kind of prophesy fulfilled. In *L'An 2440* (published in Amsterdam, 1771), the writer Louis-Sébastien Mercier had imagined waking up after a 672-year nap to find the world perfected, and redeemed. Among the wondrous things he discovered in his imagined future world was a monument to a slave revolutionary who had led a revolt that led to freedom. "I saw on a magnificent pedestal a negro, his head bare, his arm outstretched, with pride in his eyes and a noble and imposing demeanor." At the foot of the monument was this inscription: "To the Avenger of the New World." Happily stunned, Mercier questioned those nearby and learned that the "surprising and immortal man" depicted in the statue had freed the world from "the most atrocious, the longest, and most insulting tyranny of all," that of "odious slavery." The man had led a violent revolt, acting as an "exterminating angel" who "came like a storm" upon "a city of criminals," the world of the slave-holders. "The soil of America," wrote Mercier, "drank the blood that it had been awaiting for so long," and the "bones" of the ancestors of the oppressed slaves "seemed to stand up and shake with joy."[6]

The striking passage was copied and expanded by Denis Diderot in several editions of a multi-volume history of European colonialism edited by the Abbé Raynal, the *Histoire philosophique et politique dans les deux Indes.* The widely read work was banned in France (a fact which only helped it gain readers), but was published in various places across Europe throughout the 1780s, as well as in translation in the Anglophone world. If Mercier's prophetic text was written from an imagined future, Diderot's was written firmly from the present, issuing a call and a warning. "All that the negroes lack is a leader courageous enough to carry them to vengeance and carnage. Where is he, this great man, that nature owes to its vexed,

W. TH. RAYNAL,

*Lid van de Koninklyke Maatschappye te Londen
en van de Akademie der Weetenschappen en Fraaje
Letteren te Berlyn.*

C. N. Cochin. ad Viv. del.   Th. Kening, sculp.

M. Schalekamp, Excud.

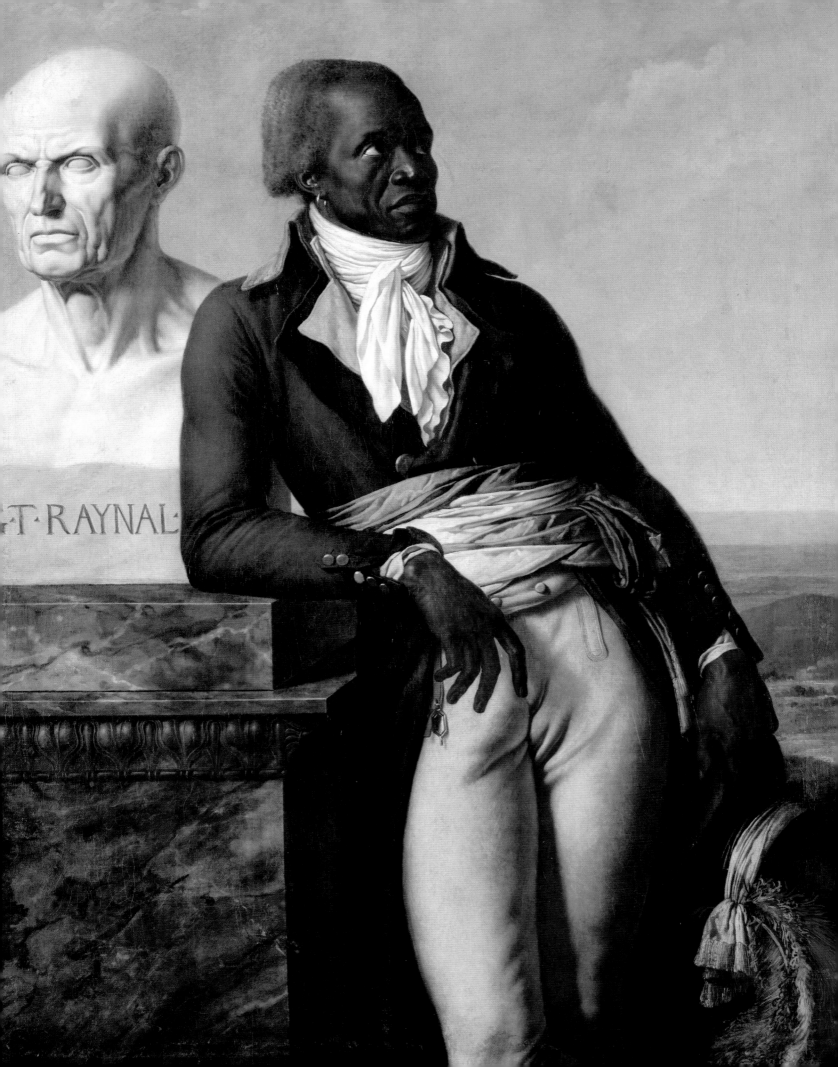

T. RAYNAL

oppressed, tormented children? Where is he? He will appear, do not doubt it. He will show himself and raise the sacred banner of liberty." In some versions of the text, the promised hero was described as a "Black Spartacus." And the prediction was that he would not only win, but become a hero for leading a violent revolt. Monuments, like the one imagined in Mercier, would be constructed to celebrate the "hero who reestablished the rights of the human species" both in the New World and the Old.[7]

This famous prophetic passage from Raynal was clearly on the mind of the painter Anne-Louis Girodet, a disciple of David, when he painted a portrait of Jean-Baptiste Belley in 1797. Since his arrival in Paris in 1793, Belley had continued to serve as a representative for Saint-Domingue, defending the project of emancipation against its many critics and enemies. In 1795, he confronted a particularly virulent and racist attack against emancipation by another representative by telling another part of his own story. "I was born in Africa," he announced, going on to denounce the racism that refused to accept the equality and citizenship of blacks in the French colonies.[8]

Belley clearly cut a striking figure in the political world of Paris in the 1790s, and the portrait painted by Girodet registers and, in a way, fixes our vision of what his presence there meant. The painting has been the subject of ongoing debate among scholars. Some have emphasized the ways in which it exoticizes and sexualizes Belley, while others see it as a dignified and impressive portrait, unique for the way in which it featured a well-known individual of African descent. As striking, of course, is the way it represents a commentary on the play of prophesy and realization. While Raynal's role as a writer whose text warned of the arrival of a black revolution is acknowledged in the painting, it is Belley who is of course foregrounded, centered, the core of the story. He leans comfortably, perhaps even arrogantly, in the tricolor sash—the same symbol that had been ripped off him by the infuriated mob in Philadelphia—as a representative of the French nation, but also of Africa. His earring, an ornament that he may well have carried but which was also a common symbol placed on African figures in eighteenth-century painting, highlights his particularity.[9]

Belley's expression is difficult to read. What is he thinking? What is he looking towards? Perhaps ahead to an uncertain future, considering what is to come? Or maybe back, to his own memories? As we look at his mysterious expression, we can think of it as an invitation to contemplate the particular place the African-born held

OPPOSITE Anne-Louis Girodet de Roussy-Trioson (1767–1824). *J. B. Belley, député de Saint Domingue à la Convention*, 1797. Oil on canvas, 62⅗ × 43⁷⁄₁₀ in. (159 × 111 cm). Châteaux de Versailles et de Trianon, Versailles, France. Photo Credit: Erich Lessing / Art Resource, NY.

in the remarkable events of the Haitian Revolution. How did their experiences in various African societies shape their perspectives and actions?

***

By 1789, about two-thirds of the slave population of the thriving French colony of Saint-Domingue was African-born. Since the enslaved made up approximately ninety percent of the population, this meant that people born in Africa were the largest group on the island. While some among this population had been put on slave ships in Africa as children, many of them were captured as young men and women. And many of the men had likely been captured because they were soldiers, fighting in a series of late eighteenth-century wars that took place in West and Central Africa, in some cases sustained and encouraged by the Atlantic slave trade itself. These men, then, were what John Thornton has dubbed "African veterans," having survived warfare in Africa but often lost their freedom, and their homelands, because of it. Whether they had been soldiers or not, all the Africans who arrived in the Caribbean during the late eighteenth century carried with them a set of political, ideological, and military experiences that had involved them in struggles over the meaning of power, representation, service, loyalty, virtue, and rights. These experiences shaped their vision of, and action within, the plantation world of the Caribbean and in the revolution that unfolded there in the 1790s.[10]

On arrival in Saint-Domingue after the brutal Middle Passage, these Africans had to find their way in a very strange and new world. The social organization of the plantation colony of Saint-Domingue likely seemed peculiar, to say the least. It was a colony in principle controlled by invisible powers seated across a vast ocean, separated by a several-months' journey from those they supposedly commanded, with a rigid but conflicting administrative structure. It was populated by emigrants who both reconstituted some aspects of French life and produced new forms of sociability among themselves, even as they perfected and expanded the forms of terror and violence directed at their slaves. For almost all the arrivals, the particular work of sugar cultivation, to which most would have immediately been put to work, would have been something completely new, even though agricultural labor would not have been. Undoubtedly, the forms of confinement, punishment, and surveillance that had been established by the late eighteenth century in Saint-Domingue would have been shocking in their intensity and oppressiveness.

Mixed in with the unfamiliar, though, would have been the familiar. Arrivals who were from or had spent time in the coastal areas of West and Central Africa would have found many things in the port towns of the Caribbean that were somewhat familiar, from the hustle and bustle of trade in goods and people on the docks, to the groups, some of them of mixed European and African descent, who participated in and defined the dealings in the market-driven world of such towns. The ships they saw, of course, would have been essentially the same—in some cases, quite literally the same—as those that gathered in the slave-trading ports of Africa. The sailors who manned the ships, and who came ashore when they docked in harbor, would frequently have traveled to Africa, and some among them even were themselves people of African descent, or African-born, both free and enslaved.

And despite the very heterogeneous composition of the African population, the form of the slave trade meant that there were significant concentrations of people from particular regions in Africa within Saint-Domingue. Many would have found at least some possibility for communication with others, and shared language, performance and religious traditions, artistry, and political thought. For the enslaved field workers on large sugar plantations, the experience both of social control and of solidarity and sociability would have taken place within a world made up almost entirely of other enslaved people, for the *commandeurs* who oversaw the labor were themselves slaves. But through Sunday travels to markets in port towns they would have also had contact with the world of merchants, sailors, soldiers, and planters in the towns. Artisans and domestics, meanwhile, especially those in urban areas, would also have been in regular contact with a range of people in the population. The distance between plantations and towns was, throughout Saint-Domingue, relatively small, although the coffee plantations that multiplied in the mountainous areas were more isolated. On many of these, built during the second half of the eighteenth century, the population of slaves from the Kongo region was quite large. Among the languages spoken in Saint-Domingue, French was important but not the dominant tongue. The Kréyol language, established well enough by the mid-eighteenth century that there were local plays written in the language, was perhaps the most commonly spoken language on the island, but African languages, especially Kikongo tongues, were probably nearly as ubiquitous.

The religion that emerged in Saint-Domingue during the eighteenth century represents a powerful system of thought that *both* maintained connections with Africa *and* reflected on and refracted the experience of exile. In the midst of the brutalities of the plantation world, in the cane fields and sugar mills, as well as in the thriving towns of Saint-Domingue, a remarkable process of cultural production unfolded over the course of the eighteenth century. Though obviously the thought and practice of the enslaved left few written traces, the religion of Vodou itself in many ways constitutes an archive of, and a reflection on, its own production. Among the songs sung in the religion in the twentieth century are several that refer in one way or another to the Middle Passage itself, such as a song called "Sou Lan Mè"—"On the Ocean"—which narrates the experience of being put in chains. "They took our feet/ They chained our wrists/ They dropped us in the bottom of the ship." The song is sung in the present tense, so that those who sing it in a sense return to the ship itself. But they also look forward to a time of reaction, perhaps revenge, calling on one of the *lwa* in Vodou— Agwé, governor of the sea—back in Africa as support. "Agwé in Oyo/ There's a time when they'll see us," the song calls, suggesting that at some point the slaves will come back at the slave traders. As the song continues the ship sails into a storm, and threatens to sink. "In the bottom of the ship," the song declares, capturing a sense of unity in the midst of terror, "we are all one."[11] Another song, transcribed by an ethnographer in the 1950s, also presents a powerful articulation of the way in which diverse enslaved people found a certain unity, or at least understanding. The singer repeats, "I am creole-congo," bringing together the terms used for American-born and African-born slaves, suggesting that between the two could be continuity, even sameness, rather than conflict.[12]

For the majority of those who lived in Saint-Domingue before and during the revolution and who had been born and raised in Africa, the social world and conflicts in the Caribbean likely seemed in some ways either a parallel to or a literal extension of conflicts taking place in Africa itself. Their experience of enslavement, after all, had begun in their African homelands, the product of specific local conflicts and relations of power. The social and intellectual experiences they had as individuals and members of communities in crisis and transformation within Africa must have informed their vision of both the Middle Passage itself and of the enslavement they experienced in Saint-Domingue. The scattered references to Africa we find in the archives of the Haitian Revolution suggest that it was a regular point of reference in political debates, though unfortunately these references are often superficial and give us little detail about precisely what they signified. The archive of Haitian Vodou (notably in its songs), however, is replete with complex engagements with and references to the shifting meanings of Africa, of various affiliations with groups within Africa itself, and with the problem of maintaining a connection to those affiliations in the midst of a new context. Since this religion was in many ways deeply shaped, even formed by, the process of revolution, that archive itself speaks directly to the question of what the political philosophy of the revolution was.[13]

Such religious practices were part of a larger social world that, by its very existence, militated against the plantation order. Masters strove to reduce the enslaved to the status of laboring machines, their lives organized by the demands of plantation work. But the enslaved were human, and they negotiated, pushed back against, and found ways to work around the insistence that they be nothing but embodied labor power. As in other slave societies, *marronage* (running away) was a fundamental part of daily life. Particularly what contemporaries and some historians have called "*petit marronage*,"— short-term flight from the plantation rather than permanent escape, which sometimes ended with capture and punishment and sometimes with a negotiated return—was crucial in laying the foundation for revolution. For along with the mobility allowed the slaves on Sundays to sell in local towns the produce grown in their garden plots, *petit marronage* opened up the possibility for the creation of cross-plantation community and collusion. If the uprising of 1791 succeeded in Saint-Domingue, it was because its leaders were able to make use of and mobilize such cross-plantation networks in order to plan a massive, coordinated attack.[14]

***

How did the slave insurgents in Saint-Domingue succeed in doing what no one else in history has? Since the beginnings of plantation slavery, of course, some slaves had rebelled, and in some cases succeeded in winning independence for themselves as maroon communities. But only in Saint-Domingue did a slave revolution lead directly to the abolition of slavery in the society in which it took place. There are, of course, many ways to answer this question, and many factors that combined to make the revolution succeed. There was, importantly, the organizational brilliance of the leaders who came together in Saint-Domingue, as well as the military abilities that both the leaders and the rank-and-file fighters carried with them and developed as they went. But theirs was also a political victory, one based on a successful challenge to colonial governance and, ultimately, an alliance with the government of Republican France.

What was the political ideology of the slave revolutionaries? From early on the slave insurgents in Saint-Domingue repeatedly invoked the language and texts of the French Revolution as they issued their demands. They sometimes spoke of the "Rights of Man," and made reference to the Declaration of the Rights of Man produced by the French National Assembly in 1789. They also, however, drew other kinds of political language and symbols, some of them seemingly at odds with this Republican language. Indeed, insurgents often used symbols of the French king, and frequently evoked the royal authorities of France and, later, Spain, in making their demands. This fact has long preoccupied historians, who have sometimes been tempted to read the use of royal symbols as a sign that the revolutionaries themselves were, in effect, royalists who conceived of political power and governance as necessarily being linked to the power of a king. Some also have suggested that the focus on royal authority is a reflection of experiences within Africa, where many of the enslaved would have lived in societies ruled through some form of royal authority.

Did the insurgent use of royalist language and symbols represent a fundamental contradiction with their use of the symbols of Republicanism? Not necessarily. In fact, rather than signifying a fragmented or contradictory set of political ideologies, the cohabitation of these forms provides us with an insight into the particularities of the Caribbean political culture embodied in the slave revolution of 1791–93. Indeed, to analyze the political culture of the insurgents in terms of dichotomies defined according to the specific European political context of the time is to obscure the complex realities of the Caribbean political context. Both royalist and republican discourses were deployed, indeed subsumed, by insurgents in the articulation of their central goal: a reform, and eventually, an abolition of slavery. By laying claim both on the authority of the king and on the promises of republican rights emanating from the evolving metropolitan power structure, slave insurgents intervened in a long-standing conflict between colonial planters and the metropolitan administration, taking advantage of a new virulence in this conflict and ultimately deepening it.[15]

Indeed, as they evoked the figure of the French king, they also were often thinking about kingship itself in complex ways, a fact highlighted most forcefully in a famous proclamation by the insurgent Macaya in 1793. Having rallied to the Republican commissioners in June of 1793, Macaya refused the offer to join them permanently in August of that year. "I am the subject of three kings: of the King of Congo, master of all the blacks; of the King of France who represents my father; of the King of Spain who represents my mother," he announced. "These three Kings are the descendants of those who, led by a star, came to adore God made man." If he "went over to the Republic," he concluded, he might be "forced to make war against my brothers, the subjects of these three kings to whom I have promised loyalty." Through this fleeting source, we learn a great deal. For Macaya, loyalty to a king was not exclusive, clearly, for one could be the subject of three kings, something difficult to imagine at least for the theorists of royal power in Europe. As importantly, one could have loyalty to the subjects of three kings, creating a rich patchwork of complicated affinities and loyalties that rendered war and conflict particularly complicated. It also suggests that Macaya's own vision of the political organization of the world in which he lived spanned Europe, Africa, and the Caribbean. As such, the quote can serve to spur us to think historically in parallel ways, redrawing our map of the period as well.[16]

Evocations of the king on the part of insurgents were often combined quite comfortably with the use of Republican symbols, often evoking both the King and the National Assembly as authorities who they hoped would hear their demands. Biassou, for instance, wrote in late 1791 of his willingness "to serve his King, the nation and its representatives." This was logical enough, since at the time both were centers of authority in Paris. But the combination of royalist and republican symbols continued into 1793, when one insurgent flew a tricolor flag decorated with fleurs-de-lys. Over the course of 1793, however, as the conflict between republicanism and royalism became superimposed in a clearer way onto the conflict between proslavery masters and sympathetic republican administrators, many insurgents came to throw their lot in with the Republic and embrace its symbols.[17]

In the process, of course, they were transforming the Republic to which they were adhering, pushing forward the claims towards universal rights that had been articulated in France but always with a clear caveat—sometimes articulated openly, sometimes not—that allowed for the denial of rights to most of the population of the Caribbean. It is with regard to the question of what political adherence meant that the perspective from Saint-Domingue can, again, help us rethink some of our assumptions about the functioning of politics during this period. The affiliation of the enslaved insurgents of Saint-Domingue with the French Republic was an intense one, and yet it also was predicated upon a particular kind of agreement that was forced on the Republic by the insurgents themselves. They adhered to the French Republic only insofar as that political body adhered to their demand for emancipation. It was, on one level, an adherence based on a radical vision of the principles of natural right written down in the Declaration of the Rights of Man and Citizen in 1789—principles which many of the enslaved may, of course, have discussed, thought through, and debated without having read or heard of the document itself—in which the right to insurrection against tyranny was seen as a basic right. For most of the revolutionaries in Haiti, the right to freedom from slavery was the foundational political code, the root of political adherence. So it was that they could forcefully transfer their loyalties from an insurrection directed against France (with Spanish aid) to a revolution and war fought by France, against its Spanish and English enemies, once France embraced freedom.

And so it was that, when France stepped back from its side of the agreement, threatening to take away that freedom, the allegiance to the principles of Republicanism shifted, taking the form of allegiance to a new nation called Haiti, one created out of conflict with France. This was not the kind of allegiance, of course, that bureaucrats and leaders in France particularly liked, but in a way it was a perfect embodiment of the principles that at least the Republicans amongst them had espoused. For, as Jean-Paul Marat wrote insightfully in the early 1790s, if the people of metropolitan France had the right to overthrow a tyrannical king, and a tyrannical regime, then surely the enslaved of Saint-Domingue had the right to overthrow the regime of their even more directly tyrannical masters. And surely, too, they had the right to overthrow an imperial system that sustained the power of those tyrannical masters. If the white residents of Saint-Domingue had the right to reject "laws emanating from a legislator who was two thousand leagues away" and proclaim independence, Marat wrote—as he believed they did, like the North American colonists before them— that the other groups in the colony also had, like all human beings, the right to resist oppression. The whites had made themselves "despotic masters of the mulattoes and tyrannical masters of the blacks" and if the latter wished to "overthrow the cruel and shameful yoke under which they suffer, they are authorized to use any means available," even "massacring their oppressors to the last." [18]

Ultimately, then, the Haitian Revolution represented a kind of ultimate test, and ultimate challenge, for the principles of the Age of Revolution. Out of a society in which tyranny and oppression were exercised in a particularly open and brutal way came a movement that argued not just for the right to freedom but also for a strategic and political vision in which allegiance to empires and states should be founded on an absolute adherence to a principle, in this case the principle that no one should be a slave. Achieving that vision, of course, was a challenge, not least because in the process of pursuing liberation leaders within Saint-Domingue and later independent Haiti produced and vigorously institutionalized forms of policing and sometimes violent coercion that represented a denial of the very principles of the revolution they purported to represent. For the problem of defining what freedom meant, and of finding a way to transform a society based on plantation slavery to one based on free labor, in the midst of a larger world still dominated by slavery, was the massive challenge faced by the leaders of independent Haiti.

***

Belley was not among them. Having spent several years during the 1790s in Paris defending the project of emancipation, he ultimately fell prey to its undoing. He was, in fact, among a large number of people who, having lived through the slave revolution that had ultimately propelled Toussaint Louverture to power, came to oppose him. The precise reasons for Belley's opposition to Louverture are not clear. Perhaps he disliked the authoritarian style of rule he developed, or opposed his labor policies, which involved quite draconian limits on the freedom of the ex-slaves to choose where and how they worked. Or perhaps he had his own personal ambitions that ran up against the overwhelming power of Louverture. Belley was part of the expedition that travelled to Saint-Domingue under the command of General Leclerc in late 1801, with secret instructions to destroy Louverture and his power structure. In the midst of the expedition, however, as Leclerc battled Louverture, he decided to deport Belley back to France. The former representative now became a criminal, and was imprisoned by Napoleon Bonaparte's regime. Like Louverture himself, Belley died in prison in France, forgotten and alone, in 1805. Unlike Louverture, however, he lived long enough to probably hear news of Haitian independence in 1804.

What did he think when he heard this news? Did he imagine heading back to independent Haiti? Did he think of Saint-Domingue, where he had arrived as a boy and spent much of his life, as his homeland? Or did he think back to Africa itself, where he had been born and lived through boyhood? His story ended in silence. When Toussaint Louverture died a few years earlier in his own French prison, he left a final letter, written in his hand, stuck under the bandanna that covered his head, to be discovered by his captors. And in the next years Louverture's story would, of course, become one of the most widely told and retold epics in the history of the Atlantic world. Belley's story, meanwhile, has largely been forgotten, in part because it is difficult to know precisely where to place it. He was an African born man, a former slave who became a French representative. He opposed Louverture, and the circumstances of his own imprisonment are unclear. Yet his story embodies all the complexities and contradictions of the Haitian Revolution itself, connected by the three worlds—African, Caribbean, and European—that made it what it was. And, thanks to the remarkable portrait left behind of him, he remains startlingly present as one of the most famous and recognizable images of this Age of Revolution.

Notes

1   We draw here and throughout the essay on the narrative history of the Haitian Revolution presented in Laurent Dubois, *Avengers of the New World: The Story of the Haitian Revolution* (Cambridge: Harvard Univ. Press, 2004); for passages on Belley see 157, 168–70, 194–95, 285.

2   On this process see Julius S. Scott, "The Common Wind: Currents of Afro-American Communication in the Era of the Haitian Revolution," (Ph.D. dissertation, Duke University, 1986).

3   For the account of the events in Philadelphia see *Lettre écrite à New York par les députés de Saint-Domingue, à leurs commetans, imprimée par ordre de la Convention Nationale* (Paris, 1794), 3–9. On Belley's role in defending Sonthonax and Polverel, see Thomas Madiou, *Histoire d'Haïti* (Port-au-Prince, 1989 [1847–48]), 1:178–79. For an excellent account of the election, travels, and impact of this delegation see Florence Gauthier, "The Role of the Saint-Domingue Deputation in the Abolition of Slavery" in *The Abolitions of Slavery: From Léger Félicité Sonthonax to Victor Schoelcher, 1793, 1794, 1848*, ed. Marcel Dorigny (New York: Berghahn Books, 2003), 167–79. See also "Procès verbal de l'Assemblée électorale des députés du nord de St. Domingue," 23 September 1793, Archives Nationales, Paris (hereafter AN), C[181], 84.

4   M. J. Mavidal and M. E. Laurent, org., *Archives parlementaires de 1787 à 1860, première série (1787–1799)* (Paris, 1962), 84:276–285.

5   Madiou, *Histoire*, 1:222–28.

6   Louis-Sébastien Mercier, *L'an deux mille cent quarante: Rêve s'il en fût jamais* (1771; reprint Paris, 1977), 127.

7   Guillaume Thomas Raynal, *Histoire philosophique et politique des établissements et du commerce des Européens dans les Deux Indes* (Geneva, 1780), 3:204–05.

8   Dubois, *Avengers of the New World*, 194–95.

9   For extended interpretations of the painting see Darcy Grimaldo Grigsby, *Extremities: Painting Empire in Post-Revolutionary France* (New Haven: Yale Univ. Press, 2002), chap. 1 and Helen Weston, "Representing the Right to Represent: The Portrait of Citizen Belley, Ex-Representative of the Colonies, by A.L. Girodet," *Res* 26 (Autumn 1994): 83–100.

10 John Thornton, "African Soldiers in the Haitian Revolution," *Journal of Caribbean History* 25, nos. 1–2 (1991): 58–80.

11 The song is recorded on Wawa & Rasin Kanga, *The Haitian Roots 1* (Brooklyn: Geronimo Records, 1998).

12 Bibliothèque Haïtienne des Pères du Saint-Esprit, Port-au-Prince Haiti, Odette Menesson-Rigaud Papers, Box 1, Folder 15.

13 There is much more to be learned here. Building on the work of scholars such as Joan Dayan and Karen McCarthy Brown, for instance, scholars might tie together historical developments in Africa and Haiti by linking them to the traces left within Haitian Vodou. See Colin Dayan, *Haiti, History, and the Gods* (Berkeley: Univ. of California Press, 1998) and Karen McCarthy Brown, *Mama Lola: A Vodou Priestess in Brooklyn* (Berkeley: Univ. of California Press, 2001).

14 The classic work on marronage in Haiti before the Revolution is Jean Fouchard, *Les marrons de la liberté* (Paris: Editions de l'Ecole, 1972); a more recent reconsideration of the question, which makes a critique of Fouchard's thesis, is in David Geggus, *Haitian Revolutionary Studies* (Bloomington: Indiana Univ. Press, 2002), chap. 5; Carolyn Fick, *The Making of Haiti: The Saint-Domingue Revolution from Below* (Knoxville: Univ. of Tennessee Press, 1990), emphasizes the importance of *petit marronage*.

15 For more on this see Laurent Dubois, "'Our Three Colors': The King, The Republic and the Political Culture of Slave Revolution in Saint-Domingue," *Historical Reflections/Réflexions Historiques* 29:1 (Spring 2003): 83–102 and *Avengers of the New World*, chaps. 4 and 5.

16 Pamphile de Lacroix, *La Révolution de Haiti* (Paris: Kharthala, 1995 [1819]), 167; John Thornton, "'I am the Subject of the King of Kongo': African Ideology in the Haitian Revolution," *Journal of World History* 4 (1993): 181–83.

17 Biassou to Commissioners, 23 December 1791, AN DXXV 1, Folder 4, No. 20; Moniteur générale … de Saint-Domingue III: 104 (28 February 1793), p. 419.

18 *L'Ami du Peuple* No. 624 (December 12, 1791) in Jacques De Cock and Charlotte Goëtz, *Jean-Paul Marat: Oeuvres Politiques, 1789–1793* (Brussels: Pole Nord, 1993), 3788.

Liberty in Black,
White, and Color:
A Trans-Atlantic Debate

Jeremy D. Popkin

Passage des 11 jours du pilliage de la ville du cap françois aux bourg du aux du cap arive le 20 juin 1793
les naigre aprain avoire manacre une partie des blanc on pillie la ville e tou brullé e se sont revetu de leurs vetem
et de ceux de la commédie et on porte leurs pilliage dans les plaines

OPPOSITE J. L. Boquet. *Pillage du Cap Français, Saint Domingue en 1793*, ca. 1795. Engraving on paper. The John Carter Brown Library at Brown University, Fr795 B7627 oversize.

I f visitors from outer space had looked down on the Atlantic Ocean on July 14, 1793, they would have seen an outbreak of red, white and blue bunting in three regions along its shores. In France, citizens of the new ten-month-old republic marked the fourth anniversary of the start of the Revolution. In the cities of the United States, local residents joined with French visitors to salute the occasion. And in the French colony of Saint-Domingue, the holiday was celebrated by newly freed black slaves, along with the French republican officials who had just granted them their freedom and soldiers sent from the metropole. From afar, it might have seemed as if the anniversary of the storming of the Bastille had created a trans-Atlantic community of free people that united citizens of France, the United States, and the future nation of Haiti, whether they were white or black, all of them sharing republican values and dedicated to liberty.

Had these visitors from afar descended to ground level, however, they would have found many divisions among the disparate groups observing the fourth anniversary of the storming of the Bastille. In France's capital of Paris, they would have learned that the idea of commemorating July 14 was considered somewhat suspect. By 1793, true patriots and friends of liberty saw August 10, the anniversary of the violent overthrow of the monarchy in 1792, as the real birthday of French liberty. The events of July 14, 1789, after all, had left King Louis XVI on his throne, and many of those who had been hailed as heroes at the time, such as General Lafayette, George Washington's close friend, were now regarded in France as counterrevolutionary traitors. In any event, on July 14, 1793, Parisians were too shaken by Charlotte Corday's assassination of the revolutionary journalist Jean-Paul Marat, which had taken place on the previous day, to do much celebrating. In the western French region of the Vendée, there were no celebrations of July 14 at all in 1793. In March of that year, a violent rebellion had broken out in that area, supported by Catholic peasants who claimed that the Revolution had brought them not liberty but oppression. To them, liberty meant the freedom to worship as they always had, to keep their sons at home rather than sending them to join the army, and to prevent wealthy townspeople from buying up the lands belonging to the church and the local nobles that the Revolution had confiscated and offered for sale. Meanwhile, in Lyon, France's second-largest city, July 14, 1793 was celebrated by local republican officials who denounced the revolutionary government in Paris as a demagogic dictatorship dominated by an urban mob. In an elaborate ceremony with parades and speeches, the Lyonnais insisted that they were the real supporters of liberty, and that the Jacobin government in Paris had created a new form of tyranny.[1]

Across the ocean, in the Caribbean colonial city of Cap Français, the celebration of July 14, 1793, took place against a backdrop of blackened ruins. Known as "the Paris of the Antilles," Cap Français had been burned to the ground just three weeks earlier, during a violent struggle between supporters and opponents of the republican civil commissioners sent from France to impose the revolutionary doctrine of racial equality among free people in the colony. During that struggle, the civil commissioners, Léger-Félicité Sonthonax and Etienne Polverel, had taken a daring step, one that the revolutionary legislature in France had refused to consider: they had offered freedom to any black slaves who would take up arms to fight on their behalf. (The Convention had not only refused to discuss slavery: on July 16, 1793, in response to complaints from white slaveholders in France, it voted to recall Sonthonax and Polverel and put them on trial.) Thanks to the support of the newly freed blacks, Sonthonax and Polverel had won the battle against their assailants, but the city had been burned to the ground. Most of Cap Français's white population and a good number of free people of color—an important minority in the colony—had fled to the United States. The crowd who listened to Sonthonax's and Polverel's patriotic speeches about liberty on July 14, 1793, consisted of one hundred whites, two hundred free men of color, and six thousand blacks, many of whom had been slaves just three weeks earlier.[2]

While the blacks in Cap Français were celebrating their recent emancipation, other commemorations of liberty were taking place in the United States. Americans were grateful to France for its aid during the war of independence, and enthusiasm for the French revolution was strong. The French "appear to have been destined to give lessons to the world by the wisdom of their new institutions," an American poet, Joel Barlow, wrote after a stay in Paris in 1791.[3] "Celebrations of the French Revolution engulfed the festive calendar of the early American republic, overwhelming the annual rites commemorating the anniversaries of Independence Day and the president's birthday," one recent historian of the early Republic has written.[4] By 1793, however, as the French Revolution became more violent, Americans who had fought together to win freedom from the British and to create a free government were becoming deeply divided about whether the cause of American liberty required support for the French. To many of those who participated in these debates, the issues seemed simple. For Edmond Genet, for example, the young French diplomat sent to the United States to obtain support for his country from the Americans whose freedom France had helped win just ten years earlier, there was just one worldwide struggle between liberty-loving republicans and aristocratic royalists. When the American president George Washington insisted that his country would remain neutral in the war between France and its enemies, Genet denounced him as an aristocrat and tried to appeal directly to the American people. The French minister had many American supporters. James Madison, for instance, wrote that Washington's declaration of neutrality "wounds the popular feelings by a seeming indifference to the cause of liberty."[5]

Other Americans, however, were not so certain that supporting France was the best way of defending liberty. Critics answered Genet by arguing that defending freedom required that the United States decide for itself where its national interests lay; being republicans did not require them to enlist in a crusade on behalf of another country just because it shared their form of government. In any event, was France truly a country of liberty? In Charleston, South Carolina, in July 1793, an opponent of French radicalism printed a poster denouncing the local celebration of Bastille Day and the "detested Villains" in France who had killed their king.[6] By summer 1793, the United States had become the home of many refugees fleeing their strife-torn homeland. Some had even fought for American independence during the war against Britain. All told stories of a country where freedom of religion was violated by a campaign against public worship, where landowners were forced to flee because they had once had aristocratic titles, and where losers in revolutionary political conflicts faced arrest and even death because of their views. Even Americans sympathetic to the French cause were horrified by the news of the execution of Louis XVI, the French king who had sent his troops and ships to support the cause of American independence. The news of the burning of Cap Français, which reached the United States in early July 1793, added to American concerns. In American publications, "French revolutionary violence and the violence of slave rebellion appeared to flow together in a common river of blood," as one recent scholar has put it.[7]

While some Americans had become hesitant to celebrate French liberty by July 1793, the several thousand refugees from Cap Français who had just arrived in the port cities of the East Coast a week earlier, fleeing the city's destruction, were determined to do so.[8] But the freedom they celebrated had nothing to do with the freedom just granted to the slaves in the island they had fled. To hear them tell it, the commissioners Sonthonax and Polverel, who had just freed thousands of slaves, were not liberators but conspirators, agents of the British paid to destroy France's valuable colony and wreck its national economy. According to French law, the fleeing colonists were émigrés, citizens who had deserted their country when it needed them to help defend liberty. Precisely for that reason, the Saint-Domingue exiles used the occasion of Bastille Day to reaffirm their French patriotism. In Baltimore, the French consul J. F. Moissonnier watched nervously as sailors from the French ships, men who had fought against the blacks in Cap Français, swaggered down the street, wearing tricolor ribbons and armed with heavy sticks, ready for a fight if anyone said anything against France.[9]

American slave owners, many of them enthusiastic supporters of Thomas Jefferson's Democratic-Republican party and of the French Revolution, joined in these cheers for French liberty, even as they shuddered at the thought that "French Negroes" from the Caribbean, some of whom had accompanied their masters in the flight from Saint-Domingue, might spread dangerous ideas among American slaves. Just weeks after the anniversary of Bastille Day was celebrated in Norfolk, the Virginia legislature called up a militia unit to protect nervous citizens of Portsmouth who complained about the presence of blacks who had supposedly taken part in the "insurrection in Hispaniola."[10] Meanwhile, American blacks looked on with admiration as the first free blacks arrived from Saint-Domingue. And, ironically, black slaves from Saint-Domingue who had accompanied their masters took inspiration from the abolition laws in some of the northern states to claim their freedom. At the same time, however, friends of the white refugees from Saint-Domingue assured them that the United States truly was a free country, where they would "enjoy the peace which our republican government, founded as it is on the rights of man, assures to all its inhabitants." One of the proofs of this freedom, as the Philadelphia merchant Stephen Girard assured arrivals from the Caribbean, was that even though they could not keep their slaves in the state of Pennsylvania for more than six months, "it is…quite easy to forward them from here to any southern state on this continent, where they are sold just as in St. Domingo."[11] The members of the Pennsylvania Abolition Society had their hands full protecting the rights of newly arrived blacks from Saint-Domingue from their masters.[12]

While differing views of slavery caused some disagreements between French and American enthusiasts for liberty, other issues also divided them. One major difference between American and French concepts of the liberty celebrated on July 14, 1793, had to

do with the role of religion. In France, in July 1793, public religious observances had largely been banned; the Catholic Church was accused of supporting the counterrevolution. One of the things the French official Sonthonax took pride in was that he had freed the blacks of Saint-Domingue from religious superstition. "No priest sullied the ceremony with his presence," he boasted in his report to the French National Convention about the observance of July 14 in Cap Français.[13] In the United States, however, the celebration of liberty went together with religious sentiments. In Norfolk, Virginia, French refugees and citizens of one of America's most important slave states joined together on July 14 to honor "the Great King of kings, by whose wise interposition this virtuous people have been delivered from slavery and oppression."[14]

Liberty obviously meant very different things to those who celebrated July 14 in the different parts of the Atlantic world in 1793. One of the most extraordinary exchanges about the meaning of liberty at that moment took place in the Caribbean colony of Saint-Domingue. On one side was the French revolutionary commissioner Léger-Félicité Sonthonax, sent to the island in 1792 to restore order and impose French revolutionary principles on the white slaveholders. On the other was the black former slave Toussaint Louverture, the most articulate of the leaders of the black insurrection that had shaken the colony since August 1791. Sonthonax had been chosen for his mission because he was known to be an opponent of slavery. In 1790, he had published an article in a Paris newspaper looking forward to the day when "you will see a curly-haired African, relying only on his virtue and good sense, coming to participate in the legislative process in the midst of our national assemblies."[15] As much as he was an opponent of slavery, however, Sonthonax was also a French revolutionary patriot. Keeping France's most valuable overseas colony was as much of a priority for him as improving the condition of the blacks who generated its wealth. Furthermore, Sonthonax understood that he was merely the agent of a government that represented the will of the French people. If freedom was to be given to the slaves, it could only be done in accordance with a law passed by the people's deputies, the National Convention. Neither the slaves themselves, nor Sonthonax acting on his own, had the authority to take such a step.

Until the summer of 1793, slavery was legal in the French colonies, just as it was in most of the states of the new American republic. The National Convention, although it had declared that the principles of French republicanism were liberty and equality, had specifically promised that these ideas would not be applied in the colonies without the consent of the free populations there. At the time of their arrival in Saint-Domingue, Sonthonax and his fellow republican commissioner Etienne Polverel had publicly sworn to maintain slavery and to crush the slave insurrection that had been shaking the colony since August 1791. Even as they became increasingly convinced that the white colonists were "aristocrats of the skin" who would never accept the principles of the Revolution, Sonthonax and Polverel were careful not to challenge the institution on which the colony's economy depended. On May 5, 1793, they even took the extraordinary step of reissuing the *Code Noir*, the slave code drawn up under Louis XIV in 1685. At a moment when revolutionaries in France were pulling down statues honoring "Louis le Grand," Sonthonax and Polverel were reasserting one of the Sun King's most despotic laws.

Sonthonax and Polverel stuck to their policy of maintaining the laws authorizing slavery until June 20, 1793, when they were nearly overwhelmed by an attack launched by the whites in Saint-Domingue's main city of Cap Français, who opposed their policy of favoring the colony's free people of color, a group that had been granted rights by the French legislature in April 1792. Outnumbered by the attackers, Sonthonax and Polverel took a drastic step: they offered freedom to any black slave who would join their army. By June 21, hundreds of blacks from Cap Français, who had accepted their status until this moment, along with several thousand armed black insurgents from the countryside, had joined the commissioners' forces. With their help, Sonthonax and Polverel were able to drive the white attackers onto the ships in the harbor, which then sailed for the United States. The commissioners had won the battle, but they now were surrounded by the black fighters they had armed. Their offer of freedom originally extended only to men of military age willing to join the army; they had to decide whether to broaden it to include the much larger population of slaves on the rest of the island. They also had to try to win over the armed black insurgents who had risen up against their masters and who had been living outside of white control since the beginning of the slave uprising in August 1791.

Before the crisis of June 20, 1793, the civil commissioners had been confident that if they ever decided to offer freedom to the blacks, it would be gratefully accepted. Sonthonax had boasted "that he could in an instant…create four hundred thousand soldiers for the Republic" by announcing the abolition of slavery in Saint-Domingue.[16] But when the commissioners made their offer of freedom on June 21, most of the black insurgents rejected it. Because the offer only applied to men willing to join the French army, blacks who were not in the physical condition to fight or who had wives and children who would still be considered slaves did not see the commissioners' offer as worth accepting. Many black soldiers, especially those who had risen to the rank of officers in the insurgent armies, decided that they would be better off joining France's Spanish enemies: the Spaniards had offered to incorporate the black units into their own army and to pay black officers handsome salaries, at a time when the French colonial authorities were so short

NEW YORK. ABOUT 1790.

Presented to D T Valentine, by Edw Crommelin, 195 Prince St New York.

of cash that they had not even been able to pay their own white troops.[17] The most adamant of the black leaders was Toussaint Louverture, who responded to the news of the commissioners' freedom offer by announcing that he and his men would "shed the last drop of their blood to defend the Bourbons to whom they have promised unswerving loyalty to the death."[18]

Sonthonax and Polverel had assumed that the rebellious blacks were "simple men" who did not know how to think for themselves, but Toussaint Louverture was certainly capable of forming his own ideas. Toussaint had started life as a slave, but he had succeeded in obtaining his freedom well before the start of the French Revolution in 1789. His success was a reminder that, oppressive as it was, the slave system did provide chances for a few blacks to obtain legal freedom. After his emancipation, Toussaint joined the class of "free people of color" in the French colony. He could now own property, defend his interests in court, and pass his freedom and his earnings on to his children. For a few years, he owned a small plantation of his own with a half-dozen slaves; later he went back to work for his former owner, Bayon de Libertat, with whom he apparently had friendly relations.

Like many free people of color, Toussaint had reason to regard the revolutionary movement that started in France in 1789 with misgivings. The French revolutionaries resoundingly proclaimed that "all men are born and remain free and equal in rights," but they were equally emphatic in defending the rights of the whites in their overseas colonies, who were allowed to elect deputies to the revolutionary assembly in France and to form their own colonial assemblies, from which free men of color were excluded. In a French version of the idea of "states' rights," the constitution drawn up by the French National Assembly in 1791 explicitly left any reform of the status of either slaves or free people of color up to the whites in each colony. As a member of the class of free people of color, Toussaint also had a stake in the colonial system. By 1789, he seems to have sold his own slaves, but many free people of color owned plantations or, like Toussaint, worked for white plantation-owners. Members of this group embraced the idea of freedom and equality for themselves, but they were often hesitant about the idea of freeing the entire slave population. The most prominent spokesman for this group in Paris, Julien Raimond, indignantly denied rumors that he was in favor of abolition. "One can hardly imagine that I would want to suddenly ruin my whole family, which owns between 7 and 8 millions in property in Saint-Domingue," he wrote in 1792.[19]

Toussaint Louverture's role in the first months of the violent slave insurrection that broke out in Saint-Domingue's North Province, the home of the colony's largest and most productive plantations, in August 1791 remains shrouded in mystery. Only when the first wave of violence had subsided and when the leaders of the revolt had begun to try to negotiate with the whites does his name begin to appear in the documentary record. Although he would stand out among the black leaders for his consistent opposition to slavery—other black leaders sometimes raised money for their troops by selling black captives into slavery in the neighboring Spanish colony of Santo Domingo—Toussaint also distinguished himself from the outset by his moderation and his willingness to work with whites. A white colonist taken prisoner by the insurgents early in the movement recalled that he owed his life to Toussaint, who stepped in to keep a more violent black general from having the white captives executed. Toussaint insisted that "we could not, and ought not to be thus sacrificed, without being imprisoned, and calling a court martial upon us"; in other words, he demanded that the blacks set up a legal system modeled after that of the whites.[20] Like Sonthonax, Toussaint was thus a man of law and order.

Toussaint Louverture was also a loyal Catholic. Throughout his career, he made a point of attending church services when he could. "He worried about the smallest details" of ritual, and often "interrupt[ed] the curé's sermon, haranguing the congregation and his soldiers," one white observer reported.[21] He was loath to accept an offer of liberty from the French, who were waging a war against the Catholic Church in their own country. Finally, Toussaint was a proud warrior who bitterly resented the fact that in January 1793, five months before Sonthonax and Polverel made their bid for his support, their troops had driven him out of the positions he had occupied after the start of the black rebellion. In the summer of that year, when Sonthonax tried to win him over to his program of emancipation, Toussaint Louverture was still smoldering about the January campaign. "You had us pursued like ferocious beasts," he wrote to the commissioner.[22]

But Toussaint and the other blacks also hesitated to accept the French offer of liberty because it came with so many qualifications. In mid-July, several weeks after the first French emancipation offer, a newspaper edited by the commissioners had published an article emphasizing the difficulties involved in abolishing slavery, from the French point of view. "A sudden universal liberty would make the African people into a people of brigands, without restraint, without laws, without government, and left to the fury of its passions," the editorialist insisted. The solution he proposed was to make the blacks earn their emancipation by giving them a free day each week to hire themselves out, "and when it will be clear that the blacks are not misusing this concession, one can give them another day, and so on up to the whole of the week."[23] When Sonthonax finally decided, on August 29, 1793, that the time had come to grant the blacks in Saint-Domingue's North Province their full freedom, he drew up a document that ran to eight pages of small type, containing thirty-eight detailed articles. The first of these announced that the famous French Declaration of the Rights of Man and Citizen would be printed and displayed throughout the territory, and a subsequent article banned punishment by whipping, but most of the document's other clauses were restrictions on the former slaves' freedom. Unless

they were serving in the army, the freed slaves were to remain on their plantations and continue working as they had before. Domestic servants caring for the sick, the elderly, or for children could not leave their positions; women were promised pregnancy and maternity leave, but their pay was set at only two-thirds of the men's level. Local officials would decide whether blacks could change plantations, and any black, male or female, who had not found a job within fifteen days of the issuance of the proclamation would be arrested.[24] To many former slaves, the freedom offered by the French looked little different from the slavery they had known before 1791.

Drawn by Henry Moses.   London, published as the act directs 4 June 1808 by Jos.ᵖʰ Collyer, Constitution Row, Grays Inn Road.   Engrav'd by H.Collyer A.R.A. Eng.ʳ to Her Majesty.

To His Royal Highness PRINCE WILLIAM FREDERIC, Duke of Gloucester &c. &c.

This Plate to Commemorate the ABOLITION of the SLAVE TRADE is by Permission

Dedicated by His Royal Highness's much obliged humble Servant Joseph Collyer.

Description. Britannia trampling on the emblems of Slavery, holding a banner Declaring the Abolition, and attending to the voice of Justice and Religion. — On the left the Trade is represented by a Ship freighted with Slaves, and the Standard on which is inscribed the sufferings of the Negroes, and on the right is a Bust of Mr Wilberforce with a scroll containing the Names of the principal Speakers in favour of the ABOLITION in both Houses of Parliament &c.

To the French commissioner Sonthonax, these regulations were no violation of freedom, but rather the necessary price to be paid for it. In his speech at the Bastille Day ceremony in Cap Français on July 14, 1793, he told his black audience to remember that "in France, the people are free and they work; remember that liberty does not consist in being idle; without work, there is neither leisure nor happiness." [25] A month later, when he announced that he was preparing to issue an edict of general emancipation, he said that "the sudden passage to liberty has to be planned in such a way that it will not rupture the bonds on which all societies are based, so that agriculture will not suffer, so that the earth will yield enough produce to nourish the warriors employed in fighting the enemies of the Republic." [26] Proud as he was of his contribution to bringing freedom to the former slaves, Sonthonax worried that they would not understand the obligations that went along with it. And he was far from certain that they were ready to adopt the new institutions that the French had created to protect their liberty. Two months after issuing his emancipation decree on August 29, he confessed to his colleague Polverel that the blacks were not enthusiastic about the new republican government he had given them. "The idea of a king is simple. It can be understood by the most stupid of Africans; even the most sophisticated of them cannot conceive of the idea of a republic," he wrote.[27]

While Sonthonax was trying to make the newly freed blacks understand the necessity of accepting the restraints he imposed on them, Toussaint Louverture was outlining a very different notion of freedom. While Sonthonax was trying to combine liberty with republican order, the black general argued that revolutionary France was a scene of violence and disorder. "It is not possible that you fight for liberty and the right of man, after all the cruelties that you commit every day," he wrote to one of the free colored supporters of Sonthonax who tried to win him over. "No, you only fight for your interests, and to satisfy your ambition." [28] In another letter, addressed to the "Perfidious republicans," he said, "you try to convince us that justice and the Republic assure us liberty, in the midst of a free people among whom reigns a perfect equality. Did the Republic need to shed so much innocent blood to establish itself?"

Like the French peasant rebels of the Vendée, Toussaint insisted that real liberty meant living in accordance with religious principles and submitting to the authority of a legitimate ruler, such as the king of Spain. "You try to make us believe that Liberty is a benefit that we will enjoy if we submit ourselves to order," Toussaint concluded, "but as long as God gives us the force and the means, we

OPPOSITE Joseph Collyer (1748–1827) after Henry Moses. *Abolition of the Slave Trade*, June 4, 1808. Engraving on paper, 13½ × 10⅖ in. (34.29 × 26.37 cm). Photographs and Print Division, Schomburg Center for Research in Black Culture, The New York Public Library, Astor, Lenox and Tilden Foundations, PR.X.081, #485329.

will acquire another Liberty, different from that which you tyrants pretend to impose on us."[29] Toussaint Louverture would eventually switch sides and embrace the rhetoric of French republicanism; "We are republicans," he wrote in a proclamation in June 1795, "and consequently free according to natural right. It can only be kings…who dare to claim the right to reduce to slavery men like themselves, who nature has made free."[30] His vision of liberty always remained a conservative one, however. The constitution he issued for Saint-Domingue in 1801 maintained the abolition of slavery, but it also subjected the population to a system of forced labor, banned all political organizing, and imposed Catholicism as the state religion.[31]

As the many different observances of July 14 in 1793 and the differing visions of liberty sketched out by Sonthonax and Toussaint Louverture in Saint-Domingue during that summer demonstrate, liberty meant very different things to people in different parts of the revolutionary world. Even two men who sincerely hated slavery, as both Sonthonax and Toussaint Louverture did, could find themselves fighting on different sides. The three revolutions in North America, France, and the Caribbean often shared common symbols and used the same slogans, but they articulated the meaning of those symbols and words in very different ways. Whether liberty could be brought about by violent means or only by peaceful reforms, whether it needed to be consecrated by religion or freed from religious "superstition," whether it implied the abolition of slavery or the protection of property, including slave owners' chattels: these and other issues were the subjects of violent disputes. Instead of sending the world one message about the meaning of liberty, the celebrations of July 14, 1793, in the United States, France, and Haiti revealed how differently people in different circumstances could interpret that term.

Notes

1   Louis Trenard, *La Révolution française dans la région Rhône-Alpes* (Paris: Perrin, 1992), 404.

2   On the events of June 20, 1793, in Cap Français and their historical significance, see Jeremy D. Popkin, *"You Are All Free": The Haitian Revolution and the Abolition of Slavery* (New York: Cambridge Univ. Press, 2010).

3   Cited in Esther E. Brown, *The French Revolution and the American Man of Letters* (Columbia: Curators of the Univ. of Missouri, 1951), 82.

4   Simon P. Newton, *Parades and the Politics of the Street: Festive Culture in the Early American Republic* (Philadelphia: Univ. of Pennsylvania Press, 1997), 120.

5   Madison to Thomas Jefferson, 19 June 1793, cited in Stanley Elkins and Eric McKitrick, *The Age of Federalism* (New York: Oxford Univ. Press, 1993), 358.

6   *Columbian Herald*, 23 July 1793, cited in Newman, *Parades and Politics*, 133.

7   Rachel Hope Cleves, *The Reign of Terror in America: Visions of Violence from Anti-Jacobinism to Antislavery* (New York: Cambridge Univ. Press, 2009), 63.

8   On the arrival of the Saint-Domingue refugees, see Ashli White, *Encountering Revolution: Haiti and the Making of the Early Republic* (Baltimore, Md.: Johns Hopkins Univ. Press, 2010).

9   Moissonnier to Genet, 16 July 1793, in Library of Congress, Genet papers, reel 5.

10 Letter from Portsmouth, Virginia, 21 August 1793, cited in Winston C. Babb, "French Refugees from Saint-Domingue to the Southern United States, 1791–1810" (Ph.D. diss., University of Virginia, 1955), 60.

11 Stephen Girard, letters of 7 July 1793 and 28 August 1793, in American Philosophical Society, Stephen Girard papers, reel 10. I would like to thank Ashli White for providing me with these references.

12 Gary B. Nash, "Reverberations of Haiti in the American North: Black Saint-Dominguans in Philadelphia," *Pennsylvania History* 65 (1998): 54.

13 Procès-verbal of celebration of 14 July 1793, in Archives Nationales (hereafter AN), D XXV 19, d. 186; Sonthonax to Convention, 30 July 1793, in AN, D XXV 5, d. 52.

14 *Philadelphia General Advertiser*, 29 July 1793 (Norfolk, 16 July).

15 *Révolutions de Paris*, 18–25 September 1790, cited in Robert Louis Stein, *Léger-Félicité Sonthonax: The Lost Sentinel of the Republic* (Rutherford, N.J.: Fairleigh Dickinson Press, 1985), 21.

16 Admiral Cambis, ship's log of *Jupiter*, entry for 19 June 1793, in AN, D XXV 54, d. 521.

17 Proclamation of Joaquin Garcia, 29 June 1793, in Antonio del Monte y Tejada, *Historia de Santo Domingo*, 4 vols. (Santo Domingo: Imprenta de Garcia Hermanos, 1890–92), 4:50.

18 Copy of letter from Toussaint Louverture and Moyse, 25 June 1793, in AN, D XXV 20, d. 200.

19 Raimond, letter of 18 June 1792, in AN, D XXV 13, d. 127.

20 Gros, *Historick Recital, of the Different Occurrences in the Camps of Grand-Reviere [sic], Dondon, Sainte-Suzanne, and others, from the 26th of October, 1791, to the 24th of December, of the same year* (Baltimore, Md.: Adams, 1793), cited in Jeremy D. Popkin, *Facing Racial Revolution: Eyewitness Accounts of the Haitian Uprising* (Chicago: Univ. of Chicago Press, 2008), 150.

21 Michel-Etienne Descourtilz, *Voyages d'un naturaliste* (Paris: Dufort, 1809), cited in Popkin, *Facing Racial Revolution*, 278.

22 Toussaint Louverture, letter of 8/27 August 1793, in AN, AA 55, d. 1511.

23 *Affiches américaines* (Cap Français), 11 July 1793.

24 "Decree of General Liberty," in Laurent Dubois and John D. Garrigus, eds., *Slave Revolution in the Caribbean: A Brief History with Documents* (Boston and New York: Bedford/ Saint Martin's, 2006), 120–25.

25 Procès-verbal of celebration of 14 July 1793, in AN, D XXV 19, d. 186.

26 Sonthonax, speech of 25 August 1793, in AN, D XXV 5, d. 52.

27 Sonthonax to Polverel, 27 October 1793, in AN, D XXV 44, d. 420, cited in Stein, *Sonthonax*, 98.

28 Sonthonax to Chanlatte, 27 August 1793, in AN, CC 9 A 8.

29 Letter signed "Toussaint L'Ouverture, Général des armées du Roy, approuvé par tous nos Chefs et tous nos soldats royalistes," 27 August 1793 (dated at beginning "8 August 1793"), in AN, AA 55, d. 1511.

30 Toussaint Louverture, letter of June 13, 1795, in Gérard Laurent, *Toussaint Louverture à travers sa correspondance (1794–1798)* (Madrid: Industrias Graficas España, 1953), 182.

31 "Constitution d'Haïti du 3 juillet 1801," http://webu2.upmf-grenoble.fr/Haiti/Const1801.htm; for a partial English translation, see Dubois and Garrigus, *Slave Revolution in the Caribbean*, 107–10.

A Vapor of Dread:
Observations on Racial Terror and Vengeance in the Age of Revolution

Vincent Brown

V.

SOULÈVEMENT DES NÈGRES
à la Jamaïque.

en 1759.

Dessiné par le Jeune.   Tom. III.   Gravé par David.

OPPOSITE François-Anne David (1741–1824). *Soulèvement des Nègres à la Jamaïque, en 1759.* Engraving, 5¾ × 3½ in. (14.7 × 8.7 cm). From *Histoire d'Angleterre, Tome troisième.* Paris: F. A. David, ca. 1800. The John Carter Brown Library at Brown University, E784 D249h.

 uring the Age of Revolution, images of black violence encircled white colonists in the Americas. Across the borders of empires, people fixated on reports and renditions of slave rebellions, wondering what they might mean for the future of European imperial enterprises. In rare cases, someone might see a just cause in slave uprisings. In 1780 Denis Diderot prophesied a righteous insurrection against slavery in a passage he wrote for Abbé Raynal's history of European colonialism. He was aware of the armed groups of self-governing former slaves in Surinam and Jamaica, where imperial officials had been forced to sign treaties respecting their emancipation, and Diderot warned the French to be afraid of their own slaves. "All that the Negroes lack is a leader courageous enough to carry them to vengeance and carnage," he wrote. "The American fields will be intoxicated by the blood that they have been awaiting for so long, and the bones of so many unfortunates piled up for three centuries, will shake with joy.... Then *The Code Noir* will disappear, and *The Code Blanc* will be terrible if the victors consult only the law of revenge!"[1] This very prospect filled whites in slave societies with dread.

One can see white fears visualized in engravings such as *Soulèvement des Nègres à la Jamaïque, en 1759*, published in François-Anne David's *Histoire d'Angleterre*. In the depiction, black insurgents have burst into a dining hall and are in the process of killing the men while the women flee. In the foreground, a muscular black man lifts a cutlass high in the air, ready to deliver a killing blow to a white man whom he has by the collar. This man appears to be begging for mercy. Just behind and to the right of him a rebel is in the act of thrusting a blade through the neck of another white man. To the left, obscured by a dining table, lies a dead man. We can only see his feet, but a black killer looms over him too. The background is teeming with slaves brandishing swords and spears.

The image almost certainly refers to the Jamaican slave uprisings of 1760–61, in which some sixty whites were killed. In his 1774 *History of Jamaica*, Edward Long estimated these insurrections as "more formidable than any hitherto known in the West Indies."[2] That the image gets the date wrong—there was no major disturbance in Jamaica in 1759—is irrelevant to its significance. Properly understood, *Soulèvement des Nègres à la Jamaïque, en 1759* refers not so much to a specific event as to a general fear of black revolt. The image encapsulates racial panic as a genre of emotive representation. In this way it speaks to something broadly shared in the Atlantic world, wherever people were interested in the maintenance of slavery, and whenever black violence seemed to threaten white supremacy. Published in France in 1800, just when Toussaint Louverture had mastered the island of Hispaniola, recently home to the most profitable European colony in the world, the image encompassed the trans-Atlantic geography of slavery and signified the deepest anxieties of the entire period between the mid-eighteenth century and the end of the Haitian Revolution.

***

In the last quarter of the eighteenth century two great upheavals shook the Atlantic empires of Great Britain and France. The American and the Haitian revolutions threw the imperial Atlantic world into chaos, killing and dislocating tens of thousands, depriving European powers of prized colonial possessions, disrupting established political orders and patterns of commerce, and finally, creating the first two independent nation states in the Americas. The participation of slaves in the revolutionary movements in North America and the Caribbean presented a grave challenge to the plantation system, which had become the foundation of European empires in the Americas. Frightened to the core, slaveholders and imperial officials responded to the threat by enhancing the brutality of slavery and then taking measures that would engulf the Atlantic world in waves of genocidal violence.

The panic that swept over the slaveholding classes during the era of revolution was not without precedent. One historian has written that eighteenth-century apprehension of slave revolt "oscillated between protracted stretches of near-complacency and brief spasms of near-paranoia."[3] And yet fear pervaded the slave societies of the Americas like a fog. Hanging like a mist about every interracial interaction, swirling up at night when black men, women, and children gathered beyond the surveillance of white people, crawling along the ground beside runaways, who considered whether their only true escape from slavery might be the death of their masters, a gaseous dread blanketed every American colony where slaves were held in thrall. For whites, the feeling might dissipate in the light of day—as they supervised rigid work routines and tallied signs of compliance—only to congeal again when confrontation threatened. Then barely suppressed anxieties could be swept up into storms of hysteria, as violence finally cleared the haze. Of the bonds that connected the different slave societies, fear was the least tangible and most durable. Repression, fear's faithful adherent, was the most apparent link—and also the most brittle.

ABOVE J. Merigot after J. Bourgoin. *The Maroons in Ambush on the Dromilly Estate in the parish of Trelawney*, 1801. Engraving. National Library of Jamaica.

In some respects, the difference between the fear experienced by slaveholders and the enslaved can be viewed as the difference between predictable and unpredictable terror. Slaves had always to fear the outbursts of slaveholders. The wrong look, word, or gesture from a slave might be enough to provoke a violent response. Acts of independence, which could be interpreted as rebelliousness, could provoke deadly reactions. So the enslaved lived with the certainty that terrible and terrifying things would happen; they were part of the routine. For slaveholders, it was the *un*certainty of slave violence that made it so feared. Colonists strove for predictability in a capricious environment, a consistency that might allow them to imagine the profit of their efforts, and propel them over the inevitable quirk of bad fortune. For this they needed an almost mechanized obedience from their slaves. Yet while the enslaved might be cowed into submission, they could never be made into mere extensions of the master's will. And when they occasionally used their enduring capacity for unauthorized action against the interests of slaveholders, hurt them or killed them, the response was shocked disbelief. It was the terror inspired by the sudden reminder that power does not guarantee security.

As surprising as it may seem, slaveholding planters, among the most powerful people in the world at the time, were also deeply vulnerable—and they felt their insecurity intensely. Like everyone, they were subject to the dangers of the natural world. Plantations, the economic engines of the British and French empires, thrived in climates that were threatening to human health.[4] Although, by the mid-eighteenth century, mortality rates had fallen dramatically from their seventeenth-century levels in the Chesapeake Bay region, settlers in the Carolinas and the Caribbean continued to see great numbers of people killed annually by disease. In the West Indies, a storm or a root fungus could destroy crops, plunging planters deep into debt. A drought might lead to famine, reducing and straining the plantation workforce. Colonists were vulnerable as well to the vagaries of imperial prerogative: incessant naval warfare scrambled trading routes, creating uncertainty in the timing of long-distance transactions; taxation policy could swing against the interests of colonial property holders; the chessboard strategies of metropolitan officials might conflict with local interests.

Slavery itself presented the greatest danger. In the most productive parts of the Americas, whites were surrounded by majorities of alienated, oppressed workers with little obvious stake in maintaining the existing order. In Jamaica, the British Empire's most valuable colony, one reformer worried aloud about the racial composition of the colony: "By the Poll-Tax in 1740," he notes, "it appeared that the Negroes were ten times more in Number than the white Persons." Writing after the discovery of a recent rebellious conspiracy, he feared that the colony was in danger of being "over-run, and ruined by its own Slaves."[5] And there was the more intangible apprehension of losing one's claim to European standards of civility, taste, and manners in a torrid zone of license and brutality. Regional differences in racial demography moderated these anxieties—whites in Virginia and Maryland could feel a bit more secure than those in the South Carolina Lowcountry or the Caribbean—but historians have observed that while some whites might grow complacent in the comfort of their majorities, they "were never free from anxiety, never entirely convinced of their slaves' intentions," and so none could be certain of their safety.[6]

As vulnerable as everyone was in these societies, there was a compelling reason to maintain them: slavery was enormously profitable. Anxiety competed with avarice to command the motivations of whites in slaveholding societies, and greed generally maintained the upper hand. Wherever in the Americas Europeans figured out how to exploit enslaved labor, their enterprises flourished. Economic, military, and political importance correlated strongly with the number of slaves in a territory, because after landholding, slaveholding was the most important source of wealth and it was slave labor that made land productive. Generally, the more slaves a colony had, the more profitable it was for its owners and operators. The extravagant wealth offered by the plantation societies conferred an exhilarating sense of superiority to property holders, and even commoners could achieve a status that would have been impossible to attain in the home countries. The stakes were too high to seriously reconsider the prevailing inequalities, so the master class did everything it could to make them absolute.

Slave society was organized to make slaveholders invulnerable: their persons were to be beyond violation. This required that white people be held in perpetual awe. The planter and politician Bryan Edwards, who published the first widely read English language account of the slave revolution in Saint-Domingue, knew that terror was the fundamental principle governing slave societies. In the 1801 edition of his history of the British West Indies, he acknowledged, following Montesquieu, that "in countries where slavery is established, the leading principle on which the government is supported is fear: or a sense of that absolute coercive necessity which, leaving no choice of action, supersedes all questions of right."[7] The laws conceived to govern the enslaved were instruments of this logic, even if they occasionally tried to soften it.

British and French slave codes developed from different legal traditions, but maintained some common features compelled by similar circumstances. In 1685, the metropolitan government in France decreed the comprehensive *Code Noir* for the colonial empire. While it was influenced by Roman canon law, like the Spanish *Siete Partidas*, the code was developed in consultation with officials in the West Indies specifically for the Americas, rather than being a holdover from medieval tradition. It meant to replace the piecemeal legislation that had been accumulating since the mid-seventeenth century, when enslaved black workers were coming to outnumber whites in plantation colonies increasingly committed to sugar production.[8] British slave laws developed in a more ad hoc fashion, adapting to meet the needs of colonists as they grew

LE
CODE NOIR,
OU
RECUEIL
DES RÉGLEMENS
rendus jusqu'à présent.

Concernant le Gouvernement, l'Administration de la Justice, la Police, la Discipline & le Commerce des Négres dans les Colonies Françoises.

Et les Conseils & Compagnies établis à ce sujet.

A PARIS,
Chez L. F. Prault, Imprimeur du Roi, quai des Augustins, à l'Immortalité.

M. DCC. LXXXVIII.
AVEC PRIVILEGE DU ROI.

enmeshed in Atlantic slavery. Models crafted in Barbados in 1661 provided flexible precedents for Jamaica, South Carolina, and other colonies, while Virginia's laws proceeded on a parallel course. The *Code Noir* generally stipulated more state protections to the enslaved than their British counterparts, though in practice and over time, what connected the two legal regimes was the importance of white solidarity to the intimidation of the black population. In 1771, the French crown made it clear that:

> It is only by leaving to the masters a power that is nearly absolute, that it will be possible to keep so large a number of men in that state of submission which is made necessary to their numerical superiority over the whites. If some masters abuse their power, they must be reproved in secret, so that the slaves may always be kept in the belief that the master can do no wrong in his dealing with them.[9]

Perhaps to an even greater degree than in the French Caribbean, masters' power in British America meant white power. In Jamaica, the law considered that the "'crime of encompassing and imagining the death of any white person, by any slave or slaves,' should be deemed and adjudged a crime of as high nature as the crime of murder, and should be punished as such."[10] It was a capital offense for slaves even to contemplate the death of whites.

More important than the laws that governed slaves was the absence of restraints upon the routine brutality of slaveholders. Their coercive power was largely unquestioned, and slaves knew that they had little formal protection from punishment, rape, torture, or even murder. The overseer Thomas Thistlewood of Jamaica often made one slave defecate into another's mouth for the mere offense of eating sugarcane without permission. Without legal limits, he penetrated the women of his choice. Once he was pleased to receive by courier the head of a runaway named Robin. As a warning to others he "put it upon a pole and stuck it up just at the angle of the road in the home pasture."[11] Warwick Francis of South Carolina saw one enslaved boy tied "on a wooden spit so near the fire that it Scorch him well and basted with Salt and Water the same as you would a pigg."[12] While some of these tortures might have been technically illegal, the perpetrators were rarely punished for fear of undermining the social order. In 1788 the Saint-Domingue planter Nicolas Lejeune was indeed tried upon the testimony of his own slaves (inadmissible in the British context) for torturing two female slaves, ultimately to their

OPPOSITE *Le Code Noir, ou Recueil des Réglemens*. Paris: Chez L. F. Prault, 1788. New-York Historical Society, Y1788.FRA.

deaths.[13] His defense was straightforward: convicting him would lead to a breakdown in authority of the master class, embolden the enslaved, and lead to servile revolt. This argument carried the day, and Lejeune was never punished.[14] Although the extremity of slaveholder violence was attenuated in places where whites were in the majority and felt less embattled, the principle was similar wherever slavery was enforced.

It is easy to be shocked. But that elemental response crowds our ability to understand the elemental feelings of the people who lived in such societies, who made homes for themselves in the cold embrace of physical and psychological brutality. Certainly, they might have imagined that these repressive measures were underwriting global security, making the world safe for civilization, commerce, and Christianity. More importantly, slaveholders and others—even including those slaves who somehow managed to avoid the worst brutalities of enslavement—hoped merely to survive, improve their status among their fellows, and perhaps leave a legacy of their brief existence. For this they required some continuity, even of a ruthless sort. But as most people knew, the cruelty of the system, which made fear so pervasive, also made it likely that at least a few slaves would respond in kind, if ever they thought that they could get away with it. And the very tools that made plantation agriculture work, like a machete or a cane knife, could be instruments of havoc when the enslaved rose up in revolution.

***

When powerful people are violated, when they discover that they are not immune to the kinds of violence they purvey, they register the most profound shock, and their shudders of vengeance are terrible to behold. Revenge: in the hands of the powerful, it is not a reaction so much as a re-affirmation of first principles, a warning to the weak that they are meant to remain subject to the whims of the powerful into infinity. So it was with the reaction to slaves' participation in the revolutionary movements of the era. Slaveholders responded to the shock of violation with extravagant

By his Excellency the Right Honourable JOHN *Earl of* DUNMORE, *his Majesty's Lieutenant and Governour-General of the Colony and Dominion of Virginia, and Vice-Admiral of the same:*

A PROCLAMATION.

AS I have ever entertained Hopes that an Accommodation might have taken Place between *Great Britain* and this Colony, without being compelled, by my Duty, to this most disagreeable, but now absolutely necessary Step, rendered so by a Body of armed Men, unlawfully assembled, firing on his Majesty's Tenders, and the Formation of an Army, and that Army now on their March to attack his Majesty's Troops, and destroy the well-disposed Subjects of this Colony: To defeat such treasonable Purposes, and that all such Traitors, and their Abetters, may be brought to Justice, and that the Peace and good Order of this Colony may be again restored, which the ordinary Course of the civil Law is unable to effect, I have thought fit to issue this my Proclamation, hereby declaring, that until the aforesaid good Purposes can be obtained, I do, in Virtue of the Power and Authority to me given, by his Majesty, determine to execute martial Law, and cause the same to be executed throughout this Colony; and to the End that Peace and good Order may the sooner be restored, I do require every Person capable of bearing Arms to resort to his Majesty's S T A N-DARD, or be looked upon as Traitors to his Majesty's Crown and Government, and thereby become liable to the Penalty the Law inflicts upon such Offences, such as Forfeiture of Life, Confiscation of Lands, &c. &c. And I do hereby farther declare all indented Servants, Negroes, or others (appertaining to Rebels) free, that are able and willing to bear Arms, they joining his Majesty's Troops, as soon as may be, for the more speedily reducing this Colony to a proper Sense of their Duty, to his Majesty's Crown and Dignity. I do farther order, and require, all his Majesty's liege Subjects to retain their Quitrents, or any other Taxes due, or that may become due, in their own Custody, till such Time as Peace may be again restored to this at present most unhappy Country, or demanded of them for their former salutary Purposes, by Officers properly authorised to receive the same.

GIVEN under my Hand, on Board the Ship William, *off* Norfolk, *the 7th Day of* November, *in the 16th Year of his Majesty's Reign.*

D U N M O R E.

G O D   SAVE   THE   K I N G.

Mais, par un rapprochement fatal, le même jour qui avait signalé à Saint-
Domingue la soumission de Toussaint Louverture, vit débarquer à la Guadeloupe trois mille cinq cents hommes arrivés de Brest. L'année précédente, le
mulâtre Pélage avait proclamé l'indépendance de cette île, et embarqué sur un
bâtiment neutre le capitaine-général Lacrosse, surpris et enlevé au moment où
il visitait ses avant-postes extérieurs. Bientôt les noirs s'étaient emparés de la
révolution de Pélage ; et ce fut contre eux que le général Richepanse, qui com-
mandait cette expédition, aidé des secours de Pélage, dut employer une valeur
tant illustrée à la bataille de Hohenlinden. Après avoir anéanti la rébellion,
Richepanse succomba, dans les premiers jours de septembre, à ce terrible fléau
dont le retour périodique, silencieusement attendu par les noirs de Saint-Domingue, devint tout à coup, ce même mois, le signal d'une fermentation sourde
dans les ateliers et dans les bataillons coloniaux. On cessa de rendre les armes,
on les cacha avec soin ; des insurgés, sous le nom de nègres marrons, se rassem-

blèrent sur les mornes aussitôt que la fièvre jaune reparut. Ce redoutable auxi-
liaire de l'affranchissement du sol d'Haïti, moissonna avec une effrayante rapi-
dité la brave armée, qui n'eut bientôt plus pour casernes que des hôpitaux, que la
mort vidait chaque jour. Le général en chef était allé, avec sa femme et son
fils, respirer pendant quelque temps l'air salubre de l'île de la Tortue, où il
avait fait établir un hôpital de convalescents; un impérieux devoir le rappela

OPPOSITE *Maroons*, in *Histoire de Napoléon*, by M. de Norvins. Paris: J. Pinard, 1839. New-York Historical Society, XS DC203.NA.

displays of violence. They mutilated the disobedient; they used ritual execution to give their authority a sacred dimension; they visited extraordinary torments on the bodies of rebels before and after death.[15] These were practices of domination, to be sure, but they were also expressions of what the historian Peter Silver has in another context called a "sense of indignant vulnerability" or "violent self-pity."[16] For the threat posed by slave revolution represented not only a disturbance to property and order, but also the horrifying vision of a carefully calibrated and hard-won way of life collapsed in a heap.

One can sense the fear inspired by the tumult of Atlantic slave revolution by surveying the circulation of panic. Philip D. Morgan has described a rhythmic sequence that characterized the response to slave violence in colonial Virginia and South Carolina: "first, a short burst of intense suspicion, more than likely out of proportion to the real dangers; second, a cathartic show of force; and finally, a return to normalcy or near-complacency."[17] In the age of revolutions, this rhythm pulsed throughout the Atlantic world, but with a difference. Increasingly, the suspicions of conspiracy were vindicated by events. The uprising of slaves in Jamaica in 1760 and 1761, during the global Seven Years' War between Britain, France, and Spain inspired comment in the newspapers in London, Boston, and Philadelphia (and in France, it was remembered as late as 1800 in engravings such as *Soulèvement des Nègres à la Jamaïque, en 1759*). As they read such reports, slaveholders watched their slaves closely, tried to screen them from news of trouble elsewhere, and punished disobedience more forcefully than usual. During the American Revolution, Lord Dunmore's efforts to use runaway slaves against their insurgent masters in Virginia sent shudders even through many of the most staunchly loyalist slaveholders. Despite the eventual use of armed slaves by both sides of the conflict, great care was taken to keep black people in submission.[18] Caribbean masters, who had shared some of the North American colonists' grievances over imperial policy, were ultimately too frightened of their enslaved majorities to contemplate independence from the United Kingdom. Indeed, West Indian slaveholders were grateful for the presence and protection of British armed forces.[19] They must have felt vindicated when the French Revolution swept through the region, as slaves and former slaves were driving global upheavals and winning recognition of their freedom from metropolitan officials. Planters within and beyond the Francophone Americas followed the news with horror. Drawing upon translated French reports, Bryan Edwards offered Anglophone readers one of the first descriptions of the revolution in progress, recounted as an unmitigated series of disastrous black atrocities.[20]

CONSTITUTION

DE LA COLONIE FRANÇAISE

DE SAINT-DOMINGUE.

Du 17 Août 1801, (29 Thermidor an 9.)

Les députés des départemens de la colonie française de Saint-Domingue, réunis en assemblée centrale, ont arrêtés et posés les bases constitutionnelles d'un régime de la colonie française de Saint-Domingue, ainsi qu'il suit :

TITRE PREMIER.

Du Territoire.

ARTICLE PREMIER.

Saint-Domingue dans toute son étendue, et *Samana*, *la Tortue*, *la Gonave*, *les Caïemites*, *l'Ile-à-Vache*, *la Saone*, et autres îles adjacentes, forment le territoire d'une seule colonie, qui fait partie de l'Empire français, mais qui est soumise a des lois particulières.

2. Le territoire de cette colonie se divise en départemens, arrondissemens et paroisses.

TITRE II.

De ses habitans.

3. Il ne peut exister d'esclave sur ce territoire; la servitude y est à jamais abolie. Tous les hommes y naissent, vivent et meurent libres et français.

4. Tout homme, quelque soit sa couleur, y est admissible à tous les emplois:

5. Il n'y existe d'autre distinction que celle des vertus et des talens, et d'autre supériorité que celle que la loi donne dans l'exercice d'une fonction publique.

La loi y est la même pour tous, soit qu'elle punisse, soit qu'elle protège.

A

Slaveholders across the Atlantic world tightened restrictions on those slaves they could still control, on free people of color, and on the movement of seditious people and ideas. Many yearned for the great cathartic show of force that might allow them a return to normal times.[21]

In 1802, as Napoleon Bonaparte prepared to send a military expedition to the Caribbean in hopes of restoring Saint-Domingue and Guadeloupe to their former opulence, Simon Taylor of Jamaica considered the prospects of the imminent French campaign. Taylor, one of the richest men in the British Empire, an experienced merchant, planter, and politician, understood the moment to be a "very critical time in this Part of the World." He had gotten wind of the massing of troops in France and Holland, but he worried that no one had any idea about the intentions of Toussaint Louverture or his generals, "whether they will resist the Troops sent out or not, or will submit and give up the island quietly." Drawing upon his lifetime of experience in the Caribbean, he advised his friends that if the black revolutionaries resisted, it would take "200,000 of the best Troops in Europe" to bring them to heel. "The Art of War is very different in the West Indies to what it is in Europe," he averred, and if conditions were favorable to Toussaint, then "the Whole force of France can not dispossess him." He was even more concerned that Bonaparte was publicly promising to endorse the freedom of former slaves in exchange for loyalty to France. "If that is his reall Intention it will serve only as a signall to all the Negroes in the other Islands to revolt & murder their Masters and the White Inhabitants, for they will rationally say that by so doing the Negroes in those Islands have acquired their Freedom, and therefore they must do the same to acquire theirs." Only a campaign of genocide would set things right. "There is one and only way to make St. Domingo again a Sugar Colony as well as Guadeloupe," he concluded, "and that is by extirpating the present race of Negroes in them and resettling them with new Negroes from Africa and making it Death to propagate Sentiments of the Abolitionists or the Doctrines of Les Amis de Noir." This was his advice to all who would listen: "I am confident there is no other Medium...but by extirpating the present generation of Negroes."[22]

Without prompting from Taylor, the French seem ultimately to have reached the same conclusion. From its inception in 1791, the servile revolt in Saint-Domingue was undoubtedly violent, but it was not the indiscriminate indulgence portrayed by writers like Edwards. The warfare of the insurgents was, rather, strategic and tactical, as even Simon Taylor recognized when he pondered their likely response to the expedition of 1802. Rebel leaders had been acutely aware of how they were portrayed, and sought to mitigate negative impressions of their struggle by containing the bloodshed and remaining open to negotiation. Widespread violence was "periodic and interspersed with periods of relative calm."[23] However, not long after the French force led by Bonaparte's brother-in-law Charles-Victor-Emmanuel Leclerc arrived on the island, the Revolution entered a final brutal phase. A series of French victories, in which they won over some rebel leaders and forced the surrender of others, proved to be Pyrrhic. Reduced by battle and disease, confronting an intractable resistance from dispersed bands of insurgents, and unsure of the loyalty of the black troops in their ranks, the French scorched the earth in desperation. After Leclerc's death, his successor Donatien-Marie-Joseph Rochambeau escalated a campaign that had become explicitly genocidal. As if Simon Taylor had been whispering in his ear, Rochambeau explained in December 1802 that it was necessary to "exterminate all the armed Blacks, the farm laborers and their chiefs and, to use a metaphor, cut the legs off everyone else: without this we will lose our colonies, and any hope of ever having any."[24]

This course of action was a disaster. France's remaining black troops defected in increasing numbers. Jean-Jacques Dessalines, who had earlier turned against the insurgents, now deserted the French and pursued his own policy of counter-terror against them. By the end of 1803, he could claim victory for the former slaves, but his experience of the white supremacist way of warfare had convinced him that the slaves' vengeance must be total. When he declared independence for the new nation of Haiti on New Year's Day, 1804, he called for the annihilation of the whites:

> Native citizens, men, women, girls, and children, let your gaze extend on all parts of this island: look there for your spouses, your husbands, your brothers, your sisters. Indeed! Look there for your children, your suckling infants, what have they become? … I shudder to say it … the prey of these vultures … What are you waiting for before appeasing their spirits? … Remember that you had wanted your remains to rest next to those of your father after you defeated tyranny; will you descend into their tombs without having avenged them? No! Their bones would reject yours.[25]

Massacres of white planters and their families would follow.[26]

***

One can recognize, without minimizing the importance of anyone's suffering, that all vengeance is not equal. The revenge of the enslaved was born of the hope that they could put an end to routine fear. The violent reactions of slaveholders were ultimately cynical attempts to continue that terror. And yet the outcomes of each may have been similar. Even after slavery, a colony organized by fear evolved into a nation governed by it, as a long succession of dictatorial regimes prevented the Haitian population from enjoying the fruits of their emancipation.[27]

These local governments were aligned, in this way, with the response to the Haitian Revolution on the part of the slaveholding powers of the nineteenth century, who spurned the new nation in an effort to make the world safe for slavery. U.S. President Thomas Jefferson had for several years feared those he called the "cannibals of the terrible republic," and established a policy of diplomatic isolation toward Haiti that would last until 1862.[28] France, which did manage to reestablish plantation slavery in Guadeloupe, actively considered sending another invasion force to Haiti, but was mindful enough of the success of the black insurgents to demur. The French withheld acknowledgement of Haitian sovereignty until 1825, when the Haitians agreed to pay a large indemnity for having deprived France of its former colony. The new relationship was to be, according to an 1820 memorandum, "a new type of colonization, without the inconveniences and expenses."[29] Historian Johnhenry Gonzalez observes that "Haiti was the first modern nation to find itself in an essentially neocolonial relationship with its former colonial metropole," indeed, "the first of many to eventually trade formal colonial subjugation for rule through foreign debt and economic control."[30]

Meanwhile, general fears of black violence had taken enduring forms, as they helped to define the supposed opposition between savagery and civilization. The "horrors of Santo Domingo," as condensed in the writings of people like Bryan Edwards and Mary Hassal, were invoked again and again beyond the Francophone world by proslavery advocates confronting the challenge of abolitionism in the United States, in the debates over emancipation and its aftermath in the British empire, even in the imperial reaction to the 1857 mutiny in British colonial India.[31] It can even be said that reactions to slave revolt connect "eighteenth-century images of black violence to modern stereotypes about black and especially black male criminality."[32] Racial fear has in this way provided a handy justification for denying black peoples' claims to political power. Since the Age of Revolution, in the former slave societies of the Atlantic world, black freedom struggles have often been viewed in the terms of ferocious abandon, onslaught, riot, and carnage rather than as organized political movements with identifiable aims, strategies, and tactics. If you wonder why, it is largely because a vapor of dread still clings to our thoughts and feelings, evoking the law of revenge.

Notes

The author wishes to thank Malick Ghachem, Ajantha Subramanian, and the editors of this volume for comments and suggestions on earlier drafts of this essay.

1 Guillaume Thomas François Raynal, *Histoire philosophique et politique des établissements et du commerce des Européens dans les deux Indes* (Geneva: Pellet, 1780), vol. 3, book 11, chap. 24 as quoted in Laurent Dubois and John D. Garrigus, eds., *Slave Revolution in the Caribbean, 1780–1804* (New York: Bedford/St. Martin's, 2006), 56.

2 For contemporaneous accounts of the uprisings and their aftermath see Edward Long, *History of Jamaica* (London: T. Lowndes, 1774), 2:447–72, quotation on 462; Bryan Edwards, *The History, Civil and Commercial, of the British Colonies in the West Indies* (London, 1801), 2:75–79; also see Michael Craton, *Testing the Chains: Resistance to Slavery in the British West Indies* (Ithaca, N.Y.: Cornell Univ. Press, 1982), 125–39; Richard Hart, *Slaves Who Abolished Slavery: Blacks in Rebellion* (Kingston: Univ. of the West Indies Press, 2002 [1985]), 130–56.

3 Philip D. Morgan, *Slave Counterpoint: Black Culture in the Eighteenth Century Chesapeake and Lowcountry* (Chapel Hill: Univ. of North Carolina Press, 1998), 386.

4 See Vincent Brown, *The Reaper's Garden: Death and Power in the World of Atlantic Slavery* (Cambridge, Mass.: Harvard Univ. Press, 2008).

5 Anonymous, *An Essay Concerning Slavery and the Danger Jamaica is expos'd to from the Too great Number of Slaves, and the too little Care that is taken to manage Them, and a Proposal to prevent the further Importation of Negroes into that Island* (London: Charles Corbett, at Addison's-Head, over-against St. Dunstan's Church in Fleet-Street, 1746), 18.

6 Morgan, *Slave Counterpoint*, 398.

7 Bryan Edwards, *The History, Civil and Commercial, of the British Colonies in the West Indies* (London, 1801), 3:36.

8 Dubois and Garrigus, eds., *Slave Revolution*, 49.

9 As cited in Elsa V. Goveia, "The West Indian Slave Laws of the Eighteenth Century," in Hilary Beckles and Verene Shepherd, eds., *Caribbean Slave Society and Economy: A Student Reader* (New York: The New Press, 1991), 359.

10 "An Act for the Better Order and Government of Slaves, article XXIV, 1696," *Acts of Assembly Passed in the Island of Jamaica from 1681 to 1737, inclusive* (London, 1738); *Journals of the Jamaican House of Assembly*, Vol. 3 (20 December 1744), 673.

11 Diary of Thomas Thistlewood, 9 October 1752, quoted in Douglas Hall, *In Miserable Slavery: Thomas Thistlewood in Jamaica, 1750–86* (London, 1989), 30. For the fullest examination of Thistlewood's career in Jamaica see Trevor Burnard, *Mastery, Tyranny, and Desire: Thomas Thistlewood and His Slaves in the Anglo-Jamaican World* (Chapel Hill: Univ. of North Carolina Press, 2004).

12 Morgan, *Slave Counterpoint*, 393.

13 The testimony of slaves was also inadmissible under French law at the time, except in situations where there were no white witnesses to a capital crime (as in the Lejeune case) or for the purpose of clarifying the circumstances of a case.

14 Laurent Dubois, *Avengers of the New World: The Story of the Haitian Revolution* (Cambridge, Mass.: Harvard Univ. Press, 2004), 56. For a thorough discussion of the Lejeune affair see Malick Ghachem, *The Old Regime and the Haitian Revolution* (Cambridge, Eng.: Cambridge Univ. Press, 2011), chap. 4.

15 Vincent Brown, "Spiritual Terror and Sacred Authority: Supernatural Power in Jamaican Slave Society," revised and reprinted in Stephanie Camp and Edward E. Baptist, eds., *New Studies in the History of American Slavery* (Athens, Ga.: Univ. of Georgia Press, 2006), 179–210.

16 Peter Silver, *Our Savage Neighbors: How Indian War Transformed Early America* (New York: W.W. Norton, 2008), 94.

17 Morgan, *Slave Counterpoint*, 387–88.

18   Douglass Egerton, *Death or Liberty: African Americans and Revolutionary America* (New York: Oxford Univ. Press, 2009); Philip D. Morgan and Andrew Jackson O'Shaughnessy, "Arming Slaves in the American Revolution," in Christopher L. Brown and Philip D. Morgan, eds., *Arming Slaves: From Classical Times to the Modern Age* (New Haven: Yale Univ. Press, 2006), 180–208.

19   See Andrew Jackson O'Shaughnessy, *An Empire Divided: The American Revolution and the British Caribbean* (Philadelphia: Univ. of Pennsylvania Press, 2000).

20   Bryan Edwards, *An Historical Account of the French Colony in the Island of St. Domingo; Comprehending a Short Account of its Ancient Government, Political State, Population, Productions, and Exports; A Narrative of the Calamities Which Have Desolated the Country Ever Since the Year 1789, With Some Reflections on their Causes, and a Detail of the Military Transactions of the British Army in that Island to the End of 1794* (London: J. Stockdale, 1797); *A Particular Account of the Commencement and Progress of the Insurrection of the Negroes in St. Domingue, Which Began in August Last* (London: J. Sewell, 1792); Dubois, *Avengers of the New World*, 111; Samuel Conrad Scott, "The Enlightenment of Bryan Edwards: Slavery, Fear, and Historical Writing in the Eighteenth-Century Atlantic" (History Department Senior Thesis, Harvard University, 2008), 88–98.

21   Dubois, *Avengers of the New World*; Laurent Dubois, A *Colony of Citizens: Revolution and Slave Emancipation in the French Caribbean* (Chapel Hill: Univ. of North Carolina Press, 2004).

22   Simon Taylor to George Hibbert, February 1802, Taylor Family Papers, Institute for Commonwealth Studies, I/D/25; Simon Taylor to Henry Shirley, February 1802, Taylor Family Papers, Institute for Commonwealth Studies I/D/26.

23   Laurent Dubois, "'Unworthy of Liberty?' Slavery, Terror, and Revolution in Haiti," in Isaac Land, ed., *Enemies of Humanity: The Nineteenth-Century War on Terrorism* (New York: Palgrave Macmillan, 2008), 45–62, quotation on 46.

24   Rochambeau as quoted in Dubois, "'Unworthy of Liberty?'," 58.

25   "The Haitian Declaration of Independence, January 1, 1804" in Dubois and Garrigus, eds., *Slave Revolution in the Caribbean*, 189.

26   Dubois, "'Unworthy of Liberty?'," 59. For the final campaigns of the revolution see Dubois, *Avengers of the New World*, 280–301.

27   Mimi Sheller, *Democracy After Slavery: Black Publics and Peasant Radicalism in Haiti and Jamaica* (Gainesville: Univ. of Florida Press, 2001); Michel-Rolph Trouillot, *Haiti: State Against Nation: The Origins and Legacies of Duvalierism* (New York: Monthly Review Press, 1989); David Nicholls, *From Dessalines to Duvalier: Race Colour and National Independence in Haiti* (London: Macmillan Education Ltd., 1996).

28   Thomas Jefferson to Aaron Burr, 11 February 1799, in Dubois and Garrigus, eds., *Slave Revolution in the Caribbean*, 161.

29   Nicholls, *From Dessalines to Duvalier*, 64.

30   Johnhenry Gonzalez, "The Ashes of Empire and the Caribbean Origins of Neo-Colonialism: The Effects of the Haitian Revolution on European Ideas about Slavery and on French Imperial Policy" (History Department Senior Thesis, Harvard University, 2006), 80, 81.

31   Scott, "The Enlightenment of Bryan Edwards," 114–27; Mary Hassal [Leonara Sansay], *Secret History: Or, The Horrors of St. Domingo, In a Series of Letters Written by a Lady at Cape François to Colonel Burr* (Philadelphia: Bradford & Inskelp, 1808).

32   Scott, "The Enlightenment of Bryan Edwards," 127. The Haitian Revolution is among the phenomena listed as "slave crime" by Ulrich Bonnell Phillips, *American Negro Slavery: A Survey of the Supply, Employment and Control of Negro Labor as Determined by the Plantation Regime* (Baton Rouge: Louisiana State Univ. Press, 1969 [1918]), 454–88.

One Woman, Three Revolutions: Rosalie of the Poulard Nation

Rebecca J. Scott and
Jean M. Hébrard

he events we call revolutions look very different depending on when and how they come crashing into a given life. People who found themselves in the greater Caribbean in the last decades of the eighteenth century felt the shock waves of three such revolutions—those that gave rise to the United States of America, the French Republic, and the nation of Haiti. This was particularly true for men and women living in the port towns and cities, connected by webs of trade both to a plantation hinterland and to the ports of other colonies and nations. It was also particularly true for those whose status was that of slaves, and for those whose status balanced precariously somewhere between slavery and freedom. Over the course of these three revolutionary movements, the very possibility of holding property in persons would be called into question, though only in the Haitian revolution would slavery itself be definitively overturned.[1]

For some of the African men and women held as slaves in the Caribbean, these were not the first revolutions that they had encountered. In the mid-1770s, for example, in the region of Fuuta Tooro, along the Senegal River, a sector of the Islamic clerical elite denounced the ruling warrior aristocracy of the Denianke and forced into public debate the question of the legitimacy of selling fellow Muslims to Europeans as slaves. The continuing Atlantic trade in captives from the Senegal River Valley had stimulated armed conflict, and raiding parties and contending armies were taking into captivity even the families of the most sanctified of religious leaders. Abdulkaadir Kan, a religious scholar, joined in building a powerful movement to overthrow the Denianke in the name of a renewed and purified adherence to the teaching of the Qur'an. By the 1780s Kan, who now held the title of Almamy [Imam] of Fuuta Tooro, controlled a long stretch of the river and forced French slave traders to concede that they would not take captives from his domains down river and into the Atlantic trade. Neighbors and rivals who refused the authority of the Almamy nonetheless continued to raid into his territory and transport captives by other routes for deportation to the Americas.[2]

The people of Fuuta Tooro, along with others who spoke the Pulaar language, were referred to by the French as the Foules or the Poules (from the word "Pullo"), a term that in the Americas was often rendered as Poulard. When we find a young woman held as a slave in Saint-Domingue being referred to as "Rosalie nation Poulard," it is thus an origin in Senegambia that is implied.[3]

OPPOSITE Agostino Brunias (1728–1796). *Free West Indian Creoles in elegant dress,* ca. 1780. Oil on canvas, 12⅛ × 9¾ in. (30.8 × 24.8 cm). Yale Center for British Art, Paul Mellon Collection. The Bridgeman Art Library International.

RIGHT *Vente par Marthe Guillaume à mongol de la N^sse Rozalie, January 14, 1793.* Notary Lépine, File 6C-119, Jérémie Papers, Special Collections, George A. Smathers Libraries, University of Florida, Gainesville.

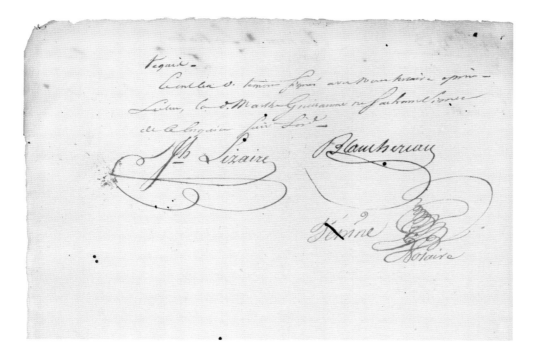

TRANSCRIPTION

14 Jer 1793
Vente par marthe
Guillaume a mongol
De la Nsse Rozalie

Au nom de La Nation

Par-devant le Notaire en la Sénéchaussée de
    Jérémie
y résidant paroisse Saint Louis, ile et cote
    française de
St Domingue En amérique soussigné, en la
    présence des
Témoins ci-après nommés et aussi soussignés

Fut présente En personne Marthe Guillaume
Citoyenne demeurant en Cette ville.

Laquelle a par ces présentes Vendu, Cédé et
    Transporté
dès maintenant & a perpétuité au S. Jn Bte
    mongol
citoyen, demeurant en Cette ville, ici présent
    & acceptant
une négresse Nommée Rozalie nation poulard
âgée d'environ vingt six ans.
Vu visitée par l'acquéreur qui a déclaré en être
    satisfait.

Cette vente faite entre parties pour le prix et
    Somme
De Deux mille quatre cent livres, que la
    venderesse
A déclaré avoir eues de l'acquéreur comptant
    avant
ces présentes dont quittance

Transportant la d. venderesse à l'acquéreur son
droit de propriété qu'elle avait sur la d. Rozalie
de laquelle elle s'est dévêtue et dessaisie au
    profit
du d. S. Mongol qu'elle a vêtu et saisi,
    consentant qu'il
fasse et dispose du sujet comme bon lui
    semblera
et déclarant l'acquéreur en avoir pris livraison
    dont décharge.

Fait & passé à Jérémie en l'étude L'an
Mil sept cent quatre vingt treize & le quatorze
Janvier à midi en présence des sieurs Jh Lizaire
& Blanchereau dom. en cette ville témoins
    connus & requis.

Et ont les d. témoins signé avec nous notaire
    après
Lecture, la d. Marthe Guillaume ne sachant
    signer
de ce enquise suivant la loi.

[Signatures]
Jh Lizaire
Blanchereau
Lépine notaire

The notary who designated her in this way did so in an act recorded for Rosalie's owner, Marthe Guillaume Aliés, a prosperous free black woman who generally signed with a heavily inked single nickname: *Martonne*.[4]

To uncover the history of Rosalie of the Poulard nation, we must also attend closely to those who claimed her as a slave. Marthe Guillaume, herself born of African parents who escaped the grip of slavery, had become a *marchande*, a woman authorized to trade in her own name. And trade she did, buying, selling, improving, and renting out real estate, buying and selling slaves, and loaning money at interest. We can thus situate Rosalie in the early 1790s as an enslaved member of a substantial household on the central Place d'Armes in Jérémie, one dominated by a black woman of imposing wealth and local influence. Although vulnerable to sale at any time, Rosalie was outside the immediate orbit of the sugar economy, located instead in a town that served a coffee-growing hinterland.[5]

Rosalie of the Poulard nation was both an unpaid laborer and part of an intricate web of relations of clientage and protection that Marthe Guillaume had developed over the years. Indeed, Rosalie may have been a somewhat favored member of that network. When Marthe Guillaume went to a notary to draw up a last will and testament in 1793, she initially declared that Rosalie should be freed upon her death. Upon reflection, however, Martonne revised the

Oxanne, Delineavit.   N. Ponce, Direxit.

VUE DE LA VILLE DE JÉRÉMIE.

Isle S.ᵗ Domingue.

A.P.D.R.

Ville haute.   Pointe de Jérémie.
Ville basse.   } Batterie.

ABOVE Nicolas Ponce (1746–1831). *Vue de la Ville de Jérémie*, in *Recueil de Vues des Lieux Principaux de la Colonie Française de Saint-Domingue*. Paris: M. Moreau de Saint-Méry, M. Ponce, M. Phelipeau, 1791. William L. Clements Library, University of Michigan, FF1791.

will, dropping the reference to this manumission, and instead selling Rosalie to one of her neighbors, a man of color who worked as a butcher. Rosalie's first promise of legal freedom had lasted for only a week, the time it took Marthe Guillaume to return to the notary and change the draft.[6]

It was thus as an enslaved woman held by successive free persons of color that Rosalie of the Poulard nation faced the first phase of the Haitian Revolution. The Revolution had begun with claims of rights made by free persons of color, and then exploded in 1791 into an uprising of enslaved laborers on the plantations of the northern plain. It rapidly expanded to the south, leading to desperate battles and complex alliances. Those who claimed ownership of Rosalie were doubly implicated in the core questions of the revolution: What would be the civil status of free persons of color, and what would be the future of the holding of property in men and women? For free people of color who sought respect and civil standing that they believed to be theirs by right, slaves were both potential allies and potential enemies—particularly when white planters chose to arm some of their slaves to fight against the increasingly assertive forces led by free men of color.[7]

For the trader Marthe Guillaume, these questions hit very close to home. Her daughter Marie-Anne Aliés had married into the Azor family, a network of property-holding free persons of color in the town and hinterland of Jérémie. Already in August and September of 1791 leaders among the free people in the south, among them Noël Azor, had taken up arms to pursue guarantees of their own civil standing and political privileges. Many white property-owners were enraged at this presumption, and a tangled set of conflicts had ensued, shadowed by struggles over the authority of the Civil Commissioners sent to Saint-Domingue by the French Republic, an authority which the white elite of Jérémie categorically refused.[8] The claims of free men of color were heard in Paris, but the Colonial Assembly, controlled by conservative white colonists, denied the legitimacy of the April 1792 French decree that granted political rights to free men of color. André Rigaud, a gifted military leader and free man of color from the south, maneuvered to secure those rights through alliance with the emissaries of the French Republic. By spring 1793, it looked as though this concession would be followed by steps toward the abolition of slavery. In turn, white planters in the south intensified negotiations with the British aimed at shifting their allegiance to a competing imperial power that might provide a more secure guarantee of slavery and of property.[9]

During the American Revolution the British had used declarations of freedom for selected slaves as a means of undercutting their patriot rivals, but the king and his advisors had no lasting commitment to emancipation as a matter of general colonial policy. On the contrary, the continued prosperity of slaveholding planters in the British colony of Jamaica was directly threatened by the revolutionary tumult in Saint-Domingue, and an intervention in the French colony could be justified on the grounds of local security as well as the longstanding Continental conflict with the French. In September of 1793, just as declarations of emancipation by the Republican Civil Commissioners sent by France were to have taken effect in the south, redcoats landed at Jérémie. They rapidly secured the surrounding area, and for the next five years the formal legal structures governing both slavery and the rights of free persons of color in Jérémie would be those imposed by the British. Republican forces led by General André Rigaud still held power at Les Cayes just to the south, however, and British authorities hesitated to provoke Jérémie's free people of color by enforcing the most draconian of the restrictions recommended by their planter allies.[10]

For Rosalie of the Poulard nation, this meant that the second promise of legal freedom—that of the French Civil Commissioners, later ratified by the Convention Nationale in Paris—would come to naught. The ever-adaptable trader Marthe Guillaume, by contrast, continued her business activities, and even rented out rooms to a translator working for the British. She did, however, return to the question of the status of Rosalie of the Poulard nation, whom she had at some point reacquired from her neighbor the butcher. This time, Marthe Guillaume decided on a full manumission, or *affranchissement*, while she was alive, rather than the fragile instruction to heirs in a testament. And so in December 1795 Marthe Guillaume went again to a notary, this time to memorialize her intention to emancipate Rosalie, *négresse de nation Poulard*, said to be about twenty-eight years old, and her commitment to acquiring the necessary approvals from the appropriate authorities—in the event, the English governor Williamson.[11]

This was more easily said than done, however. Governor Williamson's advisors among the French colonists urged him to decline all requests to authorize individual manumissions—there were too many free people of color already, they insisted, and freeing women was a particular affront to property, for it denied slaveholders the ownership of any subsequent children. Governor Williamson refused the permission to manumit requested by Marthe Guillaume, leaving Rosalie in an entirely uncertain status—not claimed as property by her putative owner, but possessed of no legally valid manumission paper.[12]

By 1796, Rosalie seems to have been living as a more or less free woman, and to have entered into an intimate union with a relatively impoverished Frenchman from one of the outlying districts, the coastal community of Les Abricots. His name was Michel Vincent, and he was a notably unsuccessful colonist. Son of a notary from Le Mans, he had managed to acquire a royal monopoly on butchering in the town of Les Cayes, but lost it again. Marriage to a rich widow had yielded him no lasting benefits, for the widow's notary secured her property to children of an earlier marriage. He moved into the coffee region of Jérémie and Les Abricots to try his luck one more time, but the few traces he left in the local notarial records suggest

GENERAL ANDRÉ RIGAUD, CHIEF OF THE MULATTOES.

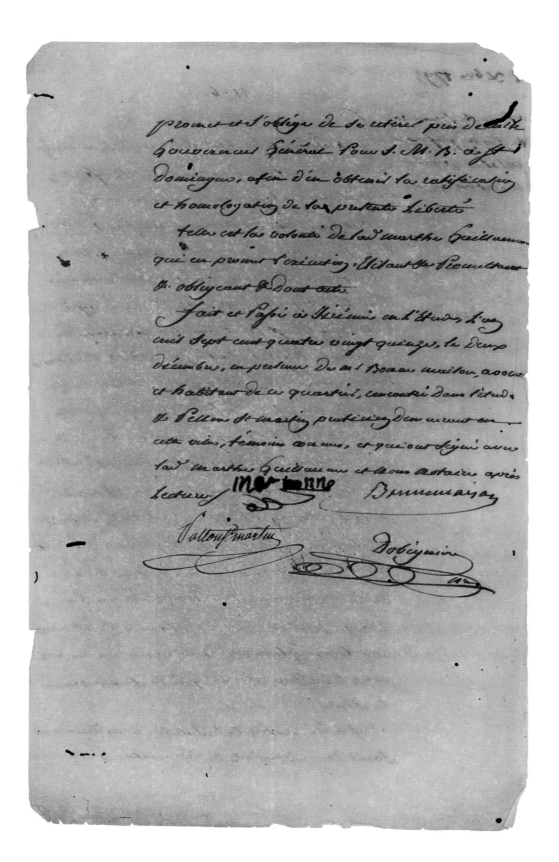

2 Xbre 1795

affranchissement
de la négresse
rosalie par
marthonne
Exped[ition]

N° 1176

Par devant le Notaire du Roi au Siège
de Jérémie résidant en la d. ville soussigné,
en présence des témoins ci-après nommés

Fût présente la nommée marthe Guillaume
Négresse libre demeurant en cette ville
laquelle désirant donner à la nommée
Rosalie, négresse de nation Poulard âgée
d'environ vingt huit ans, son esclave, des
preuves de la satisfaction qu'elle a des bons
services qu'elle lui a toujours rendus, de sa
fidélité, du zèle et de l'attachement qu'elle
lui a donnés, et ne croyant pouvoir le faire
plus convenablement que par le don de la
Liberté, [déclare par] ces présentes affranchir
de tout esclavage et Donner la Liberté, à la dite
rosalie, négresse Poulard, âgée de vingt huit
ans son esclave, pour en jouir ainsi que
les autres affranchis de la Colonie, à la
charge pour elle de se conformer strictement
aux lois, règlements et ordonnances rendues
pour les affranchis ou qui le seront par
la suite.

afin de mettre la d. Rosalie à même de
Jouir de ce bienfait, la dite marthe Guillaume
promet et s'oblige de se retirer près de M. le
Gouverneur général Pour S. M. B. de St
Domingo, afin d'en obtenir la ratification
Et homologation de la présente liberté.

Telle est la volonté de la d. marthe Guillaume
qui en promet l'exécution Elisant et Promettant
& obligeant et Dont acte.

fait et Passé à Jérémie en l'Etude, l'an
mil sept cent quatre vingt quinze, le deux
décembre, en présence de m. [s] Bonnemaison,
     avocat
et habitant de ce quartier, rencontré dans
     l'étude,
& Vallon St Martin praticien Demeurant en
cette ville, témoins connus, et qui ont signé
     avec
La d. marthe Guillaume et nous notaire après
Lecture.

[signatures]
Martonne
Bonnemaison
Vallon St Martin
Dobignies

only indifferent success. Michel Vincent's union with Rosalie of the Poulard nation may have afforded the widowed Michel an unpaid housekeeper and sexual partner, while providing Rosalie with a degree of security and some distance from the place of her prior enslavement.[13]

In 1798 Republican forces under generals Toussaint Louverture and André Rigaud succeeded in forcing the British to withdraw from the colony, and the full legal abolition of slavery decreed by the French Republic finally took effect in the region around Jérémie. In law, Rosalie was now indisputably a free woman. Children born to her would share that freedom.

At the baptism of her next child, Rosalie was designated "Marie Françoise *dite* Rosalie *négresse libre*" (Marie Françoise called Rosalie, free black woman), suggesting that she herself had by this date (1799) acquired a baptismal name. The child was named Elisabeth *dite* Dieudonné and declared to be a "natural child," one born outside of marriage. Michel Vincent nonetheless signed the document and acknowledged his paternity.[14]

Before their daughter Elisabeth had reached the age of four, war again engulfed the countryside as a French expeditionary force arrived to challenge Toussaint Louverture and his revolutionary allies. First Consul Napoleon Bonaparte aimed to humble the black generals, restore slavery and reimpose a regime more friendly to the interests of white colonists. The expedition was initially successful in occupying the port towns, but despite the French capture of Louverture, those who resisted the invading forces eventually gathered strength. Revolutionary soldiers under the authority of Jean-Jacques Dessalines set out in the spring of 1803 from Les Cayes to try to take the port of Jérémie back from the French. En route they would pass through Les Abricots, the settlement where Michel and Rosalie lived with their children.[15]

The war carried an immense risk for Rosalie and the children, whether they stayed or fled. Michel Vincent was making plans to leave—alone—for France. If Napoleon's forces were to win, slavery might be reimposed on those whom the revolution had freed. Everywhere else in the Caribbean, moreover, slavery remained in force. The decrees of the early Republican Civil Commissioners, the military achievements of Toussaint Louverture and André Rigaud, and the ratification of abolition by the Convention Nationale were all seen by other colonial powers as threats, not legitimate transformations of law. Perhaps to persuade Rosalie to remain with him until he departed, Michel Vincent prepared an unofficial manumission paper that might serve her as proof of freedom once he left. Writing without the assistance of a notary, but drawing on the language that was conventional in such documents, he declared that Marie Françoise called Rosalie, "black woman of the Poulard nation," and her four children were his slaves, and that he hereby freed them all. He promised that if she chose to stay with him, he would pay her wages. With this document in hand, Rosalie might also have some chance of persuading authorities elsewhere that she was a free woman.[16]

In June of 1803, the troops of Dessalines were approaching Les Abricots, "flaming torches in their hands." In the chaos that ensued, Michel Vincent's plan to leave for France came to nothing, and he joined in a confused evacuation. As fire and warfare approached the coastline at Les Abricots, boats in the harbor took some of the desperate refugees on board, while other men, women, and children fled on foot toward Jérémie.[17]

Despite the threat from British ships patrolling the Caribbean, ragged flotillas made a run for it from Jérémie and Les Abricots across the Windward Passage to Santiago, Cuba. Spanish authorities on the island of Cuba extended hospitality to the white refugees, but found the prospect of admitting black men from a colony in revolution thoroughly alarming, and tried to bar their entry. Women and children of color seemed somewhat less threatening, particularly those whom the Spanish perceived as loyal domestic servants. One way or another, Michel, Rosalie, and one or both of their daughters reached Santiago safely. There is no record of what became of their boys.[18]

In the burgeoning slave society of Cuba, Rosalie depended for her freedom on the continuing consent of Michel Vincent, and on the fragile, un-notarized manumission paper that he had drawn up in their last days in Saint-Domingue. When Michel Vincent's health began to fail, Rosalie approached French officials in residence in Santiago and asked them to recopy her improvised freedom paper into their records, thus leveraging up its strength. Viewing her as a French *citoyenne* (citizen), they were willing to treat the document as legitimate, and to provide her with a certified copy. Soon Michel Vincent was dead, however, and she was on her own in a foreign colony where the welcome accorded to the Saint-Domingue refugees was increasingly precarious.[19]

Crisis would come in 1808, again at the hands of Napoleon Bonaparte. Napoleon, now Emperor, had launched an expedition into Spain. When thousands of Spaniards resisted the imposition of French rule, some Spanish colonists in Cuba began to consider the French Saint-Domingue refugees to be enemies as well. A certain avarice toward their wealth soon combined with realpolitik, and in

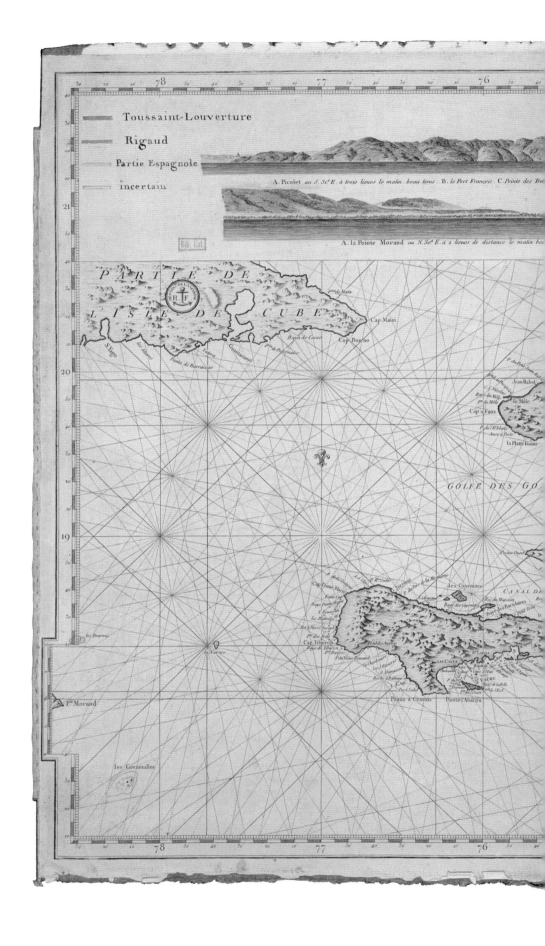

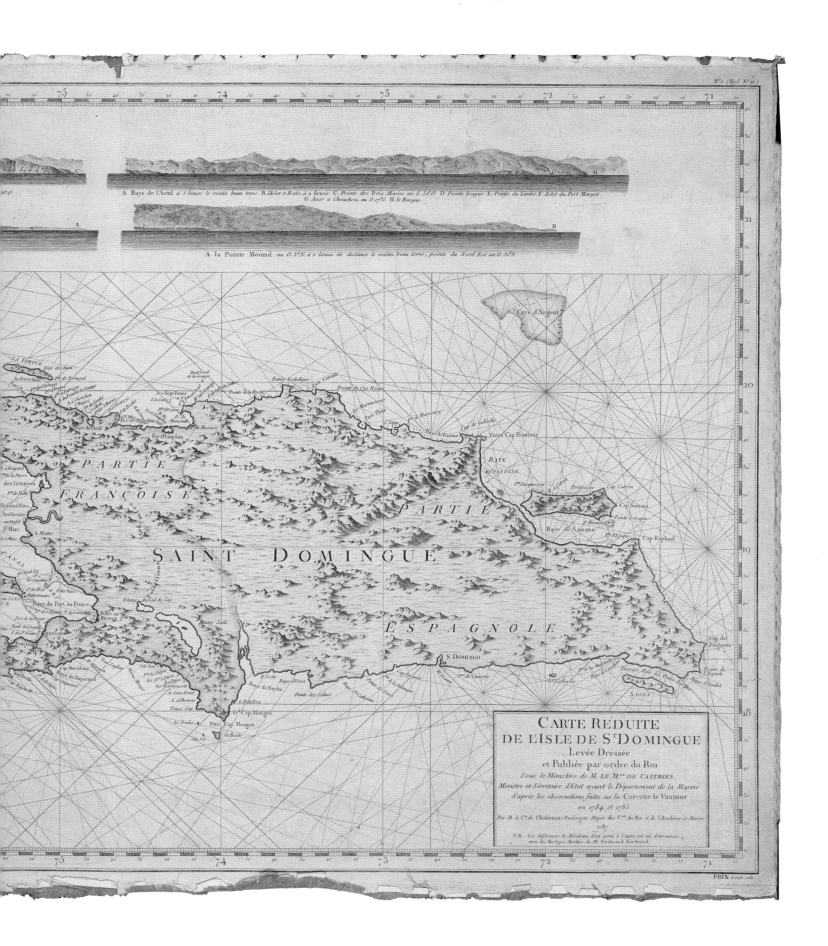

A. Baye de l'Acul à 3 heues le matin beau tems B. Islet à Rate, à 2 heues. C. Pointe des Trois Maries au S. 3¼ O. D. Pointe Icaque E. Pointe du Limbé Y. Islet du Port Margot
G. Anse à Chouchou, au O. ¼ S. H. le Borgne

A la Pointe Morand au O.5ᵈ N. à 2 lieues de distance le matin beau tems, pointe du Nord Est au O. 3½ N.

CARTE RÉDUITE
DE L'ISLE DE St DOMINGUE
Levée Dressée
et Publiée par ordre du Roi
Sous le Ministère de M. LE Mᵃˡ DE CASTRIES,
Ministre et Sécretaire d'Etat ayant le Département de la Marine
d'après les observations faites sur la Corvette le Vautour
en 1784 et 1785
Par M. le Cᵗᵉ de Chastenet-Puiségur Major des Vᵉˢ du Roi et de l'Académie de Marine
1787
N.B. Les differences de Meridiens d'un point à l'autre ont été déterminées
avec des Horloges Marines de M. Ferdinand Berthoud.

PRIX trente sols

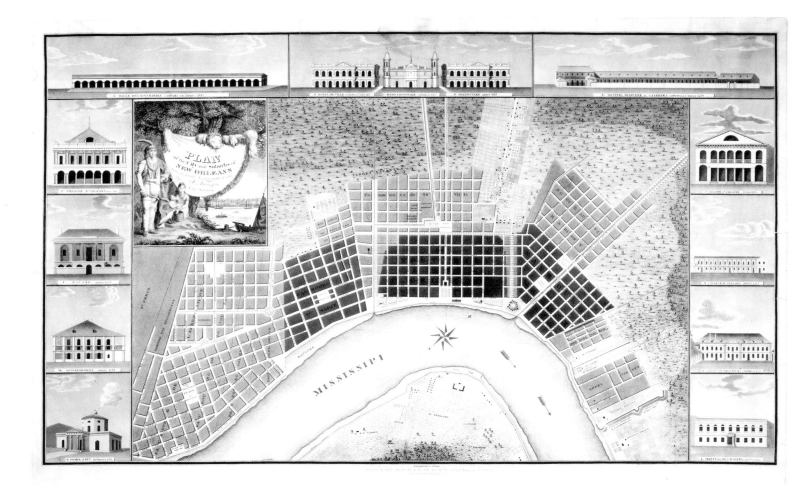

1809 Spanish officials ordered the Saint-Domingue refugees in Cuba to divest themselves of their property and depart.

Most of the ships willing to take refugees were headed for Louisiana, the slaveholding territory recently acquired by the United States and governed by an emissary appointed by Thomas Jefferson. Rosalie and Michel's daughter Elisabeth, now ten years old, had in Santiago come under the protection of her godmother, a woman of color called the Widow Aubert, who lived with a Belgian carpenter. The Widow Aubert made the passage to New Orleans, and took Elisabeth with her. But for Rosalie, an African woman whose freedom was fragile, New Orleans signified danger. She apparently did not board one of the boats headed for Louisiana, where she would again run the risk of re-enslavement.[20]

Once in New Orleans, Rosalie's daughter Elisabeth found a measure of security as a free woman of color. The Widow Aubert's carpenter companion left Elisabeth a small dowry in his will, and at the age of twenty-three she married a man of color named Jacques Tinchant, who was also a carpenter. They had several children, and Jacques gradually expanded from carpentry to become a builder, acquiring small plots of land on which to construct the wood-frame houses that were so much in demand in the expanding city.[21]

It is Elisabeth's 1822 marriage contract that reveals what had become of Rosalie, for she is described in that text as Rosalie Vincent, currently "living in Saint-Domingue." Presumably on one or another of the very small boats that still traded lumber and goods across the Windward Passage from Santiago to Jérémie, Rosalie had gone back to the island that she had fled years earlier—to the place the Widow Aubert still called Saint-Domingue, but that Rosalie would have known as Haïti. There she began her life once more, this time as Rosalie Vincent, taking the surname of the Frenchman who had never married her, and casting her lot in with the regime established by revolution.

Rosalie's Atlantic and Caribbean odyssey had been long and dramatic. Deported from Africa as a captive, she had been held in Saint-Domingue as a slave and freed in the tumult of the French and Haitian Revolutions. After fleeing to Spanish Cuba, she declined to follow the other refugees on to Louisiana, where the legacy of the American Revolution's compromises with slavery was dangerously strong. In her itinerary we can see the complexity (and often the paucity) of the choices that faced ordinary people during war and revolution, but also her discernment in moments of crisis.

***

Rosalie's journey also carries an epilogue. In 1835, Rosalie's daughter Elisabeth went to a notary in New Orleans to seek to "rectify" the name with which she had signed her marriage contract. In 1822, Elisabeth had been a young "free woman of color" living with her godmother, and she was sometimes known by her mother's baptismal name, Marie. She carried no surname, and appeared in her marriage contract with only the first name Marie and the nickname Dieudonné. Now she wished to modify that document so that she would appear with her own baptismal name of Elisabeth, the nickname Dieudonné, and a proper surname: Vincent. In support of this request, Elisabeth presented a copy of her 1799 baptismal record from Saint-Domingue, in which Michel Vincent had acknowledged his paternity. The notary agreed to the procedure. She would henceforth appear in official documents with a full proper name—Elisabeth Dieudonné Vincent—that no longer hinted at the circumstances of her birth as a "natural child" whose mother had once been enslaved. Since marriage contracts were often consulted when a married couple engaged in a property transaction, the modified record would help her establish her status and standing.[22]

When we first came across the 1835 "rectification" of Elisabeth's name in the New Orleans notarial archives, we were puzzled. The supporting sacramental record carrying the proof of Michel Vincent's paternity seemed to have appeared in New Orleans suddenly, and conveniently, many years after the marriage contract it now allowed Elisabeth to modify. Was Elisabeth engaging in the kind of social climbing that is so often attributed to free people of color in New Orleans, distancing herself from slave ancestry? If so, how had she acquired a certified copy—dated May 25, 1823, in the commune of Dame Marie, in Haiti—of the 1799 baptismal record that allowed her this maneuver?

The answer turns out to be both simple and quite remarkable. Seven months before Elisabeth's November 1835 appearance before the notary, a two-masted ship, the brig *Ann,* had landed in New Orleans after a journey from Port-au-Prince, Haiti. On its passenger list we find the name "Rosalia Vincent." The Spanish form of the name Rosalie may date back to her time in Santiago, Cuba; we know where the surname Vincent came from. It seems that Rosalie had been the one who in 1823 arranged to have a copy made of that 1799 baptismal record from the parish where Elisabeth had been born. It was many more years before she took the risk of boarding a boat in Haiti for what was by now the slaveholding metropolis of New Orleans. But when Rosalie disembarked in Louisiana in April of 1835, and passed the document along to her daughter, it became possible for Elisabeth to secure a written genealogy as well as a surname.[23]

Soon after that deed was done, there was a further task to attend to. This next event, far from distancing Elisabeth from her mother's past, pulled three generations together. Jacques and Elisabeth had a new baby, whom they would baptize in 1836 in the Cathedral of Saint Louis in the city of New Orleans. The priest who performed the baptism recorded the name of the woman who stood at the baptismal font as godmother to the baby. And it was, as you will by now have guessed, Rosalie Vincent.[24]

Soon after the baptism of their son Juste in 1836, Elisabeth and Jacques made plans to leave New Orleans for France, hoping to start over in a place without legalized structures of subordination based on color. Their youngest son Edouard Tinchant would be

born there, in the region of the Basses Pyrénées. And it is after that same baptism of the baby Juste at the Cathedral of Saint-Louis in 1836 that the documentary trail left by Rosalie finally comes to an end. She may have passed away before the departure of Jacques and Elisabeth, or she may have found a small boat making the run back from New Orleans to Port-au-Prince or Jérémie, and lived on for a few years more.

***

Three, and possibly four, Atlantic revolutions had impinged on the life of Rosalie of the Poulard nation. The Revolution of Fuuta Tooro may have been the context for her capture and deportation, as the rivals of Abdulkaadir Kan raided into his territory to take captives. The French Revolution brought unheard-of transformations to Saint-Domingue itself, both accelerating the struggle for equal rights for free persons of color that encompassed the extended family of Rosalie's owner Marthe Guillaume, and making possible the abolitionist decrees of the Republican Civil Commissioners. The rapid extension of the territory of the United States in the aftermath of the American Revolution turned New Orleans into a prosperous port city, providing opportunities for Rosalie's daughter Elisabeth and Elisabeth's husband Jacques, though territorial and later state law constrained the rights they could exercise. In the end, however, it was the Haitian Revolution that yielded the one sure home for the African-born woman who had come to call herself Rosalie Vincent. In Haiti she was a free citizen, heir to the upheaval that had brought abolition and eventually independence to the former French colony.

As Rosalie's journey came to a close, that of her grandchildren was just beginning. In the middle of the nineteenth century, her grandsons Joseph and Edouard Tinchant would return from Europe to the Americas. And in 1863, Joseph and Edouard, who called himself a "son of Africa," would step forward in New Orleans to volunteer for the Union Army and fight in one more revolution, this time a war that would bring an end to slavery in the United States.

Notes

1   This article draws on the forthcoming book titled *Freedom Papers* by Rebecca J. Scott and Jean M. Hébrard, Cambridge, Mass.: Harvard University Press, Copyright © 2012 by the President and Fellows of Harvard College, and has been adapted by special arrangement with the publisher. The authors thank Mamadou Diouf, Laurent Dubois, Andrée-Luce Fourcand, John Garrigus, David Geggus, Martha S. Jones, Martin Klein, Paul Lachance, Richard Rabinowitz, Peter Railton, David Robinson, Julius S. Scott, Ibrahima Thioub, and Rudolph Ware for continuing discussions of these questions, but we bear full responsibility for any errors and for the idiosyncrasies of our interpretation. We are also very grateful to the descendants of the Vincent/Tinchant family now living in France and Belgium who have shared materials on the generation of Rosalie Vincent's grandchildren.

2   See David Robinson, "The Islamic Revolution of Futa Toro," *International Journal of African Historical Studies* 8 (1975): 185–221; Robinson, "Abdul Qadir and Shaykh Umar: A Continuing Tradition of Islamic Leadership in Futa Toro," *International Journal of African Historical Studies* 6 (1973): 286–303; Oumar Kane, *La Première Hégémonie peule: Le Fuuta Tooro de Koli Tengella à Almami Abdul* (Paris and Dakar: Karthala and Presses Universitaires de Dakar, 2004); and Martin A. Klein, "The Impact of the Atlantic Slave Trade on the Societies of the Western Sudan," *Social Science History* 14 (Summer 1990): 231–53. Our thinking on this movement has also been influenced by the research of Rudolph Ware and his forthcoming study, "The Walking Qur'an."

3   On the Atlantic trade in captives from Senegambia see Jean Mettas, *Répertoire des expéditions négrières françaises au XVIIIe siècle*, ed. Serge and Michèle Daget, 2 vols. (Paris: Société Française d'Histoire d'Outre-Mer, 1984); Boubacar Barry, *Senegambia and the Atlantic Slave Trade* (Cambridge, Eng.: Cambridge Univ. Press, 1998); Martin Klein, *Slavery and Colonial Rule in French West Africa* (Cambridge, Eng.: Cambridge Univ. Press, 1998); and David Geggus, "Sex ratio, age and ethnicity in the Atlantic slave trade: Data from French shipping and plantation records," *Journal of African History* 30 (1989): 23–44.

4   The document referring to her in this way is "Vente par marthe Guillaume a mongol de la N^sse Rosalie," 14 January 1793, Notary Lépine, File 6C-119, Jérémie Papers, Special Collections, University of Florida Libraries (hereafter JP, SC, UFL). Marthe Guillaume occasionally used the surname Aliés, apparently that of the father of her children.

5   Marthe Guillaume had acquired Rosalie from a man named Alexis Couba, himself born in slavery and later manumitted. For further discussion of these households, and of the region of Jérémie, see Rebecca J. Scott and Jean M. Hébrard, "Rosalie of the Poulard Nation: Freedom, Law, and Dignity in the Age of the Haitian Revolution," in John D. Garrigus and Christopher Morris, eds., *Assumed Identities: The Meanings of Race in the Atlantic World* (Published for the University of Texas at Arlington by Texas A&M Press, 2010), 116–43.

6   The initial plan to free Rosalie appears in the draft will of Marthe Guillaume dated January 8, 1793, in Notary Lépine, File 6C-116, JP, SC, UFL. For the subsequent sale of Rosalie to Jean-Baptiste Mongol, see "Vente par marthe Guillaume a mongol de la N^sse Rosalie," 14 January 1793, Notary Lépine, File 6C-119, JP, SC, UFL.

7   For a detailed discussion of the war in the south, see Carolyn E. Fick, *The Making of Haiti: The Saint Domingue Revolution from Below* (Knoxville: Univ. of Tennessee Press, 1990).

8   For the marriage of Marie-Anne Aliés and Jean-Baptiste Azor, dit Fortunat, see the entry for February 28, 1783 in the microfilmed parish register of Jérémie, SOM 5Mi/60, held at the Centre d'accueil et de recherche des Archives nationales, Paris (hereafter CARAN).

9   See David Geggus, *Slavery, War, and Revolution: The British Occupation of Saint Domingue, 1793–1798* (Oxford, Eng.: Clarendon Press, 1982); and Laurent Dubois, *Avengers of the New World: The Story of the Haitian Revolution* (Cambridge, Mass.: Harvard Univ. Press, 2004), chap. 7.

10   See Geggus, *Slavery*. The intricate and difficult maneuvering of the British authorities in the south can be followed in "Copie des lettres écrites par le Conseil privé," File T81/15, British National Archives.

11   "Affranchissement de la négresse rosalie par marthone," 2 December 1795, Notary Dobignies, File 9-218, JP, SC, UFL.

12   See the discussion of the general question under the heading *affranchissement*, on p. 69, "Copie des lettres écrites par le Conseil privé," File T81/15, British National Archives, as well as the specific decision concerning Marthe Guillaume communicated in a letter dated January 13, 1796, in the same volume.

13   At the time of his marriage, Michel Vincent had been identified as the former *fermier de boucherie*, a tax farmer, in the southern town of Les Cayes. See the parish registers of Les Cayes du Fond (1698–1782) in SOM 6Mi/37, in the CARAN. His marriage to Nicole Catherine Bouché Widow Randel is on p. 177, year 1772. See also Jean M. Hébrard, "Les Deux Vies de Michel Vincent, Colon à Saint-Domingue c. 1730–1804," *Revue d'Histoire Moderne et Contemporaine* 57 (April–June 2010): 50–77.

14   A copy of the June 12, 1799 baptismal record is enclosed in "Rectification de noms d'épouse Tinchant dans son contrat de marriage," 16 November 1835, Act 672, Notary Theodore Seghers, New Orleans Notarial Archives Research Center (NONARC). For a transcription and discussion of this document, see Rebecca J. Scott and Jean M. Hébrard, "Servitude, liberté et citoyenneté dans le monde atlantique des XVIIIe et XIXe siècles: Rosalie de nation Poulard…," *Revue de la Société Haïtienne d'Histoire et de Géographie* 83 (July–September 2008): 1–52, especially 17–26.

15   In July of 1801 Louverture had promulgated a constitution that endorsed racial equality and antislavery, while claiming more autonomy for the colony than Napoleon would tolerate. On the context for the French expedition, led by General Leclerc, see Yves Benot, *La démence coloniale sous Napoléon* (1992. Reprint ed. Paris: Éditions La Découverte, 2006), 57–98, 359. The most detailed description of events in the south is Alexis Beaubrun-Ardouin, *Études sur l'histoire d'Haïti suivies de la vie du général J.-M. Borgella* (Paris: Dezobry et Magdeleine, 1853).

16   "Enregistrement de liberté … Marie Françoise," 26 ventôse an XII, folio 35 verso, Actes déclarations & dépôts divers, 10 pluviôse an XII – 12 avril 1809, Agence des Prises de la Guadeloupe, 6SUPSDOM/3, Dépôt des Papiers Publics des Colonies, Archives Nationales d'Outre-Mer, Aix-en-Provence (hereafter DPPC, ANOM). This document is analyzed in detail in Scott and Hébrard, "Servitude," pp. 28–31.

17   The quotation is from an eyewitness account by Pierre Chazotte, discussed in Scott and Hébrard, "Rosalie of the Poulard Nation," pp. 124–25.

18   The drama of these arrivals is reflected in the records now held in the Cuban National Archives (particularly the Correspondencia de los Capitanes Generals), Havana, and in the Papeles de Cuba, Archivo General de Indias, Seville. See Rebecca J. Scott, "Reinventar la esclavitud, garantizar la libertad: De Saint-Domingue a Santiago a Nueva Orleans, 1803–1809," *Revista Caminos* (Havana) (2009): 2–13; and Olga Portuondo Zúñiga, *Entre esclavos y libres de Cuba colonial* (Santiago de Cuba: Editorial Oriente, 2003).

19   The registration is "Enregistrement de liberté … Marie Françoise," cited in note 16 above.

20   On the phenomenon of re-enslavement in New Orleans, see Rebecca J. Scott, "Paper Thin: Freedom, Re-enslavement, and Determinations of Status in the Diaspora of the Haitian Revolution," forthcoming in *Law and History Review*, November 2011.

21   For the marriage of Elisabeth Vincent and Jacques Tinchant, see Marriage contract, Jacques Tinchant and Marie Dieudonné, 26 September 1822, p. 31, Vol. 22, Notary M. Lafitte, NONARC. On Jacques' business affairs, see "Société entre Jacques Tinchant et Pierre Duhart," Act. 62, 1835, Notary Theodore Seghers, NONARC.

22   "Rectification de noms d'épouse Tinchant dans son contrat de mariage," 16 November 1835, Act 672, Notary Theodore Seghers, NONARC.

23   The ship's manifest is reproduced in "List of all Passengers taken on board the Brig Ann whereof Charles Sutton is Master at the Port of Port Au Prince and bound for New-Orleans," arriving April 20, 1835, microfilmed as part of Passenger Lists of Vessels Arriving at New Orleans, 1820–1902, USNA Microcopy 259, Roll 12.

24   Act 326, St. Louis Cathedral, Baptisms of Slaves and Free Persons of Color, Vol. 25, Part I, in Archives of the Archdiocese of New Orleans.

The 1804 Haitian Revolution

Jean Casimir

Expédition de St Domingue 1801 1804
L'Armée Coloniale de Toussaint Louverture
1/2 Brigades d'Infanterie

Soldat   Oficier Supérieur   Grenadier

d'après Lacauchie § Rolfs

H. BOISSELIER

French Saint-Domingue emerged in the eighteenth century as the last of the Caribbean plantation societies. Yet it rapidly became the most profitable of all, larger than all of them put together. Along with Dominica, the refuge of the Caribs in the Eastern Caribbean, the colony of Saint-Domingue was also more mountainous than any other in the archipelago. The new economic venture was rather difficult to police, and the colonial society never experienced long periods of peace and stability. Moreover, from 1789 onwards, conflicts and crises in France made it more difficult to govern and increased its fragility, driving it to an astounding collapse in 1803.

The Haitian nation inherited severe disequilibrium from this failed colony. The experience of independent Haiti is the history of repeated challenges to the property rights of the colonial powers.[1] Success in a struggle against property rights, the basic credo of the modern world, was simply unlikely. By the very nature of its Revolution, Haiti positioned itself from the very beginning against the major historical currents set forth by the European empires.

The Haitian Revolution is known to be the only successful "slave" revolution in the history of humanity. It is therefore an unexpected accident. The French Revolution provided a context where it could materialize, but it did not inspire nor shape the upheaval in Saint-Domingue. Haitians declared independence in 1804 as a gesture of survival. They knew that in the sister territory of Guadeloupe, where slavery also had been abolished a decade earlier, the population had suffered genocide and re-enslavement. If they surrendered, they would be re-enslaved under French dominion. They checkmated the onslaught ordered by Napoleon, and in the process displayed their wide-ranging potential for military and political organization, carrying out their own unexpected revolution. The Haitians are those who should not have existed in the eyes of the imperial power. But their contribution to human history was rejected, and in many ways still is. Without the slightest examination, it has been seen as essentially unacceptable. Indeed, it has never really even been heard as a true alternative.

The colonial social system comprised two subordinate categories apart from the whites, the original subjects of the king and later citizens of the Republic: emancipated people of African descent, both black and of mixed ancestry (known as *gens de couleurs*, translated as "people of color" or simply "coloreds" by scholars working on the Haitian context), and the enslaved, who were generally black.

OPPOSITE Félix Boisselier. *Expédition de Saint-Domingue 1801–1804, L'Armée Coloniale de Toussaint Louverture*, ca. 1810–20. Engraving. Collections Musée d'Aquitaine, Bordeaux, © Mairie de Bordeaux, photograph by JM Arnaud, inv. 2003.4.193.3. In this large series of watercolors of the soldiers of French General LeClerc's invasion force in 1802, Boisselier included images of the colonial soldiers—many of whom deserted LeClerc later and fought for independence.

LOUVERTURE

Capitan de Guardias de Biasou y despues General en Gefe de la Ysla de Sto Domingo. fue arrestado y llevado á francia.

Those in the first subordinate category perceived themselves as American colonists, that is, as integral parts of the imperial world, and as such they upheld the basic philosophy of this world. Those in the other category behaved as enslaved prisoners, and had a vision of their own. In their search for freedom, they bridged the original ethnic and racial cleavages within their group. At the end of the revolutionary period, for a very brief moment, they imposed to all social strata a conception of themselves as full human beings and no longer as layers of whites, mixed-race people, or blacks.

Underneath the imperial Atlantic history, a local history unfolded in which enslaved prisoners took charge of the revolutionary process. The oppressed of Saint-Domingue stood up as representatives for the oppressed of the Americas, and expressed a world-view that foregrounded their ethnic diversity and their anti-imperialist ideology. They flaunted the immoveable pillar of their culture: the idea that "tout moun se moun"—every person is a person, that all human beings are equal—departing radically from the stances of the American and French Revolutions, both of which accepted slavery.

The Saint-Domingue Revolution had significant costs. The Haitians, however, were not offered beforehand the possibility of weighing the pros and cons of the road ahead of them. They did what they did to survive as free people, and emerged from a sequence of unforeseeable events as any others would in their situation.

THE SOURCES OF CHANGE

In all plantation societies, the captives had to be transformed into slaves in order to fit into the categories defined by the masters. The inescapable need to militarize these societies bears witness to the resistance of the enslaved and their unrelenting search for freedom. Slave societies aimed to create a workforce that would reproduce itself, just as other social categories of planters and free subjects or citizens did. But this rarely succeeded; indeed, in the Americas, North America was one of the only areas where births outnumbered deaths within the slave population. In Saint-Domingue, as in Jamaica and other Caribbean societies, the death rates of the enslaved were massive: one million were imported into Saint-Domingue over the course of the eighteenth century and by 1791, the surviving slave population had barely reached half that number.

Against the universal militarization of plantation societies, and the attempt to enslave, there were always many forms of resistance. From the beginnings of plantation slavery there burgeoned an equal and opposite world-view—an anti-plantation culture that relentlessly challenged the dominant system. The ever-present pressure to transform the captives into slaves ran up against the enslaved's culture of defiance. This autonomous culture was, however, embedded as an oppressed culture within the more powerful and dominant institutions that surrounded it. Its existence, and indeed, its power in any plantation society, was made clear most of all by the extreme, uninterrupted use and threat of violence against its bearers. All plantation societies were militarized precisely because of this contest between two cultures.

In extreme cases of colonial success, the might of the empire could render futile the slightest dissent and prevent the oppressed culture from openly challenging the dominant one. In places where any resistance or social protest by the captives was nullified, the enslaved population survived only by reproducing itself demographically and socially as slaves. Dissent and resistance, and their effect on the colony, were ultimately minimal wherever the state secured its monopoly on violence and dictated the terms of social negotiations. But even in such cases, the oppressed culture was still always there: otherwise there would have been no reason for the omnipresence of arbitrary torture. The inexplicable violence would have no raison d'être. Such unaccountable violence thus shows how the enslaved's obstinacy persisted.

In the young colony of Saint-Domingue, the slaves differed from the other categories created by the colonial empire because they never self-reproduced as a group. In order to stabilize the colony, the French would have had to install a local authority powerful enough to compel imported Africans to integrate into the plantation society. It never achieved this assimilation, and could only reproduce the enslaved population through the slave trade. The colony could not fabricate its colonial workforce.

This also was true, however, in many other Caribbean societies. Saint-Domingue was not itself in a special category among the slave societies of the Caribbean and of America. The social forces that explain the Haitian Revolution existed everywhere, but could not express themselves successfully where the state was equipped to secure its monopoly of violence.[2]

The unsettling disequilibrium that the French Revolution fostered in its Caribbean ruling classes could have caused, and indeed nearly did cause, Saint-Domingue to fall into the hands of its imperial enemies, as did Martinique, for example. Significant sectors of white and "colored" planters conspired openly with the British and applauded their landing in the colony. Had Saint-Domingue remained firmly under rule from London or Paris, no structural changes would have emerged from the turmoil caused by the French Revolution. The impact of 1789 was different in Saint-Domingue because its enslaved were a distinct and independent pressure group.

The colonial conflicts sparked by the 1789 Revolution created a distinction between two different concepts of freedom at work within Saint-Domingue colonial society. The victory of 1804 was the outcome of a convergence of two separate movements inspired by these diverging ideas of freedom. On the one hand, the leaders

Expédition de St Domingue 1800.1804

Troupes Coloniales levées par le Général Leclerc 1801.1802

5e 9e 1/2 Brigades Coloniales : Grenadier & Officier   Dragons de la Plaine ou Dragons Coloniaux

Correspondance du Gal Leclerc. & notes du Col Nemours

H. Boisselier

DESALINES.

who signed the act of independence were free blacks and colored generals, a number of them former planters and former slaveholders. Before the revolution, they had abided by the law and reached the highest social positions in the society. With their wealth, prestige, and political influence, they had fought the administration and the white planters and demanded respect for their political and civil rights. They had no quarrel with the plantation economy as such: they promoted it and it had provided them with their fortunes. They simply claimed the equality they were entitled to as property owners.

But opposing the black and colored generals were the troops and the population at large, two-thirds of whom were African born. They had experienced a life of freedom and enjoyed their natural rights in Africa before arriving in Saint-Domingue. They could only feel repugnance at the idea that they were owned and could only be emancipated by other human beings.

In the absence of a proper monopoly of violence by the state, the defiance of the African-born enslaved population was uncontainable. The ceremony of the Bois Caïman, at least in its symbolism, and particularly the technique of all-out war used during the insurgency, demonstrate the uncompromising conflict between the slavery plantation and the world-view of the newcomers. To accuse the insurgents of being uncivilized, as many contemporaries did, as the "savages" burned down all the core structures of the plantation society, is to see that their refusal of this world was total.

The Saint-Dominguan insurgents did not assist or ally with the enemies of their local opponents, unlike the revolutionaries of British North America. The actualization of the oppressed culture made it impossible for both the French and their enemies to control the situation and to re-establish the plantation economy. Instead of leading planters and would-be planters to victory, they fought for themselves and on their own ground. At the same time, their assertiveness in pursuing their own pathway made clear the fragility of the state monopoly of violence and their ability to create a zone of defiance in the landscape.

A SELF-PERPETUATING SYSTEM

Slaves in Saint-Domingue, as anywhere else, were foreigners.[3] They had, together with their descendants, neither a past nor a future in this society. They lived in an unending present dedicated solely to the well-being of their estranged masters. Their work and their existence were one and the same thing. The bits of private lives they could enjoy belonged to them no more than did their bodies. Their strangeness was absolute; they were perfect aliens. Louis XIV's *Code Noir* of 1685 was, even in its silences, unyielding on the matter.[4]

French nationals, by contrast, were free. Their rights to own land in the colony of Saint-Domingue were established in the Treaty of Ryswick, signed twelve years after the *Code Noir*. No plantation system could emerge in the new territory if such rights were not secure. Conversely, since these rights were construed to be self-evident, from 1697 to the present day, no state responsible for law and order in the territory could restraint the ability to obtain land and cheap (and if necessary, free) labor in the economic system.

This original relationship between land ownership and some form of enslavement is central to the unfolding of Haitian history and the shape of the state after 1804. In the wake of the uprising of 1791, only the governments of Toussaint Louverture and of Henry Christophe could reactivate the plantation economy and create a governable political system. They were the only regimes, before 1915, to rely on the services of professional armies, able to enforce their harsh labor policies and to impose the respect of property rights. The 1801 Constitution of Toussaint, which was later endorsed with minor modifications by Henry Christophe, substantiated the frame for official agricultural policies:

1. The Constitution distinguished in fact between the "inhabitants" and the African born,[5] on the one hand, and between citizenship "by commonality of birth place" and citizenship "by source of subsistence," on the other.[6]

2. When it stated that all men are born equal, it did not include the African born, since this category of persons is not given and cannot claim the right to move about freely. Similarly by stating that all men irrespective of color are admissible to any employment,[7] the Constitution did not apply to the majority group placed under house arrest "pour des raisons d'État" (for the state's sake).[8]

3. By endorsing the sacredness of property rights and, implicitly, of landownership,[9] Toussaint acknowledged the rights of France as the owner of the colony to distribute land to whom it sees fit and therefore he excluded the "cultivateurs et ouvriers" from any privileges conferred by such right.

4. By establishing constitutionally[10] the need for importing new agricultural workers, Toussaint was thinking of some form

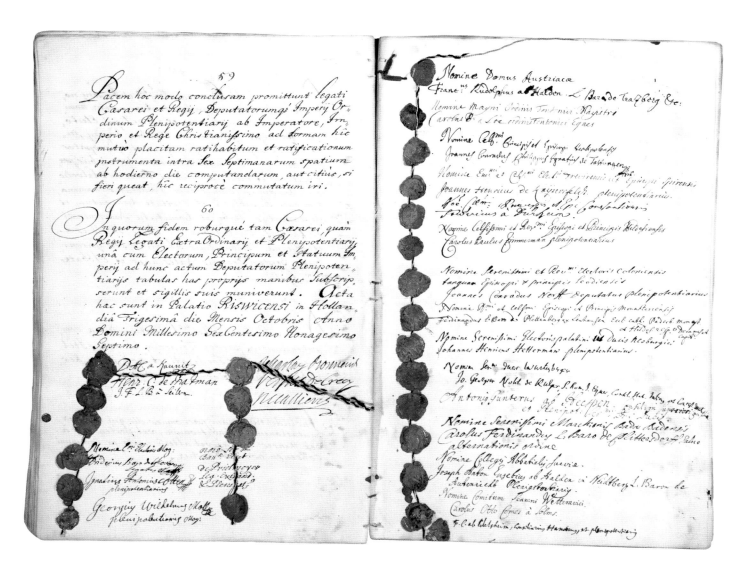

ABOVE The Treaty of Ryswick, October 30, 1697. Pen and ink on paper, French School, 17th century. Ministère des Affaires Étrangères, Paris, France. Archives Charmet. The Bridgeman Art Library International.

of slave trade to replenish the pool of semi-freed agricultural workers or indentured servants. In his mind there were two classes of persons on earth, or at least in Saint-Domingue, the inhabitants and the "cultivateurs et ouvriers."

The early oligarchy of black and colored generals of 1804 was not prepared to break up the essential pillar of Saint-Domingue's economic structure, that is, the ownership of large tracts of land. To give up such land ownership would have not only destroyed it as an oligarchy, but also would have forced it to integrate the ranks of the working people. While land ownership remained a sacrosanct premise of society, however, the harshness of enslavement was lessened from 1791 onwards, but without endangering the provision of cheap labor. In other words, the colony and later on the state of Haiti did not differ drastically from the *Ancien Régime* with respect to land tenure and employment policies. The social, political and economic preeminence of the oligarchy was and still is predicated on these two fundaments of the plantation system.

The labor force's struggle for freedom in the Haitian Revolution is inextricably linked to the question of land ownership. If, in the colonial context, the land was rightfully owned by the imperial power, then the property rights of the planters were legitimate. Small farmers, like the maroons (escaped slaves) who had set up small villages and farms in the mountains during the colonial period, were often seen as squatters to be evicted. In any event, the land they occupied was of marginal productivity and/or marginal size, but that did not qualify them to be settlers or *habitants*. The independent Haitian state inherited this attitude. In the mind of the state and of the oligarchy, such persons could not be considered legitimate economic agents. The *nouveaux libres* or emancipated slaves were therefore destined, in the minds of the oligarchy, to remain at the service and the mercy of the landowners, devoid of a means to protect their rights and to negotiate for themselves. But the *nouveaux libres* never accepted this destiny. Out of the demand for freedom from enslavement loomed not only a challenge to the rights of the planters to own the labor force, but also a demand for landownership, which in essence challenged the dominion of the state—whether French or Haitian—over the territory.

In the colony, the planters' vision of ownership rights did not deviate from that of the authorities in Paris, just as that of Virginians or Cubans fell in with prevailing notions in London or Madrid. Especially in plantation colonies, the sanctity of property rights was linked to an assumption that landless classes of non-whites would work this "sacred inheritance." Freedom conceived in the framework of the conquest of America was compatible with its efficient management of the state monopoly of violence that controlled the laboring classes.

The government of Toussaint differed from the other French colonial governments in two ways: he insisted on equality of rights for all French citizens, of all colors; and he was able to actually secure a state monopoly of violence that had eluded colonial rulers. Toussaint governed a colony that had been essentially ungovernable since 1789, in part by constantly reminding its citizens that they needed to prove that the colony could remain productive without slavery. But after 1804, once the white planters had been eliminated from the political structure, the situation changed. It was, in a sense, the opportunity

Le 1.er Juillet 1801, Toussaint L'Ouverture, chargés des pouvoirs du peuple d'haïty et auspices du Tout-puissant, proclame la

Liberté, égalité

République d'haïty

Gouverneur général, assisté des mandataires légalement convoqués, en présence et sous les Constitution de la république d'haïty.

Lith. de Villain, de Sèvres N.º 11

Expedition de St Domingue

1801   1805

Petion   Dessaline   Toussaint Louverture

Portraits de l'époque Coll. Henrin

for a change of course. But the regimes of Christophe, Pétion, and Boyer continued Toussaint's policies, agreeing on the need to coerce the rights of the workers to the full extent permitted by the state power. While they celebrated the 1804 Revolution, they were not radically opposed to the subjugation of the population of *nouveaux libres*. The inequalities condoned by the various political regimes in independent Haiti were not very different from what operated all over the Caribbean.

The independence of Haiti introduced important reforms in the management of political power, but it did not foster radical social transformations or upset the privileges of private property. It successfully destroyed the racial hierarchies among property owners and acknowledged the civil and political rights of the landed oligarchy of African descent. From this angle, the Revolution was a rather modest enlargement of the political platform of free-colored activists Vincent Ogé and Jean-Baptiste Chavannes.

What happened in 1804? Why did the plantation system fail to perpetuate itself under the guidance of the oligarchy in independent Haiti? Why couldn't Haiti revamp the plantation economy, and pursue an evolution similar to other plantation islands in the nineteenth century? Toussaint certainly had had to contend with the expedition of General Leclerc, which disrupted the full deployment of his economic policies. But what explains why the plantation system of Christophe and his successors ultimately failed?

REVOLUTION

When the news of the re-enslavement of the Guadeloupian labor force and the deportation of their leaders reached Saint-Domingue, it sparked an alliance of the Saint-Dominguan officers enrolled in the colonial army with armed insurgents: hence, the famous "*L'union fait la force*" of Alexandre Pétion's flag. Learning that the commander of the Guadeloupian expedition had exterminated 10 percent of the non-white population led the insurgents of Saint-Domingue to see that this was a question of life or death,[11] the testimony of which can be found in the famous "*Liberté ou la Mort*" of Dessalines' flag.

"Freedom or death": the Creole translation of this phrase is quite relevant: "Swa nou lib, swa nou mouri."[12] It introduced a third concept of freedom incorporating the two referred to earlier. The issue at hand ceased to be the civil and political rights of the colored and free black planters. Nor was it the conquest of the natural rights of the enslaved. "We either live free or we die" translated the need to sever all links with France in order to escape

LIBERTÉ OU LA MORT.

113

ARMÉE INDIGÈNE.

AUJOURD'HUI premier Janvier, mil huit cent quatre, le Général en Chef de l'armée Indigène, accompagné des Généraux, Chefs de l'armée, convoqués à l'effet de prendre les mesures qui doivent tendre au bonheur du pays.

Après avoir fait connaître aux Généraux assemblés, ses véritables intentions, d'assurer à jamais aux Indigènes d'Hayti, un Gouvernement stable, objet de sa plus vive sollicitude; ce qu'il a fait par un discours qui tend à faire connaître aux Puissances Étrangères, la résolution de rendre le pays indépendant, et de jouir d'une liberté consacrée par le sang du peuple de cette Isle; et après avoir recueilli les avis, a demandé que chacun des Généraux assemblés prononçât le serment de renoncer à jamais à la France, de mourir plutôt que de vivre sous sa domination, et de combattre jusqu'au dernier soupir pour l'indépendance.

RIGHT *Haitian Declaration of Independence,* January 1, 1804. On loan from the National Archives, London, CO 137/1115 folio 113–116.

genocide or deportation. It is this concept of independence from the metropolitan country (or any other for that matter) that became the common denominator, or the social contract, linking together both currents of the Haitian Revolution. Indeed, this achievement had a profound impact on the geopolitics of the Atlantic world and sent shock waves into all slave societies within it. But by itself, this did not foster internal structural modifications in Haiti, as the history of the governments of Christophe, Pétion, Boyer, and all those that followed confirm.

vrai ; mais qui n'a jamais vaincu celles qui ont voulu être libres.

Eh quoi ! victimes pendant quatorze ans de notre crédulité et de notre indulgence ; vaincus, non par des armées françaises, mais par la pipense éloquence des proclamations de leurs agens ; quand nous lasse-rons-nous de respirer le même air qu'eux ? Qu'avons-nous de commun avec ce peuple bour-reau ? Sa cruauté comparée à notre patiente modé-ration ; sa couleur à la nôtre, l'étendue des mers qui nous séparent, notre climat vengeur nous disent assez qu'ils ne sont pas nos frères, qu'ils ne le deviendront jamais, et que s'ils trouvent un asile parmi nous, ils seront encore les machina-teurs de nos troubles et de nos divisions.

Citoyens Indigènes, hommes, femmes, filles et enfans, portés vos regards sur toutes les parties de cette Isle, cherchez-y, vous vos épouses, vous vos maris, vous vos frères, vous vos sœurs ; que dis-je, cherchez-y vos enfans, vos enfans à la mamelle ? Que sont-ils devenus..... Je frémis de le dire...... la proie de ces vautours. Au lieu de ces victimes intéressantes, votre œil consterné n'apperçoit que leurs assassins ; que les tigres dégouttant encore de leur sang, et dont l'affreuse présence vous reproche votre insensibilité et votre coupable lenteur à les venger. Quattendez-vous pour appaiser leurs mânes ; songez que vous avez voulu que vos restes reposassent auprès de ceux de vos pères, quand vous avez chassé la tyrannie ; des-cendrez-vous dans leurs tombes, sans les avoir vengés ? Non, leurs ossemens repousser ient les vôtres.

5

Et vous hommes précieux, Généraux intrépides qui, insensibles à vos propres malheurs, avez rsesuscité la liberté en lui prodiguant tout votre sang ; sachez que vous n'avez rien fait, si vous ne donnez aux nations un exemple terrible, mais juste, de la vengeance que doit exercer un peuple fier d'avoir recouvré sa liberté, et jaloux de la maintenir ; effrayons tous ceux qui oseraient tenter de nous la ravir encore : commençons par les français...... Qu'ils frémissent en abordant nos côtes, sinon par le souvenir des cruautés qu'ils y ont exercées, au moins par la résolution terrible que nous allons prendre de dévouer à la mort, quiconque né français, souil-lerait de son pied sacrilége le territoire de la liberté.

Nous avons osé être libres, osons l'être par nous-mêmes et pour nous-mêmes ; imitons l'enfant qui grandit: son propre poids brise la lisière qui lui devient inutile et l'entrave dans sa marche. Quel peuple a combattu pour nous ! quel peuple voudrait recueillir les fruits de nos travaux ? Et quelle désho-norante absurdité que de vaincre pour être esclaves. Esclaves ! . . . laissons aux français cette épithète qua-lificative ; ils ont vaincu pour cesser d'être libres.

Marchons sur d'autres traces, imitons ces peuples qui, portant leurs sollicitudes jusques sur l'avenir et appréhendant de laisser à la postérité l'exemple de la lâcheté, ont préférés être exterminés que rayés du nombre des peuples libres.

Gardons-nous cependant que l'esprit de proséli-tisme ne détruise notre ouvrage ; laissons en paix respirer nos voisins, qu'ils vivent paisiblement sous l'égide des lois qu'ils se sont faites, et n'allons pas,

The first and most visible idea of freedom was an extension of the provisions for emancipation in Louis XIV's *Code Noir*, Articles 55 to 57.[13] The decree of the August 1793 General Assembly drew on these provisions, granting the *nouveaux libres* or newly freed persons treatment equivalent to that offered those manumitted according to the *Code Noir*. By pursuing this ideal of freedom, local planters sought to contain the consequences of upsetting the geopolitics and the monopoly on the best agricultural lands in the Saint-Domingue colony.

But the deep changes in the society that emerged after 1804 expressed another concept of freedom, one that denied the rights of conquest granted by the Treaty of Ryswick to France. It bore the memory of a freedom without borders, as experienced in Africa by the majority of those who survived the War of Independence. It expressed the outlook of the labor force, conveniently ignored by the *Code Noir*, and made clear that the formula of society proposed by the Western world, before or after 1789, was not intended to satisfy the needs of the working population.[14] Its successful and universal implementation would have affected the social order in Saint-Domingue and in the Atlantic Basin, and would have subverted the course of action in place since the beginning of the Renaissance. This is why the 1804 Revolution had to be stopped or contained within the confines of Haiti.

That revolution can best be defined as the transformation of an "exploitation colony," based on enslavement of the working class, into a "settlement colony," peopled by free men and women. After 1804 the Haitians, instead of producing export crops for a foreign market and using the income to acquire the goods necessary for their subsistence, produced first whatever they needed for survival and then exported the surpluses, or whatever was necessary to acquire goods they could not make themselves. This explained why, by disregarding the right of conquest granted to France by the Treaty of Ryswick, the Haitians appropriated the term *habitants*, or "inhabitants," and during the nineteenth century essentially negated the idea that the labor force of the territory was made up of "foreigners."

Haiti emerged in 1804 as the only country in the Americas that was not established by a group of Creoles—or a group of people assimilated in the Western world. During the nineteenth century, the values of its population developed out of African cultures, transformed by the experience on the plantation, and particularly by the solidarity between the various ethnic groups working together. The French metropolitan culture, with its language and religion and dominant political assumptions, was only one among many influences, the impact of which varied by region and social group. The behavior of the slave drivers calls for particular attention in this story. They were supposed to belong to the privileged group of enslaved, the cornerstone of the success of the Pearl of the Antilles, particularly in the northern region. But in fact they were precisely those who organized the August 1791 uprising: the solidarity among the different ethnic groups was more valued than the privileges offered to the *commandeurs* by the plantation society.

The most remarkable phenomenon in the nineteenth century was the creation of social institutions responsible for the establishment of a population—indeed, the creation of a people—who until then had shared only a few decades of common life. The history of the transformation of a heterogeneous group of settlers emerging from concentrations in plantation barracks to create free villages and a peasant society is yet to be documented and analyzed. But one thing is clear: the quality of life gained through this transformation was such that a population which previously could only increase through the slave trade deployed all its potential, and flourished. The plantation-oriented policies formulated by the oligarchy still contemplated increases through some form of slave trade after independence. But the self-propelled organization of the *habitants* delivered a level of well-being and a quality of life that bore no comparison to the conditions under which they had lived as slaves, and also was better than what was being experienced by people of African descent during the same century in neighboring territories.

The Haitian Revolution granted to formerly enslaved prisoners and, through them, to the worldwide history of labor, sovereignty over their time, their bodies, their space, their private lives, their community life, and, all in all, sovereignty in a world and a society of their own making. The Haitian Revolution reversed the institutions and values which governed enslavement and the modern labor market by implementing a social philosophy unknown to capitalism. Instead of preparing human resources—slaves, cultivators, or salaried workers—for economic production aimed at satisfying the needs of others, the Revolution promoted an economic production anchored in the basic needs of these very resources. It made the laborer the indisputable center of society and not a mere aspect of its economy. This laborer and his or her life story ceased to be linked to an abstract and invisible market, and the exchange of goods was made for his or her service, cancelling the primary subjugation to a supposedly worldwide vision anchored in the Western communities of nation-states.

As a result of the structural changes promoted by the Haitian Revolution, a new rhythm and calendar of production evolved. Mixed-farming replaced mono-production. New food crops more adapted to the local diet were cultivated. Rural markets became nodes of exchange and took precedence over international markets. The internal economic life overrode the needs of external powers. Reprogrammed social work came to be regulated by family units within communities assembled freely in a conviviality based on equality—and unknown to the plantation society. The isolation of extroverted colonial plantations was substituted by a new territorial organization where polarization of the hinterland by seaports was more balanced. The *lakou* (the Haitian version of the Caribbean swept yard) that constituted the basis for this regional planning was rooted in a kinship system translated into a family religion where traditions inherited from Africa were archived together with habits and traditions formulated by American communities.

In short, enslaved laborers became settlers or colonists or *habitants*, and this counter-plantation system was regulated by institutions unheard of in the West. It became operational and blossomed to its full capacity in Haiti, but the achievements of such novel institutions can be traced to some extent in all New World plantation societies. The specific contribution of the Haitian Revolution to the Atlantic world was the visibility of the system created by the enslaved in response to their wretched condition.

With the conversion of Haiti into a settlement colony, the total population multiplied between four- and five-fold, without any significant immigration. At the end of the nineteenth century, the output of the economic system was comparable to that of colonial Saint-Domingue, except for the production of sugar, and in some areas it even surpassed it. With respect to human rights, Haiti was one of the safest countries in the Americas, and certainly one where a worker, particularly if not white, could profit from his or her labor without any harassment. At its highest period of growth around 1870, the counter-plantation system was a pole of attraction for most neighboring territories.

Haiti developed an ad hoc political system, based on the regionalization of the economy. The capital city had no exaggerated preeminence, and the countryside was governed by dignitaries who would express and defend the interests of their region through private armies, holding in check the pretensions of the central government. The first two presidents of the country were from Port-au-Prince; the rest came from a wide range of areas from the most humble villages to the provincial capitals. The country experienced thirty-five years of political stability, from 1875 to 1910, with presidents alternating from the north and the south. As was the case in much of the rest of the world at the time, it was not a truly democratic system, nor was it devoid of violence, but parliament was the seat of negotiations between the provincial notables, the meeting point of the power brokers of the country.

The state often used violence in its attempts to concentrate the population on the plantation compounds. But it did not have the monopoly of violence necessary to do so—the population was armed, and well versed in strategies of resistance and escape. Indeed, the state could not even effectively implement its laws relating to the respect of private property. The members of the armed forces themselves, connected to the new society in Haiti, largely did not accept the legitimacy of these laws.

The oligarchy that signed Haiti's act of independence accepted such an arrangement under duress. The insurgencies of provincial governors bringing their private armies to the capital to negotiate conflicts with the central government repeatedly destroyed the commercial establishment, forcing the incipient national bourgeoisie always to start its activities from scratch after each achieved or aborted *coup d'état*. The nineteenth century was a nightmare for the oligarchy, which did its best to obliterate it from memory.

CONCLUSION: COUNTERREVOLUTION ENTHRONED

The Haitian oligarchy endeavored to actively silence and combat the nation's contribution to the Atlantic world. It disregarded the quality of life achieved by the masses during the nineteenth century. In its longing for the lost Pearl of the Antilles, it failed to realize that Haiti was one of the few territories of the Americas where the population multiplied without any significant immigration.

Conspiracy against the completion of popular power began with the *coup d'état* plotted against Jean-Jacques Dessalines. The phase of unrestrained counterrevolution began after his assassination in 1806 until the fall of Jean-Pierre Boyer in 1843. Then, negotiations between the rural communities and the notables were set into motion, producing a period of stability extending from 1875 to 1910.

In 1915, as in 1804, the concurrence of international power politics with internal pressures transformed the social structure of the country. Whereas in 1804, the imperial power was at odds with the masses united to the leaders of the indigenous army, the Francophile oligarchy of 1915 and the import-export interests joined forces with the United States and other imperialist powers to destroy the remnants of the indigenous army and to seal the rout of the peasantry.

The resulting demise of both the peasantry and the oligarchy begs the question: Where is the Haitian Revolution? In 1804, Haiti did not deliberately choose to depart from the proposals of the imperial powers, including the United States. An independent state fell upon the heads of the subordinated groups of Saint-Domingue, who were simply trying to survive and to shield themselves from genocide. The most radical among them challenged the notion of property rights of metropolitan France because they had literally survived only as property to be used and abused according to the dogmas of modernity. Given their African origin and their previous experience living free of any kind of bondage, it did not enter their minds that Napoleon had any right to own them, to kill them, or to people their island with new slaves. Conversely, on the basis of this same African experience, it is unlikely that they would have imagined a state-like political structure to organize their defense or survival. In alliance with the other group of free colored targeted for extermination or deportation—the officers and generals who had risen to power in the colony during the revolution—they defeated the French army and jointly inaugurated a new state they called Haiti.

The opportune alliance of the two groups who were to be exterminated or deported according to Paris's instructions was devoid of any common ideological basis. Napoleon himself, meditating upon his deathbed on the notion of his statesmanship, acknowledged that it was an unforgivable mistake not to have accepted a device to rule the colony through Toussaint's intermediary. Indeed, Henry Christophe is the only leader other than Toussaint to have enjoyed such a favorable control of state power and the only one to have reactivated the plantation economy. A similar monopoly of public violence would only be achieved by the United States occupation of 1915 and then bequeathed to the government of Haiti during the twentieth century.

While the monopoly of violence by Toussaint and Christophe explains in a large measure the success of their agricultural policies, the United States and the governments it sponsored from 1915 onwards failed to deliver even the most modest achievements in their economic endeavors. This resounding ineffectiveness makes clear that there is a distinction between the monopoly of violence and the monopoly of power.

Actions by the state after 1915 suggest some serious malfunction in the management of violence against the Haitian population. A series of gratuitous and naked abuses raised grim questions about the extent of the power exercised by the three involved states (United States, Dominican Republic and Haiti) on peasants who at best were poorly armed.[15] These abuses included the cruelty of the first and second Caco wars (1915–ca. 1925); the assassination of Charlemagne Péralte (1919), and the treacherous methods used to perpetrate this crime; the reinstatement of the practice of forced labor or *corvée*; the revolting 1937 massacre of peaceful, humble, and unarmed peasants residing within the borders of the Dominican Republic;[16]

the complicity of the Haitian government in covering up this genocide;[17] and the state-sponsored persecution of peaceful and inconspicuous Vodou believers.

Why was such indiscriminate public violence inflicted so readily on people who were considered weak and ignorant? Might it have been that there were no other means to curb their actual power other than irrational and brute violence?

A bit more than a century elapsed in Haiti from the arrest of Toussaint by the French in 1802 or the reign of Henry Christophe in 1806, to the 1915 landing of the United States Marines. The Haitian *habitants* had consolidated not only the institutions of their counter-plantation system, but also their norms of land tenure based on the family property system. The United States, with supremacy unchecked by any measure of accountability to the local population, could not re-energize plantation agriculture. The rural Haitians did not have to choose any specific course of action. The institutions they built to survive defeated the agricultural policy of the occupier and of its client oligarchy.

This constellation of dominant forces designed a policy to strangle the rural economy and to force the habitants to export their surplus labor force to the plantations organized by United States nationals in Cuba and the Dominican Republic. Gradually, Haiti—which was self-sufficient in food production—became a net importer of its means of subsistence, while quickly destroying the resources left for such purposes.[18]

At the same time, the oligarchy was sawing the branch on which it rested. It lost all support among the peasantry and since 1915 its political representatives can only achieve power if they obtain the support of the United States of America. The twentieth century was a lost century due to the obstinate attempt of the oligarchy to ignore and to disenfranchise the rural population in order to revert to the pre-independence situation when the labor force comprised essentially enslaved strangers. The country regressed steadily during the century. Its labor force does not possess nor can it reasonably achieve the training necessary for modern manufacturing; neither does it have the bargaining power which salaried personnel elsewhere are able to leverage in the quest for a decent quality of life.

Notes

1   Bernardo Vega gives an unexpected testimony of this defiant attitude of the Haitians
    when he endorsed the idea that they were, in the twentieth century, a "people not yet
    familiarized with the subtleties of the rights of private property". *Trujillo et Haïti* (1988;
    Fr. trans., Port-au-Prince: UniBank, 1995), 1:422.

2   Laurent Dubois, "'Citoyens et amis!' : Esclavage, citoyenneté et république dans les
    Antilles françaises à l'époque révolutionnaire," *Annales: Histoire, Sciences Sociales* 58
    (2003): 281–303.

3   Claude Meillassoux, *Anthropologie de l'esclavage* (Paris: Presses Universitaires de France,
    Quadrige, 1998).

4   Louis Sala-Molins, *Le Code Noir ou le calvaire de Canaan* (Paris: Presses Universitaires de
    France, 1987; 2nd ed. Quadrige, 2003).

5   For an English translation of portions of the 1801 Constitution see Laurent Dubois and
    John Garrigus, *Slave Revolution in the Caribbean, 1789–1804: A History in Documents* (Boston
    and New York: Bedford/Saint Martin's, 2006), 167–70. "Article 3: There can be no
    slaves in this territory; servitude is abolished within it forever. All men are who are born
    here live and die free and French." In fact, the majority of the population was not born
    in the territory, which suggests that they were not considered French, or indeed fully
    free, even though they were not enslaved.

6   "Article 76: Elle proclame que tout citoyen doit ses services au sol qui le nourrit ou qui
    l'a vu naître, au maintien de la liberté, de l'égalité, de la propriété, toutes les fois que
    la loi l'appelle à les défendre." ("We proclaim that all citizens owe their services to the
    land which feeds them or saw them born, and to the maintenance of liberty, equality,
    and property whenever the law calls on them to defend them.") Here again, there is a
    distinction between citizens who were born in the territory and citizens who are only
    being "fed" by it, that is those who were born in Africa.

7   "Article 4: All men, whatever their color, are eligible for all positions." "Article 5:
    There exist no distinctions other than those based on virtues and talents, and no
    superiority other than that granted by the law to the exercise of a public function."

8   "Article 16: Each cultivator and worker is a part of the family and receives a portion
    of its revenues. All change in residency on the part of cultivators leads to the ruin of
    cultivation. To repress a vice that is as damaging for the colony as it is contrary to
    public order, the governor will decree all police regulations made necessary by the
    circumstances."

9   "Article 13: Property is sacred and inviolable. All persons, either by themselves or
    through their representatives, are free to dispose of and administer what is recognized
    as belonging to them. Anyone who attacks this right commits a crime against society
    and is guilty towards the person whose property they have troubled."

10 "Article 17: Since the introduction of cultivators is indispensable to the re-establishment
    and the growth of crops, it will take place in Saint-Domingue; the Constitution charges
    the Governor to take appropriate measures to encourage and favor this increase in
    the number of hands, to stipulate and balance various interests, and to assure and
    guarantee the execution of the respective obligations that will be the result of this
    introduction."

11 Laurent Dubois, *A Colony of Citizens: Revolution and Slave Emancipation in the French
    Caribbean, 1787–1894* (Chapel Hill: Univ. of North Carolina Press, 2004).

12 Translation offered by the linguist Jacques Pierre, Professor of Creole at Duke
    University.

13 For an English translation of the portions of the *Code Noir* see Dubois and Garrigus,
    Slave Revolution, 49–54. "Article 55: Masters twenty years old will be able to manumit
    their slaves by all [legal] deeds or by cause of death, without being required to provide
    the reason for this manumission, neither will they need the permission of parents,
    provided that they are minors twenty-five years of age." "Article 56: Slaves made
    universal beneficiaries by their masters, or named executors of their testaments or

tutors of their children will be held and regarded as manumitted." "Article 57: We declare that manumissions enacted in our islands will be considered as birth in our islands and manumitted slaves will not need our letters of naturalization in order to enjoy the advantages of our natural subjects in our kingdom, lands and countries under our obedience, although they be born in foreign lands."

14   Louis Sala Molins, *Le Code Noir.*

15   See Rosalvo Bobo quoted in Léon-François Hoffmann, *Haïti, Couleurs, Croyances, Créole* (Montréal and Port-au-Prince: Les Éditions CIDIHCA et Henri Deschamps, 1990), 40.

16   "Women and children were reportedly less successful than men in escaping and hence composed the majority of those murdered". Richard Lee Turits, "A World Destroyed, a Nation Imposed", *Hispanic American Historical Review* 82 (2002): 615.

17   "[Vincent] prohibited public discussion of the massacre, and refused for a long time even to allow the church to perform masses for the dead". *Ibid.,* 622.

18   This policy is still prevalent. The *RDNP5 News* of April 12, 2010, reports under the title "Bill Clinton's Mea Culpa": "On the 10th of March, the former President of the United States, Bill Clinton, speaking to the Foreign Affairs Commission of the U.S. Senate, described the role his administration played in the exportation of subsidized food products from the U.S., taking advantage of the decrease in tariffs that was one of the conditions attached to the granting of loans by the International Monetary Fund (IMF) and the World Bank."

Curating History's Silences: *The* Revolution *Exhibition*

Richard Rabinowitz

SLAVE LABOR

SLAVERY WAS THE LIFELINE OF HUNDREDS OF COLONIAL NEW YORK BUSINESSES

- Trading in slaves

- Trading in the products of slave labor — sugar, coffee, cotton, indigo

- Harvesting, processing, and packing foodstuffs for the slave trade — rum, beef, fish, grain, cheese, butter, molasses

- Using slave labor in New York craft workshops

- Supplying slave plantations in the West Indies and North America with grain, tools, and manufactured goods

- Building, outfitting, and manning the ships that carried the trade between New York, Europe, the Caribbean, and Africa

- Borrowing, lending, and insuring vessels in the slave trade

- Advertising for the sale of slaves and for the recapture of runaways

1723
5,886 White (81.2%)
1,362 Black (18.8%)

HE FUNDAMENTAL CHALLENGE

There are plenty of challenges for historians who set out to curate an exhibition. They have to bring together the stuff to display— identifying pieces by exact date and time, finding them in dozens of repositories, and then securing their acquisition or reproduction, often by artful negotiation. They have to conjure up the right abracadabra to loosen the purses of funders and gild the words of the culture-page press with the project's importance. They have to decode official educational standards and make this project essential to the classroom teachers who will arrange for all those yellow school buses to arrive at the museum door. And, not least, the curators have to inspire designers and media producers to make the exhibition beautiful and effective, while remaining true to its interpretive priorities.

But nothing a curator does is more important than getting the story, and getting it right. That has been the Eldorado of the *Revolution* expedition.

Here we had to tell the fifty-year-long history of the eighteenth-century Atlantic revolutions in one hour. Show how they broke the unchallenged reign of monarchism, empire, slavery, and aristocratic privilege, and created the notion of universal human rights. Do it by shepherding an audience through a landscape of 3,500 square feet. Fill the space with documents in languages that many visitors probably don't know, with images and artifacts they can't immediately identify, and, most important, about subjects that they either (1) feel they should have learned better long ago ("the idea of the sovereignty of the people, oh yes,") or (2) never heard of in the first place ("there was a revolution in Haiti?"). In either case, they are frequently embarrassed by their ignorance.

As a form of scholarship, a medium of art, and an instrument of education, the interpretive exhibition is still a relatively unexamined mode of presenting history to the public—a distant relative of documentary video, site interpretation, narrative fiction in print and on film, and various kinds of performance art. Contrary to popular opinion, we do not simply disseminate, popularize, or vulgarize what scholars have written. The history exhibition uses its own tools and techniques to say something unique and unsayable in any other format.

ABOVE Telling Lives: a visitor responds booth at an exhibition at the New-York Historical Society in 2006. Photograph by Lynne Breslin Design.

OPPOSITE Visitors explore *Slavery in New York* at the New-York Historical Society in 2005–06 through a wide variety of interpretive media— graphics, multimedia and interactive devices, as well as original documents and artifacts. Photograph by Nicholas B. Paffett.

Unlike the authors of scholarly monographs, museum curators cannot assume that the members of our audience come prepared. And our visitors are much more diverse than the people who fill classroom seats at any level. We have grandmothers, and we have grandsons, and what's more, they come to our exhibitions together.

History exhibitions serve Clio, the muse of history, but they borrow the talents of her sisters as well. Our exhibitions may employ a much richer toolbox of educational and aesthetic resources than classroom teachers, or even filmmakers, writers of popular historical fiction or nonfiction, or video game designers. We can display documents actually touched, written, and worked over by major historical figures, a letter signed in Bonaparte's own hand, the camp bed that George Washington is said to have used at Valley Forge, or a desk at which members of the First Congress reviewed the proposed Bill of Rights at New York's Federal Hall.

Exhibitions can also concretize complex historical concepts with experiential learning tools. Graphic renderings, 3-D models, computer-interactives, and audio-visual presentations can slow down, speed up, reverse, and take apart historical moments, processes, and changes. Museums can stage dramatic simulations that pull visitors into decision-making or problem-solving roles. Visitors can participate in mock-dialogues with historical characters, and real conversations with one another.

What does the *Revolution* exhibition at the New-York Historical Society do, for example, that this well-illustrated book of essays does not?

BELOW Camp bed used by George Washington. Wood, canvas, iron. 27¾ × 78 × 34½ in. (70.5 × 198.1 × 87.6 cm). New-York Historical Society, Gift of Ernest Livingston McCrackan, 1871.8.

American History Workshop's method for *Revolution* was to construct the exhibition from the outside in.[1] Imagine three concentric circles, representing the Play, the Acts, and the Scenes.

1. The widest is the overall exhibition storyline. What do we want most to say about the Atlantic revolutions? Where should our narrative begin and end? Is this presentation a celebration, a story of unalloyed triumph, or is our take more ironic, even skeptical? In what sense is an exhibition about revolution timely? What is its significance for contemporary audiences? How can we make this subject appealing to possible museumgoers?

2. The middle circle is the pathway through that storyline. What narrative devices will we employ—key characters, foreground and background settings, major crises and turning points, unexpected twists, and so on? Since a history exhibition almost always tells a story that is known in a broad sense, it isn't the outcome that is likely to surprise but rather the detailed process by which the familiar outcome occurred. How will that story be told to visitors?

3. Finally, the innermost ring comprises the series of experiences visitors will have with particular clusters of historical documents, graphic panels and audio-visual elements, interactive devices, programs with docents or interpreters, and other interpretive interventions.

Though the development of the "arc" of the storyline comes first, this is not exactly a rigidly sequential exercise. To the very end of the process—the final selection of documents, the writing of texts and scripts, and the ultimate design choices—the overall narrative and the gallery divisions continue to be refined.

1. Fashioning the Story Line: A Grand Narrative Responsive to Contemporary Audiences

What should our exhibition about revolutions be? Should it be a comparative study of the three upheavals that roiled British North America, France, and Haiti? Too academic, and perhaps ultimately inconsequential: if every revolution is said to have "causes," "consequences," "military aspects," "incidents of civil violence," "new national symbols," and so on, then visitors will probably leave thinking that they pretty much resemble one another, and so what?

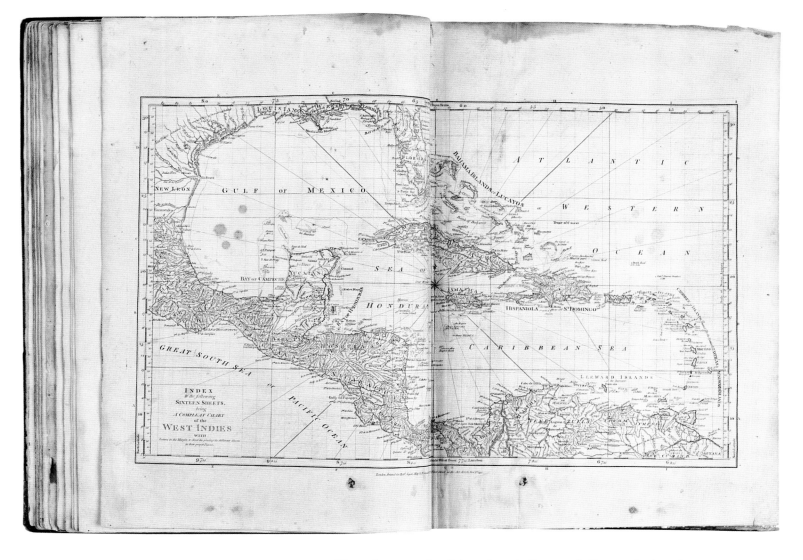

How about a tale of three heroic figures: Jefferson, Robespierre or Napoleon, Toussaint? Interesting, perhaps dramatic, but can we really see all that is important through three sets of eyes?

After many months of research, historical speculation, consultation with scholars, and ceaseless iteration, this is how the curators ultimately framed the "statement of the dramatic action"[2] of the *Revolution* exhibition:

> Visitors will explore how the people of the eighteenth-century North Atlantic world shared an evolving set of ideas about personal and political liberty. Sparked by grievances they attributed to defects in the governance of European empires, these "masterless men and women" generated and exploited a series of political upheavals and revolutions, with enormous cost in lives and treasure, that

led to major transformations in the world's thinking, even today, about freedom and slavery, hierarchical privilege and equality, national independence, and the sovereignty of the people.

Embodying both historiographical and pedagogical assumptions, this statement announced that we would consider the Atlantic world as a whole.[3] We would seek a single narrative instead of stringing together separate national histories of revolution in the United States, France, and Haiti. The actors in our story would not be Americans, Frenchmen, Britons, or Haitians—for the most part those identities are the *products*, not the antecedents, of these upheavals and revolutions. Nor did we want to attribute agency to only one class, say merchants or consumers, slaves or slaveholders. And, to be sure, we didn't want to suggest that abstractions like the "spirit of liberty," "commercial opportunities," or the "impulse to order" were the moving forces in our history. Instead, we aimed to locate the will to act in groups of people in the Atlantic, whether they came from Africa, Europe, or the Americas, and we would trace how they converged time and again to press for or against political change. Wordsworth's phrase in his 1802 sonnet to Toussaint, "a common wind," became a critical metaphor.[4] The same winds and ocean currents that carried the maritime commerce of the Atlantic transported as well the contagious ideas of liberty from one landfall to another.

Nothing in this story was inevitable, but it did have directionality. The revolutions in the United States, France, and Haiti, and the other insurrections, political contests, and military battles around the Atlantic, built upon one another and learned from one another.[5] Atlantic people were writing a collective history at the time, without a clear understanding of what was happening and without foreknowledge of the end.

By the end of the revolutionary age, however, we could assert that much had changed. At an early scholars' meeting, it was agreed that the overall arc of the exhibition would show that the age of revolutions had very dramatic consequences for the nineteenth century, and for our own day. Slavery, largely unchallenged as an aspect of the world of work in 1763, was by 1820 the subject of relentless efforts at delegitimization. Human equality, a pretty far-fetched idea in most mid-eighteenth-century quarters, came to challenge conventional assumptions of hierarchy. Empires were clearly no longer everywhere in command, fighting wars and then settling their disputes by swapping this colony for that one. A process of decolonization had begun, and "imagined communities" were on their way to becoming nation-states.

To render this enormous transformation as a single story occupying many sites around the Atlantic, with many different actors, is a tough intellectual challenge. Most histories of these revolutions, after all, have been told exclusively through the lens of a single nation's transformation.[6] We would attempt to see the Atlantic world as a whole. And, as the historian David Armitage recently complained, "narratives of the abolition of slavery, on the one hand, and of aristocracy and monarchy on the other, are almost never told in tandem." [7]

Thus, the exhibition's key interpretive strategy took shape: we would guide visitors in a tour of one Atlantic site after another, helping them to witness the process by which these massive ideological changes occurred. We would initiate our visitors into the role of Atlantic people, at a time of imperial authority emanating from the royal courts of London and Paris, and deposit them at the end as contemporary citizens of a world in which emancipation, liberty, equality, and national sovereignty had become a "new normal," though hardly an achieved reality. For many visitors, it would come as a surprise that the evolution of important political ideals came only through a series of fierce, often bloody struggles. The advance of human rights in the eighteenth century was never an easy or painless process. Imperial rivalry, almost constant global war, plantation agriculture based on enslaved labor, maritime commerce in wooden ships, the undermining of customary protections against human exploitation in traditional societies, and "line of fire" military tactics, all made this an awful, brutal era in human history. These revolutions were in no sense "velvet." Even the most high-minded documents of eighteenth-century liberty were written in the blood of combatants. And, at the end of our era, slavery, empire, and class privilege were probably stronger than they were before.

Once the endpoints of the progression had been established, we could create a pathway through the story. In an academic presentation, authors customarily maintain the same valence throughout. Each chapter is supposed to be roughly the same length as the rest and to have the same tone. But in a public interpretive presentation, like this exhibition, a more dramatic structure— creating expectations, proposing perplexities, dashing hopes, and the like—will better sustain our public's emotional engagement and thus its retention of its learning.

In a more practical vein, we have to husband our resources. An exhibition has a tight deadline, only so much space, and a fixed

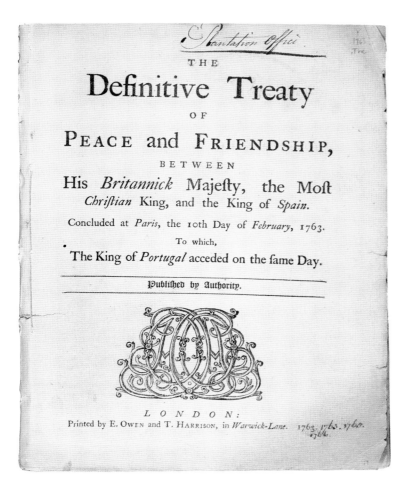

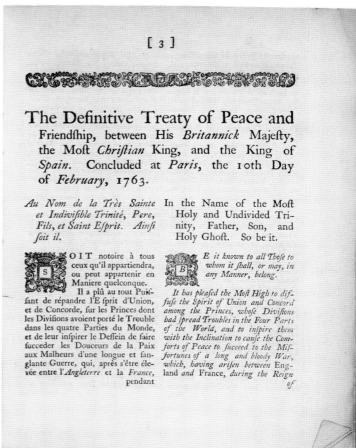

budget. We cannot stretch a wall to accommodate yet another object, or add another gallery to accommodate another argument. Obviously, our exhibition could not be a comprehensive treatment of any of the eighteenth-century revolutions. Hard choices would have to be made.

Where to focus, where to abbreviate? For American or French audiences seeing this exhibition in their home countries, we realized, the treatment of their own revolutions could not be comprehensive. The Haitian revolution, on the other hand, was so unfamiliar and yet so important that we decided to bring it to the fore, in terms of our investment of space and intellectual energy. As the most thoroughgoing of these upheavals—at least in its destruction of slavery, imperial dependency, and constitutionally sanctioned inequalities—the Haitian revolution could be viewed as the climax of the entire age of Atlantic revolutions.[8]

The basic framework was almost ready. The exhibition would be roughly chronological, moving from 1763 to 1815 or so. Timelines

ABOVE *Definitive Treaty of Peace and Friendship.* London: Printed by E. Owen and T. Harrison, in Warwick-Lane, 1763. New-York Historical Society, Y1763.Tre.

would present the "histoire des évènements." But the heart of our interpretation would emphasize transnational ideological change. We would not move from place to place but from one challenge to the Ancien Régime after another. "Liberty," though itself a changing notion, would be the central chord of the exhibition. We would center our interpretation of the revolution in British North America on the issue of national independence and popular sovereignty. Then we would shift to the emergence of anti-slavery in the Atlantic world, and particularly in Britain. At the end of the 1780s, we turn to how the gathered forces opposing racial and aristocratic privilege tore apart the French kingdom and its prize colony in Saint-Domingue.

2. Creating the Experiential Pathway: Guiding the Visitors' Encounter with the Subject

In most exhibitions in libraries or art museums, the treasures are laid out, one after another, either chronologically or in a pleasing aesthetic arrangement. Each framed document or image is the hero, so to speak, of its own story. Depending on the educational bent of the institution, the label copy for each piece may be either long or short, directed at experts or at general audiences. The exhibition's major theses are usually buried within these graphic text panels or in the accompanying catalogue.

The interpretive exhibition in the history museum is another creature entirely. The story comes first, before the checklist of objects. Original objects and documents are crucial as "actors" in the narrative. They are never simply illustrations of the events being described. Rather, original pieces (and occasionally reproductions, deployed for conservation purposes) are almost always supplemented by the museum's toolbox of interpretive devices and methods to guide visitors through a discovery of that story. Borrowing techniques from stagecraft (e.g., semi-re-created environments), from environmental design (e.g., bold graphics), and from electronic media (e.g., large-screen videos), this discovery may involve all the physical senses, including kinesthetics, and the social interplay with one's companions. Such an experiential exhibition encourages visitors to re-enact, or at least experience for themselves, the historical transformation it treats.

Then, what performative events, what experiences, could we designedly insert into the *Revolution* exhibition so as to yield a rich personal understanding of this half-century?

BELOW *Décoration de Feu d'Artifice tiré à Londres en Réjouissance de la Paix en 1763.* Paris: Chez Mondhare, 1763. William L. Clements Library, University of Michigan.

Décoration du Feu d'Artifice tiré 'a Londres en Réjouissance de la Paix en 1763.
A Paris chez Mondhare rue S. Jacque a l'Hotel de Saumur

Prospects and Refuges

From past experience, we have concluded that the most successful exhibitions are an artful interweaving of "overviews" and "immersions."[9] In overview areas, visitors use such exhibition tools as maps, charts, timelines, bold graphic elements, video animations, and the gallery's architectural elements, to gain a mastery of the place and time of the story. Overviews are aerial views of the subject. They are bright, clear, vivid, and unambiguous. The curatorial voice in an overview area is that of the senior archaeologist, briefing visitors about the importance of the site. But overviews also convey the risks of mastery—the pretensions of dominance, the failure to see what's actually happening on the ground.

By contrast, immersions bring visitors into an "eye-level"

perspective. They spark immediate encounters with individual historical characters, settings, and actions. Personal accounts, sometimes rendered aurally, are central to immersive installations. Film, video, and stagecraft provide powerful sensory environments, and attempt often to distract visitors from other people and from checking their watches. Such immersive media allow visitors to "walk in the shoes" of historical personages and to reenact historical moments for themselves. Immersions are dense, colorful, mysterious, and often ambiguous. The curatorial voice in the immersive area is that of the explorer's wise sidekick, pointing out interesting details that would otherwise be missed. Immersions incur the risk of disorientation, confusing a few trees with the whole forest and the savannas beyond.

Setting the Stage for Revolution

The *Revolution* exhibition begins with an overview, surveying the Atlantic world created by British victory in the Seven Years' War. Festooned with imperial symbols and regimental banners, resounding with anthems celebrating the Hanoverian succession, the gallery uses original and reproduction maps and treaty documents to proclaim the pretensions of the European empires in the Caribbean. Pamphlets published in London and Paris recall the French choice to trade Québec for Guadeloupe and Martinique. Models and sculptures represent the centrality of the Caribbean to the expanding commerce of the Atlantic world. Statistics render the explosion of men and women torn from the ancestral villages on four continents and thrown into the maelstrom of Atlantic mobility.

A passageway then leads "across the ocean" to the Caribbean. In dramatic contrast, visitors are immersed in a Caribbean seaport tavern, modeled after the raucous scene represented in John Greenwood's *Sea Captains Carousing in Surinam* (ca. 1752–58, Saint Louis Art Museum). Here they eavesdrop on and come face-to-face with historically documented ruffians, smugglers, corrupt officials, and other "masterless" men and women. The room quivers with scuttlebutt. Everyone is plotting something—to evade imperial regulations on trade, to foment violence, or to exploit colonial offices for private gain. Each speaks of a grievance or an oppression that must be opposed—a captain's cheating, an ex-slaveholder's brutality, a purchase of spoiled goods, the foolishness of petty regulations, an arrest for vagrancy, a betrayed promise. In effect, visitors are witnessing a wide array of overlapping spheres of protest and resistance.

This opposition of Empire, Rebel, and Loyalist sets the political tone of the exhibition, and the array of documents displayed—from royal proclamations to learned disquisitions to customs forms, newspapers, business correspondence, personal letters, court testimonies, tall tales and rumors in a dozen languages—represent the range of discourse in the Atlantic.

A Passage through Three Revolutionary Scenes

The imperial courts and the tavern have set the stage. The conditions of revolution were exposed in the mismatch of grandiose imperial pretension and inadequate mechanisms of control; in the prevalence of connivance and conspiracy that contributed to Atlantic lawlessness; in the grievances that seemed to thwart the recently broadened ambitions of the masterless masses, and the unresponsiveness of the authorities to these complaints.

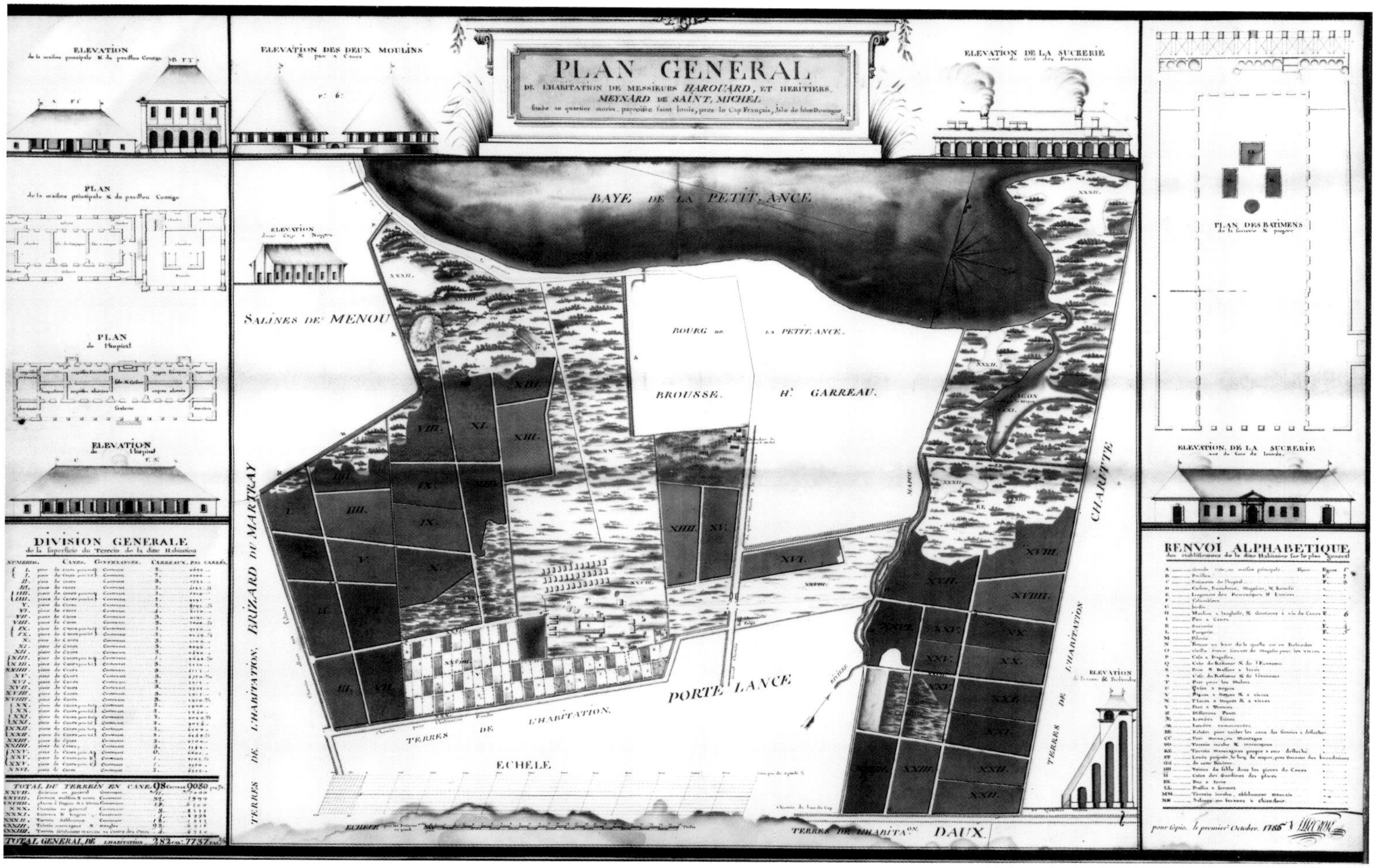
PLAN GENERAL
BAYE DE LA PETIT ANCE
SALINES DE MENOU
BOURG DE LA PETIT ANCE
BROUSSE. H.^{rs} GARREAU.
PORTE LANCE
TERRES DE L'HABITATION
ECHELE
DAUX
TERRES DE L'HABITATION BRIZARD DU MARTRAY
CHARITTE
DIVISION GENERALE
RENVOI ALPHABETIQUE
PLAN DES BATIMENS
ELEVATION DES DEUX MOULINS
ELEVATION DE LA SUCRERIE

ABOVE *Plan de la Sucrerie Saint-Michel au Quartier-Morin, près du Cap.* Copyright Jacques de Cauna Cnrs, fonds iconographique Haïti. In the left area, elevations and plans of the guest lodge and the main house; elevation and plan of the hospital; inventory of cane fields. In the center, elevations of the two mills and the sucrerie (sugar house); elevation of one of the slave quarters; map of the property; elevation of the boiler-house. On the right, plan of the buildings; front elevation of the sucrerie; and key to the property map.

Now comes the story of a half-century of revolutionary upheaval, bursting at every ocean's edge. How would we tell it? A timeline would be too thin and reductive to represent its complexity. A series of vignettes, using video or elaborate settings to represent critical moments, would be too expensive. Visitors would be wearied, we knew, by a meandering tale of one conflict after another. Designers would be delighted if some symmetry could be introduced, reducing the variability of the elements and lowering the costs of design, fabrication, and installation.

We decided on three galleries to represent the three ideological accomplishments of "liberty's arrow" in the eighteenth-century Atlantic: the notion of *national independence*, focused on the revolution in British North America; the struggle for *emancipation*, most notably embodied in these years by the campaign in Britain for abolition of the slave trade; and the *assault on hierarchy and privilege*, located in the fierce revolutionary turmoil of France and Saint-Domingue.

EMANCIPATION.

GLORIOUS FIRST OF AUGUST 1834

ENGLAND STRIKES THE MANACLE FROM THE SLAVE AND BIDS THE BOND GO FREE.

For Sale at the American Anti Slavery Office, 144 Nassau St. New York

1834

OPPOSITE Stephen Henry Gimber (1806–1862) after Alexander Rippingille (ca. 1793–1859). *Emancipation.* Engraving on paper, 1834. 13½ × 8½ in. (35 × 24 cm). Picture Collection, The New York Public Library, Astor, Lenox and Tilden Foundations, 807782.

Could these three chapters be told in the same manner? Did they follow some pattern that could assume physical form? Did we, in sum, actually have a distinct definition of "revolution" that we could apply to such different historical events? Finding the right "pattern language" for these narratives was a major milestone of the exhibition development process. Ultimately, we characterized each political upheaval as a concatenation of six elements: (1) the "common wind" that brought ideas of liberty to bear, as in the multiple translations and responses to Thomas Paine's *Rights of Man* in the early 1790s; (2) one or more "triggering events" that inadvertently set the blaze a-burning, like the calling of the Estates General in 1788; (3) qualities of the "host culture" that would shape the revolutionary struggle in particular ways, for example, the litigiousness and nearly universal literacy of the American colonies; (4) the "transformations" in the political and culture world that brought both a regime change and a new sense of nationality into being, as in the flowering of vodou in revolutionary Saint-Domingue; (5) the "culminating" event that sealed this period of change, like Parliament's closing the British slave trade in 1807; and, finally, (6) the "contribution" that these changes made to the larger story of the histories of liberty and revolution.

The designer's role is to organize these six different "actions" into a spatial sequence. This is, in effect, an architecture of revolutionary narrative.[10] Too orderly a sequence would belie the violence and disorder in our story. Too random an arrangement would undercut our claim to speak authoritatively about this history. The form of our "pattern language"[11] is based on the metaphor of a huge Atlantic storm system, in which prevailing winds (radical ideas set forth on the "common wind") met powerful cold fronts (characteristics of the "host culture") over a series of Atlantic landfalls, blew up into years of fire and rain (scenes of revolutionary upheaval and the formation of a new political culture), and then passed along the unsettled air to another landscape.

As they reenact these passages, visitors will, we hope, recognize the complex challenges facing our revolutionary forebears. As visitors glimpse the emerging familiarity of the modern world, they should sometimes measure a gain and sometimes a loss. In the exhibition's final gallery, they get to explore the "unfinished" business of eighteenth-century revolutions. The world was not delivered from evil. The French sank back into autocracy. The United States became the world's greatest slaveholding nation. The British Empire expanded and intensified its domination of remote people for another 150 years. Haiti, isolated as a pariah by the U.S. and European

OPPOSITE Napoleon Bonaparte to [LeClerc], January 14, 1801. Archives de la Département de la Marine, Service Historique de la Défense, Ministère de la Défense, Château de Vincennes, Paris, item # BB8 2721, pp. 338–44.

powers, was forced to pay reparations for all the slaves its revolution had freed. Cuba and Brazil succeeded colonial Saint-Domingue as the toxic cauldrons of slave-grown sugar and coffee.

But there were lasting achievements as well. The Spanish dominions in America caught the contagion of liberty and followed Haiti into independence in the two decades after 1804. Slavery was abolished in the British Empire by 1834, by the French in 1848, and throughout the hemisphere by 1888. In the midst of its awful civil war, which finally lifted the scourge of slavery here, the United States recognized Haitian independence. Over 150 nations have emulated the Americans in declaring their independence, most since World War II. And, almost immediately after that horrendous global conflict, the United Nations produced a Universal Declaration of Human Rights. The stirring words of 1776 and 1789 had become the birthright, if not yet the guaranteed condition, of every human child.

3. The Innermost Circle: The Immediacy of History

At the innermost circle of the curator's task, historiography and dramaturgy give way to pedagogy. Here is the "real stuff"— documents, images, and artifacts as close to you as they once were to the departed souls whose lives they record or preserve. Here is the immediacy, the pulse, of history.

Bonaparte's letter, Washington's bed, and the Federal Hall desk are now long separated from their original historical settings. The letter no longer tries to browbeat a subordinate. The bed no longer keeps the general's legs off the frozen muddy floor. But our bodies can occupy the same spaces that they do, decades and centuries after their makers and original users have passed on. That almost invariably raises shivers and provokes questions about mortality and our place in the flow of history.

Skillfully exhibited, such two- or three-dimensional documents yield a form of learning that seldom comes by reading about or even seeing pictures of such objects. Our own bodies might stretch out, imaginatively, in the space of Washington's camp bed.[12] Our hands grasp the quill pen and mimic the gesture of Napoleon's sign-off.

The art of the curator and designer is to reconstruct those moments of action in the past when these objects were present. For the historian and teacher, I would insist, it is not the thing itself but its power to evoke a human action that is most important. Things, however, do "say" much about action that language omits.[13] For one thing, they force us to acknowledge that history is made by deeds of brawn and cunning as well as by literacy and numeracy, by the skills of hand and eye and the process of social interaction

An 10.

Instructions

pour le Général
nommé Commandant Général de toute
l'Île de St. Domingue:

et

le Citoyen
chargé par le Gouvernement d'organiser
provisoirement en cette Colonie le Service Civil,
Economique, Judiciaire & Administratif.

_____

On a cru devoir réunir ici les Instructions des deux
Citoyens à qui le Gouvernement confie l'importante
mission de ramener l'obéissance, la Paix et le bon ordre
à St. Domingue; afin de leur montrer par là même
que dans leurs fonctions diverses il sera nécessaire qu'ils
soient toujours animés par un seul esprit, celui de
tendre à la plus prompte restauration d'une Colonie, destinée
à redevenir la source de la prospérité de la France sous
des mains libres, mais laborieuses.

Nous ne retracerons point ici l'affligeant
tableau des déchiremens auxquels depuis long-temps
elle est en proie. Reposons-nous plutôt sur l'idée
consolante de la cessation actuelle de la guerre intestine
qui la dévorait, et saisissons l'heureux augure que cette
circonstance nous présente d'un meilleur avenir.

C'est pour en hâter l'approche, que le Gouvernement
a fait choix du Général Divisionnaire
et du Cen   chargés, l'un de
l'emploi de la force armée, pour la défense intérieure

Leclerc —
Ce ne sont pas là
évidemment les
instructions secrètes,
mais ce pourraient
être les Instructions
patentes dont
le Ministre avant
par sa lettre du
9 brumaire
demandé au
1er Consul
de jeter les bases.
—

as much as by wit, persuasion, and precise description. Secondly, objects remind us that life is temporal, durational, and sequential. A letter excerpted in a textbook or cited in a monograph is simply an arrangement of words. An original sheet of paper with those same words is also a *series* of actions—the impulse to communicate; the choice of the pen and paper; the words considered, chosen, and inscribed; the decision to send it along, when and to whom. The Federal Hall desk is an even more complex object. Designed perhaps by Pierre L'Enfant, it is more French than English in style. Constructed of mahogany, perhaps from the about-to-explode French colony of Saint-Domingue, it is evidence of the lively trade with the Caribbean which helped New York recover in the 1780s from its wartime destruction. But, further, the desk is itself an artifact of America's political evolution—it may be one of the earliest legislator's desks ever. Recall that the colonial assemblies, and even the Parliament in London, had only benches and tables. United States congressmen, the historian Gordon Wood has taught us, were expected to answer their constituents' letters and petitions—and needed a place to wrap them with colored cord (called "red tape") and stash them away.

By itself the individual document will never, magically, communicate the historical concept we wish to convey.[14] To be honest, few historical artifacts have jaw-dropping visual power. To draw visitors' attention and to focus it, to dramatize the object or document as part of a complicated action in the political or cultural realm, we must add other historical sources and, often, interpretive interventions like maps, audio-visual presentations, interactive devices, or graphic panels.

Such a cluster, thus, is the basic experiential unit of the exhibition. It is most effective when it concisely communicates a single action in the past. A central section of the area devoted to the Haitian revolution, for example, details the brilliant campaign of Toussaint Louverture to seize the reins of the colony from 1794 to 1801. A major text panel introduces this area, which is then divided into three clusters, representing Toussaint's military ascendancy, his efforts to reinvigorate the plantation economy, and his attempt to achieve autonomy through negotiations with regional powers and by creating the trappings of a state. Since almost no three-dimensional artifacts of the Haitian revolution survive, we may choose to symbolize each of these moments with an object reproduced from an early illustration of Toussaint—his fancy feathered hat, the campaign writing-desk of his amanuensis, and podium on which he (may have) stood to promulgate his constitution.

Toussaint's use of military, political, diplomatic, and economic tactics was not, however, matched by the construction of a stable institutional and ideological basis of a new state in Saint-Domingue. Ultimately, his promulgation of a colonial constitution in 1801 revealed the weakness of Toussaint's vision, and it set in motion Napoleon's expedition to topple him from power.

For each of the clusters, we assemble manuscripts, published documents, newspapers, maps, illustrations, and pamphlets interpreting the controversies of the time. These sources, written in eighteenth-century script and in a language unfamiliar to nearly all visitors, are supplemented by transcriptions, translations, and sometimes by compilations into more accessible media. A single map of Toussaint's military campaign, marking its progress chronologically, is more useful than a dozen period maps—though some of the detail will inevitably be lost thereby.

But, most importantly, we use interpretive text panels to invite an intellectual archaeological excavation of each source document. These panels situate the documents, and link them to the themes of the specific gallery and to the exhibition as a whole. They do more. They posit that each document is only a partial lens into the past. Other perspectives, especially those of historically unrecorded slaves, women, children, and poor folk, are to some extent excluded by these documents—but also glimpsed through them. Finally, every document begs for an explanation of how and why it survived, and what that tells us about the construction of memory and history in the centuries since it was created.

Of course, not every document will accommodate this much scrutiny, nor can we devote the space and time to explore each piece in such detail. The examination of each piece, with its own story, can distract visitors from the larger narratives we seek to tell. But the key purpose of the cluster, as of the exhibition as a whole, remains: to re-people a past that has become faceless and remote.

ABOVE Lacolle, manager of habitation Codere, to Commissioner Polverel, March 20, 1794. Archives nationales, Paris, cote D/XXV, 37, 373.

BELOW Member's Desk from Federal Hall, ca. 1788. Mahogany. 31 × 92 × 15 ½ in. (78.7 × 233.7 × 39.4 cm). New-York Historical Society, Gift of the Corporation of the City of New York, 1837.4.

Our role as teachers is to help visitors re-imagine each of our sources as a site of human action in all its complexity. As an example, look with me at a document in the French National Archives. It records that in 1794, two recently emancipated women, unnamed "Affricaines," were sent to French commissioner Polverel for threatening their overseer and refusing to work in the sugar mill at night, as he insisted. "I want you to make an example" of these women, the agent wrote to Polverel.[15]

From the cool, well-lit, elegantly appointed reading room of the Archives in Paris, these two voices still reach us. They can be heard over the silencing by the authorities, over the grinding roar of the mill in that torch-lit tropical night, over the distance of two centuries and 4,500 miles. Their anguish shatters the façade of History. Through them, we can still feel the pulse of human beings. We ask, what kind of real freedom had these women attained? What kind of protest, if any, would have been appropriate for them? What power remained in the hands of the commissioner Polverel, who had himself issued the emancipation decree just a few months earlier? When we bend our ears to listen to these two protesters, when we feel their common humanity with us, we recognize that they too, like Jefferson and Lafayette and Tom Paine, are the heroes of liberty's birth. I can close my eyes and imagine them, as free women, sitting across from me on the 2 train from Brooklyn, laughing over a niece's bad taste in dresses or worrying over the recent Haitian earthquake. Or, perhaps, I can even feel their spirits mounting mine and strengthening my own commitment to justice.

From careful surveys conducted at previous exhibitions, we know that most of the thousands who see the *Revolution* exhibition will not master all its historical details. They will not be able to recite the names of Toussaint's generals or the politicians who espoused anti-slavery in Britain or France. They may not be able to distinguish "positive" from "negative liberty."

But they should understand the magnitude and interconnectedness of these revolutions. They will also experience and carry with them a link to particular people, acts, and ideas— different ones for each visitor. We expect that the complexity of the story told will strengthen their capacity to understand and embrace the complexity of their own lives. They too are the legatees of liberty's revolution and responsible for its survival.

Notes

1   The plural pronoun used in this essay accurately reflects the collaborative quality of the work. In addition to the author, key American History Workshop team members included Lynda B. Kaplan, Peter P. Hinks, Aileen Fuchs, Flora Boros, and Millery Polyné. The dramatic and visual imagination of David Layman, the exhibition designer, has played an important role in shaping the exhibition content. Beyond their editorship of this volume, Thomas Bender and Laurent Dubois persistently pressed the exhibition development toward clarity and thoroughness. Jean Casimir, a great Haitian scholar, deserves special thanks for opening his heart, his mind, and his country to the challenges of this exhibition.

2   The "dramatistic" criticism of Kenneth Burke helped us to see every document, every artifact, and every interpretive statement as an action, requiring us to specify each of Burke's famous "pentad" of elements—the Act, the Actor(s), the Agents, the Scene, and the Purpose. See *A Grammar of Motives* (Berkeley: Univ. of California Press, 1969).

3   We acknowledge the importance of the very different experience of the African, Iberian, and South American peoples in the South Atlantic.

4   "There's not a breathing of the common wind /That will forget thee; thou hast great /Thy friends are exultations, agonies,/ And love, and man's unconquerable mind." ("To Toussaint L'Ouverture"). See Julius S. Scott III, "The Common Wind: Currents of Afro-American Communication in the Era of the Haitian Revolution" (PhD diss., Duke University, 1986).

5   Robin Blackburn, "Haiti, Slavery, and the Age of the Democratic Revolution," *William and Mary Quarterly*, 3rd ser., 53 (October 2006): 643–74.

6   Perhaps the most powerful exception is David Brion Davis's epochal *The Problem of Slavery in the Age of Revolution, 1770–1823* (Ithaca, N.Y.: Cornell Univ. Press, 1975).

7   Review of *Aristocracy and Its Enemies in the Age of Revolution*, by William Doyle, *Times Literary Supplement*, August 14, 2009: 5.

8   But no historical instance is a perfect model. The revolution in British North America established a stable national government and found a way to address the problem of mixed sovereignties that had bedeviled London policy-makers in the 1760s and 1770s. But this fragile solution came only by strengthening slavery's hold on the new republic. Ultimately, the United States needed a brutal civil war to secure a permanent resolution. The new Haitian state, by contrast, saved the lives of thousands of African-born slaves from the killing-fields of sugar cultivation, but it could not fashion a political order that ensured equitable treatment of its people.

9   This distinction is derived from the "prospect" and "refuge" theory elaborated by Jay Appleton, *The Experience of Landscape* (London: Wiley, 1975).

10   By analogy, my nineteenth-century Brooklyn brownstone once operated as a narrative of domestic life as well, bringing visitors from street to doorway to vestibule, and thence either to working areas (the kitchen, storage areas, servant's quarters), to public areas (the parlor and dining room), or to more private zones (family sitting rooms, bedchambers).

11   The idea derives from Christopher Alexander, *A Pattern Language: Towns, Buildings, Construction* (New York: Oxford Univ. Press, 1977).

12   As the exhibition design developed, there was not enough space to display and interpret the camp bed. In its place, we substituted a 1780 engraving by Frenchman Noël LeMire of J. B. LePaon's portrait of Washington. The engraving shows Washington holding a copy of the Declaration of Independence. But any substitution inevitably alters the interpretation. We put aside Washington's acceptance of personal discomforts in the fight for liberty. Instead, the chief point became his adherence to the authority of Congress and the principles enshrined in the Declaration. Of course, the presence in this image of his slave, Billy Lee, complicates that interpretation.

13   Or, to say it better, language abbreviates and symbolizes much of what action (with things) communicates. See Kenneth Burke, *Language as Symbolic Action: Essays on Life, Literature, and Method* (Berkeley: Univ. of California Press, 1966), 5. Cf. Michael Oakeshott, *Experience and Its Modes* (Cambridge, Eng.: The University Press, 1933).

14   In general, art museums claim to focus on the object in itself, but they often rely upon long text labels (or catalog entries) to highlight the important details of the work, to stress its significance, and to contextualize it within an artist's career or its cultural milieu.

15   Archives Nationales, Paris, DXXV, 37, 373.

Contributor Biographies

Thomas Bender is University Professor of the Humanities and Professor of History at New York University, where he has taught since 1974. The focus of his scholarship has been on the intellectual and cultural history of the United States, as well as cities and city culture, including contemporary as well as historical studies of urbanism. These books include *Toward an Urban Vision: Ideas and Institutions in Nineteenth Century America* (1975), *New York Intellect: Intellectual Life in New York City, from 1750 to the Beginnings of Our Own Time* (1987), and *The Unfinished City: New York and the Metropolitan Idea* (2002). For the past fifteen years he has devoted himself to reframing American history in a manner that makes clearer the ways in which American history is entangled with and shares the histories of the peoples of all continents. This cosmopolitan approach has been argued and illustrated in several articles and two books: *Rethinking American History in a Global Age* (2002) and *A Nation Among Nations: America's Place in World History* (2006). Besides numerous articles in scholarly journals, he has written for a variety of magazines and newspapers, including the *New York Times* and the *Los Angeles Times*. He has been a Guggenheim Fellow; the Mel and Lois Tukman Fellow at the Cullman Center for Scholars and Writers of the New York Public Library; a Getty Scholar; and a fellow at the Center for Advanced Study in the Behavioral Sciences at Stanford University and at the Davis Center for Historical Studies at Princeton University. He was elected to the American Academy of Arts and Sciences in 1994.

Robin Blackburn teaches at the University of Essex in the UK and the New School for Social Research in New York. He is the author of *The Overthrow of Colonial Slavery* (1988) and *The American Crucible: Slavery, Emancipation and Human Rights* (2011).

T. H. Breen is the William Smith Mason Professor of American History at Northwestern University. He is also the founding director of the Nicholas D. Chabraja Center for Historical Studies. He has held appointments as the Pitt Professor of American History at Cambridge University and the Harmsworth Professor at Oxford University. He has received major research awards from the Humboldt Foundation, the Guggenheim Foundation, and National Endowment for the Humanities. Breen has authored eight books, among which are *American Insurgents, American Patriots: The Revolution of the People* (2010), *Marketplace of Revolution: How Consumer Politics Shaped American Independence* (2004), *Tobacco Culture: The Mentality of the Great Tidewater Planters on the Eve of Revolution* (2001), and *"Myne Own Ground": Race and Freedom on Virginia's Eastern Shore*, with Stephen Innes (1980).

Vincent Brown, Professor of History and of African and African American Studies at Duke University, is a multi-media historian with a keen interest in the political implications of cultural practice. Brown is the author of the prize-winning book, *The Reaper's Garden: Death and Power in the World of Atlantic Slavery* (2008), and producer and director of research for *Herskovits at the Heart of Blackness* (2009), an award-winning television documentary about the pioneering anthropologist Melville J. Herskovits. He teaches courses on Atlantic history, African diaspora studies, American revolutions, and the history of slavery, and he is currently writing about an archipelago of slave revolts that stretched from the Gold Coast of Africa throughout the Americas in the seventeenth and eighteenth centuries.

Jean Casimir teaches at the Faculty of Human Sciences at the State University of Haiti (UEH). He began his professional career as a lecturer at the National Autonomous University of Mexico (UNAM), his alma mater. He also has taught as a visiting lecturer at Stanford University, Duke University, and the University of the West Indies (UWI). He served as an official at the United Nations Economic Commission for Latin America and the Caribbean from 1975 to 1988, and was his country's ambassador to the United States and the Organization of American States from 1991 to 1997. He is the author of many publications, including *La Cultura Oprimida* (1981) and *Haïti et ses élites, l'interminable dialogue de sourds* (2009).

David Brion Davis is a Sterling Professor of History Emeritus at Yale University and Director Emeritus of Yale's Gilder Lehrman Center for the Study of Slavery, Resistance, and Abolition, which he founded in 1998 and directed until 2004. He is a frequent contributor to *The New York Review of Books*, and has written or edited eighteen books, including *The Problem of Slavery in Western Culture* (1966), winner of the Pulitzer Prize for nonfiction, the Anisfield-Wolf Book Award, and the National Mass Media Award of the National Conference of Christians and Jews; *The Problem of Slavery in the Age of Revolution* (1975), winner of the National Book Award for History and Biography, the Albert Beveridge Award, and the Bancroft Prize; *Slavery and Human Progress* (1984); *Revolutions: American Equality and Foreign Liberations* (1990); *In the Image of God: Religion, Moral Values, and Our Heritage of Slavery* (2001); *Challenging the Boundaries of Slavery* (2003); and *Inhuman Bondage: The Rise and Fall of Slavery in the New World* (2006), winner of the Connecticut Book Award for Nonfiction, the Association of American Publishers' Award for Excellence in History and American Studies, and the Ralph Waldo Emerson Award of the Phi Beta Kappa Society. Davis has also received the Society of American Historians' Bruce Catton Prize for Lifetime Achievement (2004); the Horace Kidger Award for Excellence in Teaching, Scholarship, and Service, from the New England History Teachers Association (2004); the Presidential Medal for Outstanding Leadership and Achievement, from Dartmouth College (1991); the American Historical Association's Award for Scholarly Distinction (2007); Harvard University Graduate School's Centennial Medal for Contributions to Society (2009); and two Festschrifts from former graduate students. He has been elected a member of the American Academy of Arts and Sciences, the American Philosophical Association, and the British Academy.

Laurent Dubois, a specialist in the history and culture of France and the Caribbean, is Marcello Lotti Professor of Romance Studies and History at Duke University and Director of the Center for French and Francophone Studies as well as co-director, with Deborah Jenson, of the Haiti laboratory of the Franklin Humanities Institute. He is the author of *Avengers of the New World* (2004) and *A Colony of Citizens: Revolution and Slave Emancipation in the French Caribbean, 1787–1804* (2004), which won four book awards, including the Frederick Douglass Prize. His most recent book is *Soccer Empire: The World Cup and the Future of France* (2010). He also has published two collections: *Origins of the Black Atlantic*, edited with Julius Scott (2009) and *Slave Revolution in the Caribbean, 1789–1804: A History in Documents*, edited with John Garrigus (2006). He is now writing *Haiti: The Aftershocks of History* (under contract with Metropolitan Books) and a history of the banjo (under contract with Harvard University

Press), for which he received a National Humanities Center Fellowship and a Guggenheim Fellowship. With Richard Turits, he is also currently working on a history of the Caribbean. He was the head historical consultant for the recent PBS documentary on the Haitian Revolution, *Egalité for All*, and the co-chair of the scholars committee for the New-York Historical Society exhibition *Revolution!* He recently received a Mellon New Directions Fellowship to study Ethnomusicology.

Jean M. Hébrard is co-director of The Law in Slavery and Freedom Project at the University of Michigan, where he is the Norman Freehling Visiting Professor. He also teaches at the École des Hautes Études en Sciences Sociales, where he co-directs the Center for Research on Contemporary Brazil.

Peter P. Hinks is the author of the award-winning book, *To Awaken My Afflicted Brethren: David Walker and the Problem of Antebellum Slave Resistance* (1996). He works professionally in public history and has served as the Senior Research Historian with the American History Workshop for several major exhibitions at the New-York Historical Society including *Slavery in New York* (2005) and *New York Divided* (2006). With the late professors John Blassingame and John McKivigan, he co-edited Frederick Douglass's three autobiographies, *Narrative of the Life of Frederick Douglass*, *My Bondage and My Freedom*, and *The Life and Times of Frederick Douglass* for Yale University Press. He has also completed a new encyclopedia for Greenwood Press entitled *Encyclopedia of Antislavery and Abolition*. Hinks is co-editing with Stephen Kantrowitz a forthcoming collection of essays for Cornell University Press on the history of black Freemasonry.

Cathy Matson is Professor of History at the University of Delaware and Director of the Program in Early American Economy and Society at the Library Company of Philadelphia. Her work specializes in the economic culture of the Atlantic World from 1500–1800. Matson's publications include *A Union of Interests: Political and Economic Thought in Revolutionary America* (1990), *Merchants and Empire: Trading in Colonial New York* (1998), *The Economy of Early America: Historical Perspectives and New Directions* (2005), and *The American Experiment: A History of the United States* (2008). She has written over twenty articles on American economic culture and political economy and edited numerous collections of essays. She is currently finishing a book, *A Gambler's Ocean*, about the global reach of Philadelphia's economy from 1750 to 1815.

Jeremy D. Popkin is the T. Marshall Hahn, Jr. Professor of History at the University of Kentucky in Lexington, Kentucky. He is the author of *"You Are All Free": The Haitian Revolution and the Abolition of Slavery* (2010) and *Facing Racial Revolution: Eyewitness Accounts of the Haitian Uprising* (2007), as well as several other books on the history of the French Revolution. In 2011, Wiley/Blackwell will publish his latest book, *A History of the Haitian Revolution*.

Richard Rabinowitz is one of the leading public historians in the United States. Over the past forty years he has led creative teams of scholars, curators, educators, artists, architects, designers, and institutional planners in fashioning over five hundred successful and innovative history programs at sites like the New-York Historical Society; the Lower East Side Tenement Museum in New York; the Birmingham Civil Rights Institute; the National Underground Railroad Freedom Center in Cincinnati; and other sites in thirty-three states and the District of Columbia. Since 2005, he has curated six blockbuster history exhibitions at the New-York Historical Society, including *Slavery in New York* and *Revolution! The Atlantic World Reborn*. Rabinowitz has an A.B. *summa cum laude* and a PhD from Harvard University and is the author of many works in history and museum practice. He is currently a Fellow at the Gilder Lehrman Center for Slavery, Resistance, and Abolition at Yale University.

Julius S. Scott is a lecturer in the Department of History and the Center for Afroamerican and African Studies at the University of Michigan. His research focuses on the Caribbean world in the seventeenth, eighteenth, and nineteenth centuries; slavery and emancipation; and the Haitian Revolution and its impact in Afro-America. Among his publications are "Afro-American Sailors and the International Communication Network: The Case of Newport Bowers," in *Jack Tar in History: Essays in the History of Maritime Life and Labour*, ed. Colin Howell and Richard Twomey (1991) and "Crisscrossing Empires: Ships, Sailors, and Resistance in the Lesser Antilles in the Age of Revolution," in *The Lesser Antilles in the Age of European Expansion*, ed. R. L. Paquette (1996).

Rebecca Scott, the Charles Gibson Distinguished University Professor of History and Professor of Law at the University of Michigan, teaches on the law in slavery and freedom as well as on Latin American history and on the boundaries of citizenship in historical perspective. Her book, *Degrees of Freedom: Louisiana and Cuba after Slavery* (2005), received the Frederick Douglass Prize and the

John Hope Franklin Prize. Among Professor Scott's recent articles are "Public Rights, Social Equality, and the Conceptual Roots of the Plessy Challenge," *Michigan Law Review* 106 (2008); "'She … refuses to deliver up herself as the slave of your petitioner': Émigrés, Enslavement, and the 1808 Louisiana Digest of the Civil Laws," *Tulane European and Civil Law Forum* 24 (2009); "The Atlantic World and the Road to Plessy v. Ferguson," *Journal of American History* (2007); and "Public Rights and Private Commerce: A Nineteenth-Century Atlantic Creole Itinerary," *Current Anthropology* (2007). She is a recent recipient of the Guggenheim Fellowship and a member of the American Academy of Arts and Sciences.

Bibliography
The Revolution *Exhibition*

THE OVERALL NARRATIVE OF THE REVOLUTIONARY AGE IN THE ATLANTIC WORLD

Anderson, Fred. *The Crucible of War: The Seven Years' War and the Fate of Empire in British North America, 1754–1766.* New York: Knopf, 2000.

Armitage, David, and Sanjay Subrahmanyan, eds. *The Age of Revolutions in Global Context, c. 1760–1840.* London: Palgrave Macmillan, 2010.

Bailyn, Bernard. *Voyagers to the West: A Passage in the Peopling of America on the Eve of the Revolution.* New York: Knopf, 1986.

Bender, Thomas. *A Nation Among Nations: America's Place in World History.* New York: Hill and Wang, 2006.

Blackburn, Robin. "Haiti, Slavery, and the Age of the Democratic Revolution." *William and Mary Quarterly* 3rd ser., 63 (2006): 643–674.

Calloway, Colin G. *The Scratch of a Pen: 1763 and the Transformation of North America.* New York: Oxford Univ. Press, 2006.

Gaspar, David Barry, and David Patrick Geggus, eds. *A Turbulent Time: The French Revolution and the Greater Caribbean.* Bloomington: Indiana Univ. Press, 1997.

Geggus, David P., ed. *The Impact of the Haitian Revolution in the Atlantic World.* Columbia, S.C.: Univ. of South Carolina Press, 2001.

Hunt, Lynn Avery. *Inventing Human Rights.* New York: Norton, 2008.

Klooster, Wim. *Revolutions in the Atlantic World: A Comparative History.* New York: NYU Press, 2009.

Linebaugh, Peter, and Marcus Rediker. *The Many-Headed Hydra: Sailors, Slaves, Commoners, and the Hidden History of the Revolutionary Atlantic.* Boston: Beacon Press, 2000.

Palmer, R. R. *The Age of the Democratic Revolution: A Political History of Europe and America, 1760–1800.* 2 vols. Princeton: Princeton Univ. Press, 1959–64.

THE AMERICAN REVOLUTION

Armitage, David. *The Declaration of Independence: A Global History.* Cambridge: Harvard Univ. Press, 2007.

Bailyn, Bernard. *To Begin the World Anew: The Genius and Ambiguities of the American Founders.* New York: Knopf, 2003.

Becker, Carl Lotus. *The Declaration of Independence: A Study in the History of Political Ideas.* New York: Knopf, 1942.

Breen, T. H. *American Insurgents, American Patriots: The Revolution of the People.* New York: Hill and Wang, 2010.

Maier, Pauline. *American Scripture: Making the Declaration of Independence.* New York: Random House, 1998.

———. *From Resistance to Revolution: Colonial Radicals and the Development of American Opposition to Britain, 1765–1776.* New York: Norton, 1991.

Nash, Gary. *The Urban Crucible: The Northern Seaports and the Origins of the American Revolution.* Cambridge: Harvard Univ. Press, 1986.

———. *The Unknown American Revolution: The Unruly Birth of Democracy and the Struggle to Create America.* New York: Viking, 2005.

Niemeyer, Charles Patrick. *America Goes to War: A Social History of the Continental Army.* New York: NYU Press, 1996.

Toth, Charles W., ed. *The American Revolution and the West Indies.* Port Washington, N.Y.: Kennikat Press, 1975.

Wood, Gordon S. *The Creation of the American Republic, 1776–1787.* Chapel Hill: Univ. of North Carolina Press, 1998

———. *The Radicalism of the American Revolution.* New York: Knopf, 1992.

SLAVERY AND ANTI-SLAVERY

Anstey, Roger. *The Atlantic Slave Trade and British Abolition, 1760–1810.* Atlantic Highlands, N.J.: Humanities Press, 1975.

Berlin, Ira. *Many Thousands Gone: The First Two Centuries of Slavery in North America.* Cambridge: Harvard Univ. Press, 1998.

Berlin, Ira, and Philip D. Morgan, eds. *Cultivation and Culture: Labor and the Shaping of Slave Life in the Americas.* Charlottesville: Univ. Press of Virginia, 1993.

Blackburn, Robin. *The Overthrow of Colonial Slavery, 1776–1848.* London: Verso, 1988.

Brown, Christopher Leslie. *Moral Capital: Foundations of British Abolitionism.* Chapel Hill: Published for the Omohundro Institute of Early American History and Culture, Williamsburg, Virginia, by the Univ. of North Carolina Press, 2006.

Davis, David Brion. *Inhuman Bondage: The Rise and Fall of Slavery in the New World.* New York: Oxford Univ. Press, 2006.

———. *The Problem of Slavery in the Age of Revolution, 1770–1823.* New York: Oxford Univ. Press, 1999.

———. *Slavery and Human Progress.* New York: Oxford Univ. Press, 1984.

Drescher, Seymour. *Econocide: British Slavery in the Era of Abolition*, 2nd ed. Chapel Hill: Univ. of North Carolina Press, 2010.

Edwards, Paul, and James Walvin. *Black Personalities in the Era of the Slave Trade.* Baton Rouge: Louisiana State Univ. Press, 1983.

Fladeland, Betty. *Men and Brothers: Anglo-American Anti-Slavery Cooperation.* Urbana: Univ. of Illinois Press, 1972.

Genovese, Eugene. *From Rebellion to Revolution: Afro-American Slave Revolts in the Making of the Modern World.* Baton Rouge: Louisiana State Univ. Press, 1979.

Rediker, Marcus. *The Slave Ship.* New York: Penguin, 2007.

Walvin, James. *Black Ivory: Slavery in the British Empire.* Oxford, Eng.; Malden, Mass.: Blackwell Publishers, 2001.

———. *The Trader, The Owner, The Slave: Parallel Lives in the Age of Slavery.* London: Vintage, 2008.

Wise, Steven. *Though the Heavens May Fall: The Landmark Trial That Led to the End of Human Slavery.* Cambridge, Mass.: Harvard Univ. Press, 2005.

CARIBBEAN, ESPECIALLY SAINT-DOMINGUE AND HAITI

Bell, Madison Smartt. *All Souls' Rising.* New York: Pantheon, 1995.

———. *Master of the Crossroads.* New York: Pantheon, 2000.

————. *The Stone that the Builder Refused.* New York: Pantheon, 2004.

————. *Toussaint Louverture: A Biography.* New York: Vintage Books, 2008.

Bush, Barbara. *Slave Women in Caribbean Society, 1650–1838.* Bloomington and Indianapolis: Indiana Univ. Press, 1990.

Cauna, Jacques. *Au Temps des Isles à Sucre: Histoire d'une Plantation de Saint-Domingue au XVIIIe siècle.* Paris: Karthala, 2003.

Dayan, Joan. *Haiti, History, and the Gods.* Berkeley: Univ. of California Press, 1984.

Dubois, Laurent. *Avengers of the New World: The Story of the Haitian Revolution.* Cambridge: Harvard Univ. Press, 2005.

————. *A Colony of Citizens: Revolutions and Slave Emancipation in the French Caribbean.* Chapel Hill: Published for the Omohundro Institute of Early American History and Culture, Williamsburg, Virginia, by the Univ. of North Carolina Press, 2004.

————, and John D. Garrigus, eds. *Slave Revolution in the Caribbean, 1789–1804: A Brief History with Documents.* Boston: Palgrave, 2006.

————, and Julius S. Scott, eds. *Origins of the Black Atlantic: Rewriting Histories.* New York: Routledge, 2010.

Fick, Carolyn E. *The Making of Haiti: The Saint Domingue Revolution from Below.* Knoxville: Univ. of Tennessee Press, 1990.

Fischer, Sibylle. *Modernity Disavowed: Haiti and the Cultures of Slavery in the Age of Revolution.* Kingston, Jamaica: Univ. of the West Indies Press, 2004.

Garrigus, John D. *Before Haiti: Race and Citizenship in French Saint-Domingue.* New York: Palgrave Macmillan, 2006.

Geggus, David Patrick. *Haitian Revolutionary Studies.* Bloomington: Indiana Univ. Press, 2002.

————. *Slavery, War, and Revolution: The British Occupation of Saint Domingue, 1793–1798.* New York: Oxford Univ. Press, 1982.

————, and Norman Fiering, eds. *The World of the Haitian Revolution.* Bloomington: Indiana Univ. Press, 2009.

James, C. L. R. *The Black Jacobins: Toussaint L'Ouverture and the San Domingo Revolution.* 1938. Reprint ed.: New York: Random House, 1963.

McClellan, James E. *Colonialism and Science: Saint Domingue in the Old Regime.* Baltimore: Johns Hopkins Univ. Press, 1992.

Moreau de Saint-Méry, Mederic Louis Elie. *Description topographique, civile, politique et historique de la partie francaise de l'isle Saint-Domingue.* 1797; repr. 3 vols. Paris: Société française d'histoire d'outre-mer, 1984.

Popkin, Jeremy, ed. *Facing Racial Revolution: Eyewitness Accounts of the Haitian Insurrection.* Chicago: Univ. of Chicago Press, 2007.

———. *You Are All Free: The Haitian Revolution and the Abolition of Slavery.* Cambridge, Eng.: Cambridge Univ. Press, 2010.

Sheller, Mimi. *Consuming the Caribbean: From Arawaks to Zombies.* London: Routledge, 2003.

Wimpffen, Alexandre-Stanislas. *Haiti au XVIIIe siècle: Richesse et esclavage dans une colonie française.* Paris: Karthala, 1993.

FRENCH REVOLUTION

Furet, François. *The French Revolution, 1770–1814.* Oxford, Eng.; Cambridge: Blackwell, 1996.

———, and Mona Ozouf, ed. *A Critical Dictionary of the French Revolution.* Cambridge: Harvard Univ. Press, 1989.

Hunt, Lynn Avery. *Politics, Culture, and Class in the French Revolution.* Berkeley: Univ. of California Press, 2004

Popkin, Jeremy D. *Revolutionary News: The Press in France, 1789–1799.* Durham: Duke Univ. Press, 1990.

Soboul, Albert. *A Short History of the French Revolution, 1789–1799.* Trans. by Geoffrey Symcox. Berkeley: Univ. of California Press, 1965.

EXHIBITION CATALOGS

Barringer, Tim, Gillian Forrester, and Barbaro Martinez-Ruiz. *Art and Emancipation in Jamaica: Isaac Mendes Belisario and His Worlds.* New Haven: Yale Center for British Art and Yale Univ. Press, 2007.

Common Routes: St. Domingue–Louisiana. Historic New Orleans Collection, March 14–June 30, 2006. Paris: Historic New Orleans Collection, Somagy, AGADP, 2006.

Hamilton, Douglas, and Robert J. Blyth, ed. *Representing Slavery: Art, Artefacts and Archives in the Collections of the National Maritime Museum.* Aldershot, Hants., Eng. and Burlington, Vt.: Lund Humphries, 2007.

Regards sur les Antilles: Collection Marcel Chatillon. Musée d'Aquitaine, 22 septembre 1999–16 janvier 2000. Bordeaux: Musée d'Aquitaine, 1999.

A Rising People: The Founding of the United States, 1765 to 1789: A Celebration from the Collections of the American Philosophical Society, the Historical Society of Pennsylvania, The Library Company of Philadelphia. Philadelphia: American Philosophical Society, 1976.

Index